ADVANCE PRAISE FOR

LESBIANS
RAISING
SONS

"*Lesbians Raising Sons* is a poignant and down-to-earth book that makes you think and think again about what it means to raise sons in today's world. From Wells's insightful introduction through all the honest stories, readers will be enlightened, challenged, sometimes saddened, often amused, and never bored."
— Dena Taylor, editor of *Feminist Parenting: Struggles, Triumphs & Comic Interludes*

"Lesbians raising sons is one of the hottest topics in today's society, and Jess Wells has put together indispensable reading for lesbian moms. Each contributor has a unique perspective, from Lillian Faderman to Kate Kendell, Audre Lorde to Robin Morgan. Fresh, diverse, and readable, there's something for every kind of mom, with every kind of son, in this collection. I give it my highest recommendation, and I wish I'd had it when my own son was born!"
— Phyllis Burke, author of *Family Values* and *Gender Shock*

"We have waited many years for such an insightful and loving book.... I cried. How could I not cry, reading these stories while my own son is lost from me?... In these essays, we can find insights, new questions to ponder, shared pain, mutual forgiveness, and, I hope, healing."
— Jenny Sayward, director of Lavender Families Resource Network

Also by Jess Wells

Run
The Sharda Stories
A Herstory of Prostitution in Western Europe
The Dress, The Cry and a Shirt With No Seams
The Dress/The Sharda Stories (reissue)
Two Willow Chairs
AfterShocks

LESBIANS
RAISING
SONS

AN ANTHOLOGY EDITED BY
JESS WELLS

alyson
books
LOS ANGELES • NEW YORK

Manufactured in the United States of America.
Printed on acid-free paper.

This trade paperback original is published by Alyson Publications Inc.,
P.O. Box 4371, Los Angeles, California 90078-4371.
Distribution in the United Kingdom by Turnaround Publisher Services Ltd.,
Unit 3 Olympia Trading Estate, Coburg Road, Wood Green,
London N22 6TZ, England.

First edition: May 1997

10 9 8 7 6 5 4 3 2 1

ISBN 1-55583-410-8

Library of Congress Cataloging-in-Publication Data
Lesbians raising sons : an anthology / edited by Jess Wells. — 1st ed.
    ISBN 1-55583-410-8
    1. Lesbian mothers—United States.   2. Mothers and sons—United States.
3. Child rearing—United States.   I. Wells, Jess.
HQ75.53.L48 1997   97-1109
649'.1'086643—dc21   CIP

Credits
    "Raising Sons With Emotion" by Laura K. Hamilton was previously published in *Feminist Parenting* (Crossing Press, 1994)
    "Man Child: A Black Lesbian Feminist's Response" by Audre Lorde was previously published in *Sister Outsider* (Crossing Press, 1984. Freedom, Calif.)
    "Every Mother's Son" by Robin Morgan is reprinted with permission from *The Word of a Woman*, copyright 1994 by Robin Morgan by permission of Edite Kroll Literary Agency
    "The Uncles' Club" is an excerpt from "lesbian/motherhood" by Christina Starr, previously published in *Lesbian Parenting* (Gynergy Books, 1995)
    "Outside the Inside" by Lillian Faderman was previously published in *The Advocate*, April 2, 1996
    "Marbalo, Lesbian Separatism, and Neutering Male Cats" by Ruthann Robson is reprinted with permission from *Cecile*, copyright 1991 by Ruthann Robson (Firebrand Books, Ithaca, N.Y.)
    "Or Not" by Leslie Lawrence was previously published in *Seneca Review*, Vol. XXVI, No. 2 (Fall 1996)
    "Here Comes the Groom" by Pearlie McNeill was previously published in *Beyond Blood: Writings on the Lesbian and Gay Family* (BlackWattle Press, 1995)
    "Declared Not Fit" by Minnie Bruce Pratt is reprinted with permission from *Crime Against Nature*, copyright 1990 by Minnie Bruce Pratt (Firebrand Books, Ithaca, N.Y.)
    "Children in Lesbian and Gay Families" by Susan Golombok and Fiona Tasker is reprinted with permission from *The Annual Review of Sex Research*, 1994, published by the Society for the Scientific Study of Sexuality, Mount Vernon, Iowa
    "The Men in My Life" by Lisa Orta was previously published in *The Family Next Door*, Vol. 1, No. 6 (June–July 1994) and Vol. 2, No. 1 (August–September 1994)
    "Choices" by Tryna Hope was previously published in *All The Ways Home* (New Victoria, 1995)
    "Fighting for Our Children" by Tzivia Gover was previously published in *The Advocate*, November 26, 1996.

Cover design by Bruce Zinda.

Dedicated to E.D.W.

CONTENTS

FACING LOSSES

Introduction

"Few subjects so provoke anxiety among feminists as the four-letter word *sons*," wrote pioneer feminist Robin Morgan. "Yet that subject goes to the crux of power and of patriarchy, even though it also grazes the living nerves of love."

The stories in this book are true-life adventures of lesbians raising sons in the face of power and patriarchy, of staring down the right wing's objections to our families and sometimes losing, of volunteering for the enormous, magnificent task of loving a child with every fiber of your being. It is about teaching sons the feminism that is so frequently at the root of the lesbian community, of showing them firsthand the fluidity of gender, the equality of people, the possibility of nonviolence, and the breadth of the spectrum of emotional expression. This book is about women who, in greater numbers than ever, are becoming mothers unlike any others and the sons they are raising to be men—the likes of which have never been seen on the planet before.

It is estimated that there are more than 14 million members of lesbian and gay families in America, with the overwhelming majority of children being raised by lesbians. While many were conceived and born to heterosexual mothers who later came out, there is also a current baby boom among lesbians, and it is reshaping that community, challenging concepts and constraints of the family and, perhaps most important, raising men in a completely new way.

A socially and biologically driven phenomenon is producing a disproportionate number of male children within the current lesbian baby boom. Lesbians who choose to undergo donor insemination have at least a 65 percent chance of bearing a son.

Here are the biological facts: "Male" sperm (sperm that carry a Y chromosome) weigh less than "female" sperm (sperm that carry the heavier X chromosome). Male sperm therefore swim faster, although female sperm live longer. If a woman is inseminated before an egg is discharged into the uterus, she is more apt to conceive a girl, since the male sperm reach the area where the egg should be sooner and die waiting for it.

However, lesbians who decide to have children tend to be inseminated close to the actual date that their egg is ready. Ovulation is difficult to predict mathematically, so most lesbians use ovulation-predictor kits, which tend to pinpoint only the actual day that the egg is ready.

The AIDS crisis has mandated that semen be chosen from carefully screened donors, processed, frozen, and then quarantined for six months before use. Previously frozen sperm have a longevity in the body of just one to two days, contrasted with fresh sperm, which can live for up to three or four days in the vagina. So to increase the chances of a successful insemination, lesbians tend to go through the process on the day of ovulation. In addition, since sperm is somewhat expensive, few lesbians can afford to risk inseminating days before their egg is discharged. The outcome is that lesbians more often conceive male children.

The result when viewed as part of the big picture of the lesbian and gay community? One could wax poetic about the yin and yang of it — the men facing sickness and death, the women bringing forth life, a new generation, focused on raising, rearing, and nurturing. Lesbians generating new men as their brothers fall around them.

At the same time, lesbian parents have all the earmarks of an oppressed group breaking new ground: subjected to appalling injustice at the hands of the courts; forced to educate everywhere we go, including places that are traditionally relied on for nurturance, such as doctors' offices and schools; selectively hiding our family structure for fear of recrimination and thereby struggling with the mixed messages sent to our children; saddled with pressure to see ourselves as being "as good as" our heterosexual counterparts in raising traditional children rather than acknowledging the beautiful, inherent differences in the children we bring into the world; and yet frequently able to overcome all of the obstacles and create marvelous love and stunningly healthy homes.

We are parents unlike any others, and this is most evident in the mothering of our sons. Lesbian households are raising a new generation of men who will be significantly different from their counterparts from patriarchal families. Lesbian parenting by and large incorporates strong feminist concepts. Patriarchal families teach girls what they cannot *do* and teach boys what they cannot *feel*. They traditionally teach boys to sublimate their emotions into only two areas: anger and aggression. Don't cry, don't be afraid, don't feel melancholy, don't be intimidated. Be tough when you're frightened; be silent when you're hurt. Lesbian families teach their sons to embrace the full range of their emotions. No one in a lesbian household says, "Take it like a man" or "Big boys don't cry." We have opened up more avenues for expression for our sons instead of limiting them to sports and sex. We encourage them to dance, sing, decorate, play music, sew, and do theater and imaginative dress-up as well as play football and baseball, surf, ski, and shoot hoops.

"Sensitive men" may have gotten a bad name over the past decade because they were frequently feigning mannerisms that disguised a sexist intent, but lesbian mothers are raising generations of men who have been allowed to be sensitive from birth. Widening that emotional spectrum for boys is destined to have an immense impact on the formation of the male psyche and personality. Laura K. Hamilton's "Raising Sons With Emotion" gives shape to these new ideas.

Lesbian families teach boys nonviolence. As Cheryl Deaner, founder of the All Our Families Coalition, states, "Boys really benefit from learning negotiation skills instead of using their fists to resolve conflict. In this violent society...it is especially important for boys to learn diverse ways of solving conflicts."

We also teach our sons a level of self-sufficiency and nurturance that is not found in patriarchal families. Our sons may cook, do laundry, clean, and knit. While this may seem to be a technique to ensure that they don't tie another generation of women to domestic servitude, it is also because of the high regard in which the lesbian community holds self-sufficiency. And is it not a gift to our sons to equip them to take care of themselves for the rest of their lives? We also spend a great deal of time trying to be certain that our sons learn how to nurture. Try buying dolls for your son in today's toy market, and you'll see how difficult a task that is, but the impact this could have on modern fathering goes without saying.

Sons raised in lesbian households see women in nontraditional roles when their parents are construction workers, firefighters, lawyers, doctors, and all the other jobs lesbians hold. They see women in nontraditional settings regardless of their profession: In a household of two women, the parent with the tools is a woman and the parent with the cookbook is a woman.

In fact, the fluidity of gender roles may be another of the most important contributions of lesbian parenting. We show our sons not only that women are equal and that men can cry but also that gender is not the linchpin of world order. The world is not divided by what men can do and what women can do. The world is not defined by how men and women look. Facial hair, dresses, bustiers, boots — whether one has or wears these is irrelevant. We teach our sons that self-definition is not a box their bodies put them in but an entirely individual, infinitely mutable expression of their imaginations, their psyches, and their souls. The courage required to teach boys this lesson is evident in the moving account "On the Way to the Water," in which a mother grapples with supporting her transgender toddler. In "Black. And White. And All the Colors in Between," the author challenges the world to make room for her son, whose biological mother is her partner, now a female-to-male transsexual.

And what of the infamous "gay question"? Will our sons grow up to be gay? As with the world at large, 10 percent of our children will be gay. Lesbian families, however, may be some of the only families to reflect a true 10 percent instead of the tragic condition of 2 percent gay and 8 percent tormented and suicidal from life in the closet. And it almost goes without saying that there are now four million people in the country who are much less apt to be homophobic when they grow up.

Lesbian families, more frequently than their heterosexual counterparts, embrace racial diversity. This is so partly because the lesbian community has by and large made marked progress on issues of racism. Sometimes it is because of the double hit of homophobia and racism on the part of adoption agencies: In the South, for example, multiracial children can be adopted by single mothers who are rarely given healthy white boys. This diversity is now a component of our lesbian families, and Jenifer Levin paints a stunning picture of the adoption of her Cambodian son in "Some Queer Straight Talk on Adoption."

Audre Lorde's classic piece "Man Child: A Black Lesbian Feminist's Response" eloquently shows how "raising black children — female and male — in the mouth of a racist, sexist, suicidal dragon is perilous and chancy. If they cannot love and resist at the same time, they will probably not survive."

As Grace Woodacre points out in "Back to the Village," the inclusion of the extended family and the community in the raising of children has been the method of successful child rearing for thousands of years. It is only since the invention of the nuclear family after World War II that people have begun to believe that everything a child learns should be supplied by the male and female who spawned them. Pointing out the coaches, friends, and teachers in our lives, Woodacre says it isn't necessary for one's mother to have sex with these people for them to be mentors. Lesbians may not have a man in their bed, but that is not to say that men are not present in their children's lives. In fact, research by Susan Golombok and Fiona Tasker shows that lesbians are more apt than straight women to have men in their children's lives. And Cheryl Deaner suggests that one doesn't even have to teach boys to become men: They are inherently male. The right wing's furor over the issue of the male role model is fueled by an old patriarchal adage used against all mothers but especially against lesbian mothers: The boy must sever ties with the mother to become a man. Only men make men; women make faggots. Feminists and lesbians are mounting a head-on challenge to this sexist, homophobic edict.

Of course, the nuclear family is falling apart with or without the help of lesbian families. "A 1990 U.S. Census Bureau Household Information survey found that only 9 percent of families have a full-time homemaker and only one quarter of all American families qualify as heterosexual nuclear families," *The San Francisco Bay Guardian* reported in a June 1996 feature on gay families. With a divorce rate of 50 percent, the nuclear heterosexual family is a thing of the past. Blended families or single parentage is now the norm, and with the new pressure to care for the elderly within the home, extended families are increasingly common. Black, Latino, and Asian cultures have always embraced the extended family; it is only the segment of the white community whose mouthpiece is the right wing that strives for the isolationist nuclear family and that now mourns its demise.

The right wing reacts to lesbian mothers with a vengeance for several reasons: We procreate without intercourse; we raise sons without men in the house; and we teach boys not to oppress women, to feel, and to live free of gender restrictions and homophobia. We are not raising the next generation of patriarchs, and the right wing is coming at us with the full force of its power. The conservatives have conceded that queers may congregate, drink, dance, and work like dogs without the benefit of medical coverage for our spouses, but they are marshaling all their resources to stop us from going to the next level and creating long-lasting unions, with children as our focal point. Says Kate Kendell, legal director of the National Center for Lesbian Rights: "It's all the radical right has left to hang on to, and they're going for it, big time." The horrific case of Sharon Bottoms, reported by Tzivia Gover, is just one extreme example of the right wing's agenda. More insidious, there is a move afoot to regulate access to sperm, an action that, if it weren't so necessary in this day of AIDS, would be laughable, since the male prerogative to spread semen wherever and whenever he chooses is so much a part of male culture that you can't get men to contain their ejaculate with condoms even when their life depends on it.

The right-wing threat to our parenting affects us not just where state law is hostile in custody cases. It is a constant pressure on us as parents. For example, we struggle to invent language to describe ourselves in this role-rigid world — is it two mommies, mother and parent, first-name basis? The desire to protect our children from homophobia sometimes results in teaching our children the painful lessons of living partially in the closet. And the fear that lesbians will raise their sons to be gay men results in a pressure to prove that we can raise "real boys." In the courts we still must prove that our children are not worse off for living with us, when in fact the research of Golombok and Tasker shows that "children in lesbian families reported...a greater sense of well-being (joy and contentment) than did children in heterosexual families." It is the typical pressure brought to bear on an emerging group: The contention that we are equal starts out as a pronouncement that we are the same and only later grows to a stronger position, one in which we gain equality, society honors our difference, and we introduce our language and social structure into the larger culture.

The road to lesbian parenting has been long and hard. Many of us have come through tremendous anger at the male world to be able to embrace our sons with unconditional love. My own piece, "Born on Foreign Soil," examines my fury when I was offered what felt like a blatant patriarchal setup: Cater to a man-child or don't mother.

And what will all these boys and men do to the lesbian and gay community? Laura Davis and other contributors recount the days when our sons were not welcome in our midst. Those days are over. Christina Starr's "The Uncles' Club" outlines a way for gay men to become involved. "Lesbian Divorce," by Sara Michele Crusade, shows the new face of the lesbian breakup.

A radical new agenda is being written for the community, one in which lesbians — as well as the children of the lesbian nation — are at the top of the list.

—*Jess Wells*

New Lessons

On the Way to the Water
by Sara Asch

I have two sons
One appears to be a girl
The other's probably a boy

They have two mothers
One is kind of like a boy
The other's clear she is a girl

I have two sons
They are black
Their moms are white
Three of them are Jewish
I take lessons

Our family crosses many boundaries, artificially drawn but culturally indelible. Only the courageous work of our transgender warriors on the front lines of cultural transformation have been able to blur the lines, a smudge here and there. The smudges, though, haven't reached into most of the spaces in which a family lives its daily life: the supermarket, the public school, the community center, the playground, the office, the temple, the neighbor's house.

In those public domains, away from the private sphere of home, the lines are solid and powerful. They emit a message of warning, like an electric fence or barbed wire. Cross, and risk.

Our family risks. Daily. I have a son who is apparently a girl and who, if he were old enough to read this, would be furious at me for using this male pronoun, for saying "he." He wears eleven braids that hang down his face to one side of his head. Some have reached about seven inches now. A friend of his recently counted eighty-eight beads adorning these flowing tresses.

Flowing tresses is the effect he seeks, for he has studied well the white girls with their long, straight hair. He has watched the col-

lege girls who student-teach, the video mermaids, the female hero-
ines of the silver screen. He knows how to toss his head just so, to
tuck a lock behind his ear, to suck on a strand that reaches the
mouth. And he covets the opportunity. His braids, done by his
butchish mommy with loving care, some fear, and a deep commitment to his growing spirit, are his way into that tress experience.

His white high-tops sport pink soles, pink stars, and glitter. He car-
ries around his pink ballerina-outfitted Addy doll to school. His Addy is
a cheaper imitation of the American Girl doll series, a collection dis-
played in an upscale catalog that he pores over. He knows the details
of their accessories. Addy is brown, sweet, and bedecked. She often
sits in his school cubby to wait for him, a touchstone in the day.

We dress him in solid-colored sweatpants and turtlenecks for the
winter, solid matching shorts and T-shirts in the summer. He wishes for flowered tights, for dresses with big collars, for red patent-
leather Mary Janes. He has always wanted these. We don't give in
on these requests because of our fear of a deeper scorn, the one
we think we've protected against by just allowing the pink soles,
pink socks, pinkish purple snow boots, and purplish magenta snow
coat. After all, they're from Lands' End. That's rugged, right?

4   Malik is tall and lithe, four-foot-two at age five, and he is black.
His presence in the classroom challenges the rules. As a kinder-
gartner, he has already forced the school to move its dividing lines,
to *remove* them in some cases. During the first two weeks of
school, the kids learned somehow that he is actually a boy, a fact
to them that is proved by biology, his nemesis. Six months later,
however, they still refer to him as "she" or "her." To do otherwise
would create for them a dissonance that youngsters are creative
about solving. There are other adults on the periphery (and some
closer) who also refer to him as "she." He prefers this. Initially the
teachers thought he needed to be protected from the insult of being
called a girl. They felt, however unconsciously, compelled to uphold
the misogynist social imperative to save boys from the demeaning
label and status of a girl. Then they realized that he preferred it.

The phys ed teacher, Mr. M., told the children to line up, boys to
one side, girls to the other, for races. My son stood in the middle,
a little dumbfounded that such a request was being made, then slid
himself to the girls' side. Afterward a confused Mr. M. went to the
teachers for clarification. They recommended he no longer divide
children by gender, and that was that.

While the class was learning categorization skills, they brainstormed ways to sort sneakers. Tie and Velcro, high-tops and lows, boys' and girls'. Oops. What about Malik's sneakers? They were encouraged to probe the question: How could you tell boys' shoes from girls' shoes anyway? White sneakers for girls? Hmm, that didn't work. It *had* seemed you could tell, except Malik's presence raised bigger questions. As Kate Bornstein asks in *Gender Outlaw*, "What is a man?" "What is a woman?" so did Malik require of five-year-olds to wonder, *What is a boy? What is a girl? Are sneakers a way to know?* For this year in this class at least, Malik smudges the line, and gender has been both added to the dialogue and removed as a dividing line.

These are the easy stories (with the sensitive teachers), the kinds of daily life experiences that sound great in the telling. But there are others. There are the deeply anxious, wrenching, tearful scenes as he forces his desires, his sense of self into the contortions demanded by the world outside the house...and that we, in our confused wisdom, enforce.

Swimming. If he wears a boy's suit, they will all know that he is a boy. This disturbs his sensibility, and he feels exposed. Can we, his mothers, send a black boy to the town swimming pool, full of black and white families, dressed in a girl's bathing suit, with his little genitals bumping out, so that *their* sensibilities are disturbed and *we* feel exposed? These conflicts have created wails, angst, and anger. The anger can be a knot of confusion. He is angry at me, yelling, crying, maybe hitting. I am furious at being in a situation where I am forced to support a system of oppression I abhor. I respond to his anger and my impotence with more anger...and so it goes. Until I remember his dilemma and that he is only a child and that my yelling and crying and shaking fury are not all deserved by him. We settle down. Something shifts somehow. We try not to do this in a public place, but we have.

The odd compromise so far is a boy's printed trunks with a tank top, so Malik can feel as though it's a one-piece. Missing is the joy, the pure delight on his face, when he wears neighbor Amanda's suit. Oh, once the swimming begins, there's the feel of the water, the freedom of the buoyancy, then happy is the swimmer. Something, though, is lost on the way to the water.

We talk at night sometimes, my son and I, about the ways of the world, of race, of gender, of war, and whether mama bears tickle

5

their cubs. He is only five. He knows that lots of rules aren't fair. (After all, doesn't Princess Jasmine of *Aladdin* assert, "The law is wrong"?) He announces, "When I grow up I'm going to make a law that says women can go without shirts and boys can wear dresses and girls' bathing suits."

Sometimes we role-play:

"Mommy?"

"What, baby?"

"What if the kids at the nature center ask me if I'm a boy or a girl?"

"What would you like to say?"

"I don't know."

"Can you say it's none of their business?" (Of course, *I'm* willing to snarl at them.)

"But that would be rude."

"Oh, right."

"I could say I don't care which one?"

"Do you want to practice?"

"Okay."

"Hey, Malik, are you a boy or a girl?"

"Well, it doesn't matter to me what you think."

"Hey, Malik, are you a boy or a girl?"

"Whatever you decide."

"Hey, Malik, are you a boy or a girl?"

"It doesn't matter to me, so it shouldn't matter to you."

Of course, it does matter, but in the face of questioning children (usually boys do the asking), Malik is steadfast and clear. I marvel at this capability, this practice. I also know that he will be just as likely to nudge them, annoy them, or tease them first before they even get a chance to question him.

In the bathroom Malik is quick to cover his genitals or to arrange himself in such a way that he convinces himself that he has female parts. I remember back to when I was five, to the same scene in reverse. Only I never talked to my mom about it.

I admire his courage, his tenacity in the face of powerful restriction. When he wears a pink ruffled dress and tights in the living room, twirling on his toes and spinning with glee to the violins of Tchaikovsky, I experience his pure joy. My heart soars with him. It is a joy of liberation.

Daily, however, I also experience a searing pain, a deep fear, and an immense and powerful rage. I could kill. It is energizing and catalyzing but also enervating and exhausting. I am enraged that the binary configuration of gender has placed him in a position of choosing, of maybe losing. He continues to place himself in the middle. I have to question my own reluctance to write this about him by being true to him and writing *she.* What stops me? What am I afraid of? The fact that it matters makes me wild, and I sometimes feel hopeless. But it does matter. Beaded braids matter. Whether Masai warriors wear a head full of braids is irrelevant on the playground or grocery line when questions regarding Malik's gender become everyone's business. (I'll never forget Malik, at three, sitting in the grocery cart drinking from a juice bottle, when an older woman walked up to him and said, "Aren't you a big boy to be drinking a bottle?" And he asserted rather emphatically, "I'm not a big boy — I'm a little girl!" She left.)

Pink sneaker soles matter. Carrying a doll matters after about age two. Notice that so much of this focus is on clothes, on accessories, for the performance of gender is really best available to us first as a visual experience. Appearance so forcefully defines our initial response and the society so requires a gender assignment that it always matters. At the community center, on the neighborhood sidewalk — it all matters. As Malik approaches six and seven and eight, it will matter more.

Enter race. Again, though there is some limited room for biracialism, a binary construction of black and white creates a line so difficult to cross and so loaded with a history of power imbalance that crossing the line takes a powerful heart.

At the playground I am not necessarily assumed to be Malik's mother or the mother of our two-year-old, although Adam's little basketball-loving self and sweet toddler looks keep him out of controversy for now. I am white, they are black. How can we be together? "Baby-sitting?" some of the grown-ups ask. "Foster children?" say others. For the young children, once they have ascertained that I am indeed a female *and* his mother, they come to me to clarify Malik's gender, since he has probably skirted the issue or ignored them. "Ask Malik," I have learned to say.

If she's the mother, wonder the other parents, *why would she possibly allow such a departure from our expectations for dress and appearance? Doesn't she know she's supporting his confusion?* (Read *their confusion.*) *No doubt it's the lack of a male role model.*

Then I posit to their unspoken question with my unspoken answer, *Do you think he learned this from me? I hate pink.*

This is a lot of work to do to give your kids a push on the local swings.

In our community it is important for my family to be accepted as part of the fabric, part of the texture of the neighborhood. My kids must feel safe here. So far this has been possible because we choose to live in a city where a family like ours is not a total aberration.

At the two recreation centers at which workers and children are primarily African-American, we participate with another layer of concern. It is essential for our children to experience a black and multicultural context, to feel a part of it, to grow in it. Accepting my partner and me as our kids' mothers is happening through a tremendous amount of energy on our part and the slowly expanding openness of others.

While sex-role stereotyping and homophobia are alive and well in all communities, they appear to be deeply entrenched in our town's African-American community. This contributes to our worries about Malik's level of acceptance. Fortunately there is also is a broad commitment to acceptance of different ways of being. It feels like a paradox, but it may create just enough space for our family to be. Children are loved here. Hopefully, that will go a long way.

8   What about Malik? He's moving into solid childhood now, well beyond toddlerhood, pushing the boundaries, challenging bathroom-selection mores, maintaining his close attachment to the sweetness of ballerinas and "my little flying ponies." Just today I was cutting and gluing fairy wings onto a yellow female Power Ranger he had been given by someone else. That way he could "really play with her."

How will I modulate both my fears of his being rejected or hurt and my fears about the effect of internalized self-restriction? How will I use my rage to continue our family's freedom-fighting stance at the same time that I want to bash anyone who suggests the status quo? My joy in my children's existence and their sweet, open faces fuels my fury at anyone who tries to dull their glow. How will I continue to lead my children and be led by them at the same time?

I will. We will all be led by them. As I finish this essay, I look around at the coffee shop where I write. My partner has given me the morning to do this. She took the kids downtown, where Malik has a ballet class. Adam is probably bouncing around, getting into trouble while he waits for his brother (Mister Sister to you) to finish his toe-pointing twirls. I see around me twenty-four large color prints of big trucks — fine, sparkling tractor-trailer rigs — captured by the eye of an artist who saw the spirit and power in their shiny lines. I grin because I know Adam would be running around here saying, "Trucks, big trucks, why are there big trucks here, Mommy?" Malik would notice none of them. But far off in a remote corner of one photo, taken at a truck stop, sits a Barbie doll on a toy-store counter. That he would see. His radar would have picked it up on entry, and his eyes would have lit up as he pulled me to see it, glowing all the way.

I have two sons
One is apparently a girl
One is probably a boy
Time will find us all
somewhere outside those
lines
And my sons will write poems
of their
own.

Fighting for the Rights of Mermaids
by Harriet Alpert

Soon after my forty-third birthday, my partner and I adopted our first child. We were a little surprised to find that we could specify a gender, but we declined. We did so partly because I am a superstitious, knock-wood sort and partly because we wanted to trust the process and be parents to the child who came to us. Truth be told, in our hearts I had hoped for a girl and Susan had hoped for a boy. My hope was based on a complex set of feelings. The two closest to the surface of my consciousness were that I grew up in a very female-oriented family and that I had dreams of raising a little girl whom I could support to face society in a quest to be all that she wished to be. When the call came from our lawyer, we received the thrilling news that we were about to become the parents of a newborn African-American baby boy. We were ecstatic. We had already made the decision that we were open to taking on the joys and challenges of raising a child in a transracial family, so gender issues melted away as we prepared to begin life as mothers.

Upon our arrival home with our little Aaron, friends and neighbors began a steady stream of visits. We loved the attention and support we were receiving but were surprised at some of the comments. "He's beautiful!" they exclaimed. "Look at those hands — a future basketball player." Strangers stopped us on the street to comment on our adorable baby and to ask, "Is it a girl or a boy?" They often followed with, "What country is he from?" and "Do you know much about his history?" Aaron was barely two weeks old, and race and gender had already come crashing in — on him and on us. Yet we were determined to call people on these comments and tried to come up with nondefensive responses. This is difficult for many adoptive parents, since people act as if adopted children's personal histories should be public record. It can be difficult for new parents to field some of the questions and respond without embarrassing the asker or pushing them away. For gay and lesbian parents and those in transracial families, these challenges are compounded.

We proceeded to parent Aaron with the strong belief that he could become any kind of boy he wanted to, within certain parameters. As a feminist, a former heterosexual, and a lifelong observer of relationships, I have developed some strongly held beliefs about the emotional status of men in our culture. As a psychotherapist, I have had these beliefs confirmed by sixteen years of working with clients (women and men) who are trying to heal from the effects of being shaped by a patriarchal system. One thing I was determined to ensure, if at all possible, was that my son would have access to his full range of emotions. I hoped he would be able to identify and express his feelings and that he would listen with caring and kindness to other people's expression of their feelings. That was my ax to grind, and I had mucked through the debris of male-female relationships long enough to understand the tragic consequences we all suffer as a result of men not being allowed to develop these skills from childhood.

Aaron was intense from babyhood. He was a baby who wanted to lock his big, black, coffee-bean eyes with ours the whole time he was drinking his bottle. His intensity was a joy and a challenge. On one hand, we were delighted with this people-watching, interactive little guy. On the other, we were becoming increasingly exhausted by his "I need very little sleep" brand of passion. Mornings found Susan and I offering each other everything from financial bribes (this was back when we still had savings), to promises to do each other's chores in exchange for gaining a little more sleep while the other did "play-play."

"You be the big bad wolf, and me be the three little pigs," our toddler would announce at 5:30 A.M. from behind his wall of cardboard bricks.

"You be Bambi, I'll be Faline," said Aaron the three-year-old deer as he peered from between the grasses of his make-believe meadow.

"You be Aladdin, I'll be Jasmine," we heard at age four.

"I'll be Nala, you be Simba," Aaron, at five, directed his baby brother, Elan. (Yes, it's true; when I was forty-six, we adopted a second baby boy, our own little Elan Malcolm.)

A pattern seemed to be emerging. First, and to our great dismay, we seemed to be coparenting with Walt Disney. Second, Aaron was clearly and consistently choosing to play female roles. And our attentive little guy did not miss a beat.

"How come Bambi is down in the forest with his mother and the other animals, having a party, and Prince is up on the mountain

11

looking the other way?" he asked us at age three. "How come Prince tells Bambi, 'Your mother died. You will have to walk alone'? Why can't he walk with Prince?" (Now, I have to take a break here to defend ourselves and say that we are conscientious feminists whose children do not watch television but do watch carefully monitored videos. We have a collection of nonsexist, multicultural books that can rival that of most bookstores. But although we screen and discuss ad nauseam, the mainstream culture is a huge and mighty force.)

"Do you think Belle is braver than Jasmine?" he wondered at age four.

At age five the questions became more complex: "Why does Disney (it's true — he did evoke Walt's name) make all the princesses white?" When we answered that Pocahontas wasn't white, he replied indignantly, "Pocahontas isn't a Disney — she's strong!"

Well, here we are, five and a half years into this program with two little boys presenting their own daily evolving agendas. Aaron has made it perfectly clear to us, in every way he knows how, that it is all well and good to have two moms who believe in giving their kids non–gender-specific toys, but he prefers Barbie to Tonka any day. This was less than crystal clear up to age two and a half, when he still enjoyed playing with the occasional school bus or dinosaur. About age three the ambiguity dissolved. It was "kissing dragons" and Kenya, the doll whose hair could be fashioned with lotion and beads. The fairy tales he chose to act out are those in which the heroine swoons and falls to the floor in a heap. We were astounded. These were certainly not our predispositions, but in a home where individual preference is honored, Aaron was making his known, and his moms were finding ourselves challenged on both internal and external levels.

The internal struggle centers around the work I have to do to assure myself that this child does feel good about himself, even if the self he is defining doesn't fit my projections. "It's sad that he doesn't feel good about who he is as a boy," a kind neighbor shared with me over coffee. I froze inside as I became washed with the fear that this was true. But five years of puzzling over this and learning more about my child reassures me that, in fact, he does feel good about who he is. The sadness is not about Aaron's sense of himself but more about society's unwillingness to let each of us stretch and be who we are.

12

Externally, it is a challenge to protect my son when he goes out into the world and faces potential scorn. For the past few years we have had many discussions with Aaron about what the consequences of his choices might be. He seems to have a good sense of how to protect himself and when and where to appear carrying his Angelina the Ballerina mouse replete with tutu. I grieve deeply that my child has had to learn, so young, to filter himself through our culture's harsh screen. I am simultaneously thankful that he has an inner sense of what safe choices might look like.

What I do about all this is read and process and talk. The talk is with my partner, with my friends, and with Aaron and Elan. As parents, Susan and I look at and examine our children's wishes and how they come up against society's assumptions.

Elan, our 2½-year-old, loves his teddy bears. He hugs them and talks to them and has them "go to meetings" together. He is a child who can walk through a department store and name every ball in the sporting-goods department. Aaron — who notices that his teacher's voice sounds "a little like Snow White's" and asks me whether I think that is good, given that Snow White isn't a very strong person — sees a baseball and says, "Look, a soccer ball." Same moms, same house, same toys, but two very different children.

So here we are with our two little guys, creating a new world together. They are both children who know how they feel. "Me not sad, me angry," Elan told us recently. I marveled that this two-year-old could spontaneously make a distinction that was beyond my ex-husband's scope. And I wondered whether this man too, at age two, had also known the difference. Our children both listen to other people's feelings and respond from their hearts. And, most gratifying, our children are becoming freedom fighters. On a vacation in North Carolina we were driving in the car, listening to a tape, and singing civil rights songs. "Mama," came Aaron's voice from the backseat, "do you think mermaids fight for their rights?"

"Probably," I replied.

Then we all proceeded to list the kinds of things mermaids might have to fight for.

13

Some Queer Straight Talk on Adoption
by Jenifer Levin

We're here, we're queer.

We're parents. Of sons.

We're also human.

We want our children to be healthy and strong. They cannot always be.

We work hard to make their existences pleasant, ideal. We often fail. Yet in between the angels we wish to be and the demons we fear we might become, there *we* are, standing in the mess and clutter of life — we and our sons.

In Kampong Spoe, Cambodia, where my son was probably born, people grow wet rice and dry rice, sell what they can, eat the rest, and occasionally supplement meals of rice with fruit or fish. Farther north where the Mekong meets the Tonle Sap, young Khmer Rouge cadres still materialize from the nighttime jungle to slaughter ethnic Vietnamese fishermen and send their bodies floating downriver, and things are rougher than they are in the south — especially during dry season. Then, the lake recedes. The land is dusty, baked. Children eat lizards, flying cockroaches, fried fire ants. Their bellies bloat. Their hair turns reddish gold in the sun.

In this little country destroyed by American bombs — almost as an afterthought, what our military personnel called a sideshow to the war with Vietnam — people are still very hungry, desperate, poor. Even after the lengthy, costly, unwieldy occupation of the United Nations Transitional Authority in Cambodia (under the aegis of which elections were held and a coalition government put in place).

Poor people everywhere lack access to vital resources. Bad things are always happening to them, things for which — in the absence of service delivery — there is no solution. They're often ill and in trouble. They are traumatized, depressed. In Cambodia, as in other postholocaust places worldwide, the poor especially suffer continual deprivation and loss of one sort or another. They live in an ongoing state of grief. By the time the other shoe drops, they have already mourned; they've been waiting a long time for the sound of its thudding to earth, laces and all. They are past any responsive display. They're exhausted. Westerners often mistake this for impassivity or lack of emotion.

I believe it was in such a state of grief that someone brought yet another child to a Phnom Penh orphanage. He was about two months old. Born with a minor disability (cleft lip and palate) he could not breast-feed. He was dying of starvation. It was January, the middle of the dry season, the weather hot but pleasant.

The Khmer word for January is *Makara.* In Khmer *Makara* means lobster too. Originally, though, it was a Sanskrit term; in the Indian epic the *Mahābhārata,* it refers to a pincerlike battle formation intended to flank and squeeze the enemy. Anyway, Makara is what they named the boy.

Julie and I met him three years later, during our second stay in his country. He sat on my knee in an orphanage office, mute and sad, and after a while began playing with some Tibetan prayer beads I'd strung around my neck. Suddenly a door opened eerily beneath my feet. I fell deep down into a cavern of life feeling, into a reality that had never revealed itself before. I asked him, in Khmer, to be my son.

Later that day he ran to me, shoving other toddlers out of the way, clutching my neck and shoulders with genuine ferocity. He gave his battle cry, a single sound of triumph howling out from between scarred lips: "*Ahn!*" he proclaimed, over and over. "*Ahn! Ahn! Ahn!*" It is the word in his language for *mine.*

"I guess you've been chosen," Julie said softly.

A few days later she left to return to the United States and to a home that needed toddler proofing. I stayed in Phnom Penh to adopt Makara.

Over the next several months there, much befell us. Someday I will tell him everything. About crouching on hospital floors in long lines of crouching parents and their children, waiting for medical attention while he fought to breathe. About our boat ride on the Mekong, eating ginger candy from China, waving at the Muslim Cham — an ethnic fishing people, descendants of the ancient

Southeast Asian kingdom of Champa. About our many trips to temples, our many donations to the Buddhas, our prayers to the gods and demons of all directions and places, our lighting of much incense. About riding in bicycle rickshas, stopping at little streetside cafés in the mud for *Bai saw chia muy bunlai.* About the evening he fell asleep in a bowl of shrimp soup. About the tuberculosis hospital that doubled as a garbage dump, so that all the ambulatory patients walked around holding freshly red-soaked kerchiefs in front of their mouths and noses to ward off the smell of burning trash. About the very old dried bloodstains I began to notice everywhere beneath the grime and dust — on the floors of hotels and of government offices — fruits of twenty-year-old interrogations. About my sipping tea in the posh villa of a very high government official — a former Khmer Rouge commander who had signed the death warrants of thousands before deserting Pol Pot and fleeing to Vietnam — and asking him not to oppose the adoption of my son. About looking at the hands of this man while he held his porcelain cup of tea, noticing that the fingers were small, delicate, very pale and soft; about looking into his eyes once, briefly, and seeing nothing monstrous there, nothing but a human being. About understanding that there is no devil in the world — only we humans, after all, wending our human ways — and if there is any real horror, it is that, just that. This man was cordial. He spoke with me gently. In the end he did not stand in my way.

All these things I vowed to speak of someday, when we had long mother-son talks about difficult things like good, evil, love, life, courage, human differences, adoption. In another language; in another country.

Makara and I eventually left Cambodia. We came home to Julie. We came to the land of freedom and of snow, where people walk dogs instead of eating them. My son is a citizen now. So is Henry Kissinger — who, like my son, was born in another country and who, in collusion with Richard Nixon, was responsible for the secret bombing of Cambodia. Makara became a citizen on George Washington's birthday. I find that fitting, somehow. Note: It is only fitting if you believe in karma. Which I do. Wholeheartedly.

Peace.

Two years and multiple surgeries later, our kid is very tall and strong. His feet are enormous. He has a new mouth, new teeth, and a new face. He is beginning to speak so clearly and well that strangers can now understand him. His English vocabulary is extensive; his syntax still Khmer. He will have a lot more surgery.

Makara's a popular, outgoing kid with many friends. Sometimes, though, children who don't know him yet tease him about his facial scars. I struggle with that — the question of when to intervene, when to let him fend for himself, and what skills to give him in order for him to be able to fight, like the warrior he was born as...and, like a warrior, to know when to save his strength and fight another day. He studied toddler karate last year. This year we will try jujitsu. In between we play with lots of toys, read lots of books. He also has plenty of play dates. We talk about being a person, a man — or a boy — in this world. I teach him what I know. Butch, lesbian things. Or, rather, *human* things. Like: Restraint is commendable. But nonviolence ain't always the answer. Clarity and motivation count. Honest affection is good. These things I believe.

What he teaches me: Life matters. Love matters. What we do, give, and receive now, right now — these things matter. There is nothing else for sure in this world.

You know, there are dykes who think adoption is wrong. Especially foreign adoption. They say we're tearing kids away from their cultures, ripping their mother tongues from their mouths, doing something terrible. These people invariably speak from a position of affluence and privilege. My two cents — some straight talk from this here queer: These folks are spoiled. These folks are just flapping their jaws. They should spend a few months in orphan shoes. In bare-bottomed orphan feet, I mean. Then come back and tell me more theory. Tell it to me and to my son.

As for us — well, how can I truly explain it? All I know is that everything changed when he first sat on my lap, sad-eyed, playing with prayer beads. It changed for him and for me. The world opened up. The world collapsed. Mind shrank, and heart enlarged. We are specks, really, against an awesome background of stars, but mighty specks too, in our way: motes in the eyes of the angry, blinking gods.

Raising Sons With Emotion
by Laura K. Hamilton

I guiltily dream of daughters as my twin sons sleep in the room above me. I ache for some imagined bliss of the union between related women. I crave the unique closeness I know gender provides, and I yearn to nurture a being with whom I can intuitively connect. Yet these sons are so dear, entirely whole and perfect, and I look over my shoulder as the thoughts come to mind.

I do acknowledge the reality of chasms between mother and daughter. I recognize the inherent pitfalls in that bond I long for, the danger and risk in the very relationship that offers a healing force unlike any I seem to be able to manufacture for myself. I long to explore my path and review my journey in the company of a girl child. To wander further myself, while watching her clamber over the path of her own making, appears so comforting from here. To have been in the company of a mother myself at those moments of facing sheer cliffs or jagged crevasses seems magical to me.

In parenting this pair of boys, I feel both cramped and stretched beyond my limits. I worry that my feminism and emotional base are too strong for their fledgling masculine selves. I am proud as well as concerned that they are too close to their feelings. They have emotional reactions to things I sometimes believe they "should" take in stride, though I also know this is normal for them.

I fear the depth of tenderness that one of the boys, at age seven, lavished on his stuffed bunny. Torn between protecting his instinctive parenting and fear of ridicule from the "regular" world, I carefully asked if he was sure he wanted to take it to the park. Watching him push "Bob" on the swings brought tears to my eyes.

Now, at eleven, my son has to handle, unthinkingly, questions from the astonished librarian when he asks for books on knitting and quilting. I want to scream at her sexism or sit her down to explain how similar to Legos it is; how much logic, math, and patterning it involves; as well as how much creative pleasure and sensory satisfaction there is in using yarn and fabric to make something all his own. He is entitled to all this obviously, and yet I too hesitate sometimes when he asks if he should take it along to the beach. Someone will make fun of his choices someday; do I prepare him for that?

Yet I am glad that they cry and choose their friends so carefully. I delight in their empathy and their awareness of the intuitive and unspoken dialogue. I was raised in a gender-biased society, however, and at times I admit that I cringe and compare them to "regular boys" with frogs and jackknives in their pockets, not poems and beads to string. But I love their connection with and need for creativity and conversation.

Where will they find acceptance and companionship? Have I skewed their natural maturation by my passions? Do I really have that much influence?

The love between my sons and me will never disappear. I am more sure of that than of any other truth I have found. And yet increasingly we speak two different languages. We communicate amazingly well considering that fact; love and gesture go a long way, but I can see them drifting into a haze of adolescent maleness, to places I wouldn't choose to visit even if I could. They show the pain and loneliness as they look back at me sometimes. I'm sure my loss and hurt shows too, the silent ache that throbs when I am closest to them.

19

My very feminist aunt once told me that changes in society were up to women like me, who were raising sons to be nonviolent in the face of persistent messages from the patriarchy. I feel overwhelmed by the task. This is more responsibility than I ever bargained for. I need to be sure I am not raising batterers or rapists. Even more, there are moments when I hope I am raising kind and caring male role models who feel secure enough in their sense of self that other, younger, men may someday be shaped by their gentleness and quiet strength.

But what if I am wrong? What if my efforts to break the mold result only in forming two young men who feel out of place in every group, who are isolated and solitary creatures and because of rejection and their resulting anger lash out in crazy and unpredictable ways? Can I live with that? Do mothers of baby girls whirl endlessly like this, banging themselves against the edges of "What if?"

So I dream. If she arrived, I'm aware that she might drive me wild with wishes for Barbie dolls, exasperate me with her long nails and eye shadow and then worry me with unsuitable lovers; but she would be my own kind in a certain immutable way. As I fret the years away over these boys, I dream of a daughter.

Born on Foreign Soil
by Jess Wells

"Looks like a little penis in there," the nurse singsonged as she held the ultrasound wand on my enormous belly. The rest of the amniocentesis procedure, with a fourteen-inch needle punching me in the belly, seemed to take place in slow motion. It could not be possible: I was going to be the mother of a son.

How had this happened? I had paid to have the sperm sex-selected. The sperm had been made to swim for hours, and the fastest swimmers — the "male" sperm — had been poured down the sink. It was an extra expense at a fancy lab I had considered well worth the money, since it would vastly increase my chances of having a girl. I had been planning on a girl. It was essential that I have a girl. In fact, after I had done some initial (what I thought was thorough) investigation of what it meant to have a son, I had dismissed the possibility as something that happened to other lesbians. Science would prevail, and I would be one of the lucky ones to bear a daughter, I had thought.

That day, lying on the table with an ache in my uterus, it was clear that neither science nor my preparation had been sufficient. The intensity and complexity of my reaction to spending the rest of my life raising a boy surprised me.

I was profoundly disappointed. I wept. I sobbed to my friends. I was afraid that I would not be able to go to work in the morning because I could not muster the socially acceptable response "as long as it's healthy," a lie I had been spouting (after much rehearsal) to the almost constant barrage of questions since the early days of the pregnancy. The thought of spending the rest of my life with a boy brought up memories of my family of origin, their reaction to my brother, and their response to my lesbianism. In no small measure it brought up in me a frightening rage at the patriarchy.

Based on what I had seen in my family of origin, I identified the mother-son bond as one filled with loneliness and a lack of reciprocal love. The mother-son story was a tale of resentment on one side and abandonment on the other. My mother told me stories of how my "uncuddly" brother broke her heart, and I've seen in my brother's face the damage done by an angry, controlling mother and a distant, submissive father. The prospect of raising a son proved daunting to my brother as well. Before my brother adopted his second child, he went into a deep depression and asked us to fly to Arizona to go into counseling with him. What had been the family's experience with fathering? the therapist asked, and we unraveled a story of my father being pushed out, harangued, verbally abused, then surrendering to his powerlessness and emotionally abandoning us. Sons and their parents seemed to live on distant shores. When I saw mothers and their sons on the street, this is the relationship I projected. To me, they seemed like strangers to each other. Was I going to be caught in this same lonely scenario?

When I dared voice my preference for raising a girl, I was met time and again with the pat answer, "Oh, it doesn't matter; they're the same." This simply was not defensible to me. Men and women are not the same, and neither are boys and girls. Therefore, it couldn't be true that a relationship with a boy was the same as a relationship with a girl. What did sons and mothers have in common? What could they do together? Weren't they like foreigners without language or customs to share? I am a femme, and I used to love to shop. During the early days of the pregnancy, when I thought I had done so much good work on the concept of sons, I would joke, "I'm sure it would be fine, but what could I do for a son? My sport is shopping!"

21

What surprised me in my reaction to the news was how threatened I felt. The birth suddenly seemed to be a very sexual event, and that horrified me. In my mind's eye my child was a man suddenly close to my genitals, a man breast-feeding at my nipples.

And what about the politics of it all? I worried. Wasn't I about to spawn a member of the oppressing class? Wasn't I being forced to leave a community? I had been a separatist, a punk dyke, a radical feminist. These have been my clans. I thought about all the people who claim that raising a son is "schooling the next generation of men to be sensitive and compassionate, men who know both sides of themselves, men who don't oppress women." Very laudable, I thought with a forlorn feeling. Work for society certainly interests me, but what I found frightening was how little nurturance for myself I saw in return. Sitting in the café after the sonogram, I was panic-stricken. I didn't want to join the group of lesbians spewing rhetoric about helping the "whole world, not just women." I didn't want to say all that crap about "they need us too." Where are men when the issue is breast cancer? When do they start working to stop rape? Where is their help to change the seventy-two cents on the god-damn dollar? I absolutely hate male privilege, patriarchy, and male culture. I didn't want to help fashion men. One of the reasons I had been so attached to having a girl is that I identified the struggle for women as a source of companionship. I imagined that all my work would be manifested in my caring for my daughter, that she and I would fashion a new society for women, fight for access to male privilege. So much of my life and work is dedicated to the better-ment of women. *Am I now alone in that?* I lamented.

I felt as if I were not only about to be incredibly alone but also trapped. The world seemed to be telling me that I could either raise a man or not be a mother at all. *You want this wonderful thing, you want to love this much?* the vicious spirits seemed to be saying, *then you have to do it in the service of men.* It felt like a patriarchal setup at the most basic level — not just laboring for the patriarchy but actually creating its members.

22 The other side of the equation seemed just as dismal. What about my son's isolation? Isn't he doomed to be a foreigner in my life as well? In this era men are getting in touch with the appalling absence of male mentors, the lack of fathering that has scarred them. How could I bring a boy into the world without a father? Not just with a father who would need to be trained in how to be affec-tionate and expressive, but to give him no father at all. To what kind of pain would I be subjecting him? And how would I ever be able to show him his culture? It's not enough to glibly say that male culture is all around us. There are very important aspects that are not broadcast through the dominant media. Would he be a stranger to his culture? I am a single parent. A femme. A lesbian. I don't have very many men in my life, gay or straight. Would I be forced to go looking for the nefarious "good man"? The thought of being forced to cultivate relationships with men did not please me. Not in the least.

After my shock wore off, though, I began to see that infamous "other hand." It is true that, being that I am a lesbian, the things I'm interested in doing are those most easily identified with the male world: science experiments, building things, research, libraries, bookstores, the outdoors, the seashore, and the marshes. I think I would be profoundly disappointed if, at just the age when these explorations could be tremendous, I discovered my daughter to be interested in nothing but makeup, clothing, and talking on the phone. What about glitter dolls and jewelry machines? What about diets at age twelve? These would be difficult. Now that I was considering this son thing, I could see myself sitting in the aisles of a bookstore with my rambunctious boy, scouting through science books or working at the computer while my son built something with wood and nails. *Sexist?* I wondered. I'm not saying I wouldn't strongly encourage my daughter to do these things, but we would be swimming against the mainstream, and that is always riskier. I have talked with friends who have raised both girls and boys. "In some ways," a friend said, "it's refreshing to raise boys. They're into their bodies, and sometimes that's a nice energy to be around. They're not as into their emotions, and so you just don't have the drama that you have with girls. Of course, girls can break your heart too," my friend added sadly, thinking of mutual friends whose daughters had turned to drugs and prostitution.

In fact, what I discovered as I polled every parent I could about their feelings regarding the gender of their child is that nearly every parent feels better equipped to provide for one gender over the other. It's not just lesbians who have a difficult time with the gender of their children. I've listened to straight men who are frightened of diapering their son, then after they grapple with that they are frightened of raising a daughter. I've talked with gay men who want to raise daughters because they can't do the "football thing." I have a cousin who is straight but possessed of a wonderful "boyish charm," as she calls it. She very much wanted a son because she just didn't know what she would do if her daughter got into frills and lace. Her daughter has, and she copes. She plays Barbie, she says, her most hated thing to do in the world.

The butches in my life joke that now *they* will have someone to shop with. As a femme, I am and will always be surrounded by butches. So what's one more? They are stepping forward to provide softball, football, surfing, the love of tools, the ability to fix things, skiing, kayaking, snowshoeing, cummerbunds, and boots. His Auntie Ann will teach him fishing, his Uncle Craig will show him photography and the desert, his Aunt Julie will demonstrate an appreciation for animals of all kinds, his godfather will show him what an

23

emotional man is like, while his grandfather will instruct him in woodworking and a love of the absurd. "And what do you mean, you don't do sports?" my butches challenge. Years ago I was on the San Francisco Women's Boxing Team and was damned good.

Of course this is all very stereotypical and gender-laden, isn't it? Why isn't it good enough that I introduce him to piano, dancing, cooking, and embroidery? Isn't it homophobia hiding in the feeling that those are fine if taught as secondary, balancing interests — the spice in the soup but not the soup itself?

One of the first thoughts to go through my head after the nurse mouthed her pronouncement was to worry about my family's reaction. Based on her description of my brother's babyhood, I predicted that my mother would all but ignore my son and love him less than his female cousin. Wouldn't he be an outsider to her? I couldn't bear that. Worst of all, though, I was convinced that my father would hover on the outskirts of my life, suspiciously watching for any sign of feminization, indications that I was "turning my son into a faggot." I would be under constant scrutiny, my parenting skills questioned at every turn, I surmised. What does that say about my family's homophobia? it finally occurred to me. What does that say about my concept of gayness and my own internalized homophobia that I would be worried that producing a gay son would be "failing" in some way?

Coming to terms with my child's gender, I realized that I thought of boys as being much more independent than girls and therefore more suited for my life. *It would be easier to leave the child alone in the playpen and write if that child were a boy,* I (foolishly!) thought at the time. Maybe the universe was sending me an independent child because I am a writer who requires a lot of time alone, a woman who needs a lot of "space" in relationships. My writing requires so much from me that I have very little ability to have a traditional relationship. I thought a son might fare better. My therapist says otherwise: Boys need as much attention, but society doesn't give it to them. The expectation of their independence, in fact, leaves them unnurtured and thereby dramatically nonindependent.

That made me admit that I have considered men and boys second-class citizens in my world, people who are simply not as important. In reaction to the news from the nurse, I was not as careful about my prenatal vitamins or caffeine for a week or so. Part of that

24

was suppressed anger, and part of it was because I just didn't identify the child as being as fragile or needing as much. Did I actually believe that boys are inherently healthier or more self-reliant?

Their self-reliance also seemed true for their futures, I thought. I imagined that as a middle-class white boy, my kid would need to be well-trained, with a bit of discipline and in possession of good values. Then the world would lay its riches at his feet. Opportunity would be set in front of him, and I would not have to worry quite as much about giving him access to privilege. This is simply true. Of course, I understand that it's still very hard work to equip boys to succeed; there are so many possible learning disabilities and emotional land mines, but male access to privilege is a fact in this world.

Looking back on all this nearly a year later, I am astounded how fervently I believed it all, how I felt it to the end of my fingers, and then how completely inconsequential it all became. My son is here. I am so in love with him and so bound to him that I would do anything to make his life joyous, healthy, and safe.

When he was first born, I was struck not by how male he was but by how nonhuman he seemed. With the stub of his umbilical cord, his lack of head control, and his transparent, wrinkly skin, he seemed very primal, very animalistic. His testicles were just some odd body part that had no relation to anything in the rest of the world. He was healthy. He continued to breathe through the night. He nursed, and there was an abundance of milk when he wanted it. That was all that mattered. My lover, my friends, and I spent the first few weeks of his life calling him "she," calling him "he," and confusing the gender of the dogs. None of it seemed to make any difference.

Other people were not so laissez-faire, however. Before they could say anything about his full head of hair or his huge blue eyes, they had to know whether he was a girl or a boy. During the first few weeks, the only time I thought of him as a boy was when elderly people on the street called him a "lady-killer." One older woman went on about how he was "ready to rule the world." Then I thought about some of the clothing I had received at his baby shower — sports outfits and little sailor suits. I now have very strict rules: no Disney advertisements, as little polyester as possible, no military images, no sporting visuals. As you can imagine, this makes shopping diffi-

25

cult, as it did for my sister-in-law when she refused to buy her daughter anything in pink. I have to admit that I am not radical enough to put him in a dress. (Is radicalism what is required for this?) He does have a hot pink sheet on his bed and a hot pink rhino, which caused quite a stir at my baby shower at the office. I have also been known to rip the lace collar off an outfit from the secondhand store and consider it a terrific piece of clothing for him.

Thankfully, in the months since my son's birth, several books have hit the stands debunking some of the particularly damaging mythology around parenting sons. I've come to understand that part of the perceived loneliness in the mother-son relationship has been fabricated by the patriarchy that says only men can make men. A son must break away from his mother or he will be a "sissy," a "mama's boy." Inherent in the process of raising a son, then, the patriarchy says, is the eventuality of being rejected by the child you have held so dear. A son's your son till he takes a wife, but a daughter's your daughter for the rest of her life, the proverb goes. Now that I would lay down my life for my son, I refuse to allow that loss to happen. I am beginning to see that a strong, healthy relationship between a son and his mother can exist and can last. I pray for it.

26   My family of origin has risen to the challenge. My son's grandfather, skeptical over my having a child without a father, is now a boasting, proud grandpa. His grandmother adores him. "That was the '50s, dear," she says of my brother. "Now you have a chance for a new type of relationship."

What I had not factored in in all my rageful doubt about raising a son was how much love you could feel toward your child. Parents try to describe it — it's part of the traditional verbiage that goes with families — but it has been astounding to me how deep, how desperately intense, and how completely unconditional the love is. When I was investigating day care, a woman described being a new mother as "an amazing romance," and that's just what it feels like. I can't talk of anything other than what he does and what he looked like while doing it. I am so in love that I am barely fit company.

Despite all my early fears of loneliness, I feel an almost indescribable companionship with my child. We are a team. I take delight in everything he learns. We shop for groceries together, and he rides in the sling, the top of his head just below my chin so I can lean down and kiss his hair, point out apples and odd jars with bright labels. I can see us as companions for years, me teaching him to cook, him learning to run the washing machine, us doing collage and studying the encyclopedia, me learning the rules of softball and video games. Incredibly, after all that anxiety, there is no feeling of his being the "other." He is not an outsider. He is not foreign. He is my child, my family, inextricably bound to me and me to him. Before I was pregnant I pushed a stroller down the street with my goddaughter's child in it and felt very out of place, an urban, black-leather-jacket lesbian with some weird suburban contraption in my hands. Now that the stroller holds my son, I feel like half of a team, with the other half temporarily physically challenged. I would push him in a box down the street on my knees, I tell my friends, if that's what it required for us to get from one spot to the other.

There seem to be no perceptions of motherhood that you formulate before becoming a mother that have anything to do with it at all, I surmised. The breast-feeding that I was so loath to share with a male child is now the most physically satisfying experience of my life, one that I consider a tremendous honor and privilege, especially since I am a relatively small-breasted woman and it was such a joy to see my breasts working up to par. Nursing my child is so important to me at this point that I am actually glad he doesn't sleep through the night: holding him to me at 3 A.M. is one of the best parts of my day. The breast-feeding has, quite frankly, changed me for the better because it releases prolactin, a very powerful hormone. Science discovered its power when researchers gave it to fighting cocks and they turned into little brooding hens who started making nests. That's how I feel, like a fighting cock who has suddenly been given a chance to nest. Ten years ago my idea of a good time was hanging on the sidelines of the girlbar in striped hair. Now I love to stand in my kitchen by candlelight and spoon homemade baby food into jars. Of course, not all of it is hormonal. I have spent a lot of time calming my life down, removing drama, quieting anger, getting more spiritual. Maybe the universe was giving me this opportunity because if there's one person in the world who would benefit from the task of training a child to be gentle, it might be me, I mused. I have worked on losing a fierce temper and a sharp tongue. Learning to be tender would be something we could do together. It is unacceptable to me to raise my child around self-hatred, so I make a conscious effort to be kinder to myself. My goal as a mother is to instill in my child a sense of joy, and it has meant that, as a member of the team, I work on my own sense of joy. My love for

27

my son has also given me the courage to finally go for the life I have always wanted, and I gave up a corporate job to make my living as a freelance writer in part so that I could spend more time with him.

It is true that my son is a boy and so of a different culture, but somehow that does not seem insurmountable anymore. All of this hoopla over gender and its instruction! Isn't gender rigidity at the root of sexism? Of homophobia? It's only the right wing that says a family requires codified male and female roles. Right-wing philosophy says there are two camps in the world, based on gender identity. It is the foundation of their lifestyle. The limiting concepts of gender are taught at a frighteningly early age. My son will learn love, respect, a work ethic, a sense of justice, and as much mental health as I can possibly model. For me to worry about being able to teach him gender-identified reality is to fall into their trap. Love is all it takes to build a family, says the slogan of the gay and lesbian family. Isn't it one of the most important lessons to teach a child that self-definition is a wonderful exploration that can take them anywhere up and down the spectrum of reality? Not just gender reality but that they exist along the spectrum of race and class reality, that their dreams and aspirations and talents can take them into different nooks and crannies of the broad band of life's possibilities? We make ourselves of what we are given, what we create, and what we believe. In that sense it is not a demarcation of body parts that could separate us — a split in philosophies could be as damaging. If I had a daughter who became a right-to-lifer, I would feel a chasm between us; if I had a son who nurtured the environment and his children, I would feel a philosophical bond.

It's not just lesbians grappling with these issues. Throughout my pregnancy there had been a woman at the office who was my companion. She is heterosexual but in poor health and so has had to inseminate, take tests, and do drugs — in a much more elaborate process than even I. Whenever I started feeling sorry for myself that I had to inseminate or that the world considered it an odd way to have a child, I would remember that she was plagued with this process as well. Now that she has decided to adopt, I see that she is again going through something very similar to my concern over sharing a sense of community with my child. Both of us wanted a specific thing: She wanted a healthy biological child; I wanted a healthy biological girl. She is white and so through adoption will most likely have to deal with cross-culturalism. I have a son and so will have to deal with cross-culturalism as well. So many of us — like my son — are born on what is a type of foreign soil: As a lesbian, I was born and raised in a family of heterosexuals. My niece and nephew, adopted from Korea, were born into families that couldn't raise them and are now being raised by a family that isn't of their race. Girls are most often conceived in families with men, and in my case a son is being raised in a culture of women. I have a friend who was eight months pregnant and wrote across the front of her bulging workout shirt, FAG-IDENTIFIED PREGNANT LESBIAN. Most of her friends are gay men. She gave birth to a girl.

Just as foreign a territory, so many of us are trying to be good parents after being born of and raised by people for whom nurturance, boundaries, and unconditional love are foreign concepts. How do we provide this love to our children? How have we learned to speak this foreign language to ourselves?

For that matter, even within the same family, each of us incorporates experiences that are like arriving from a foreign country. Within our family of origin, each of us has different memories of the same events, and we choose different paths in life. This foreignness is inherent in life: I am a mother for the first time and so step lightly in new territory. I bring my child of whatever gender into my life as a foreign visitor, and my child brings me into his world as his guest. He is from a different generation, a different time. He is being raised in a different location than I was. The world is a different place for him.

In fact, I have begun to see this issue as one of boundaries: Each of us is foreign to one another because each of us is an autonomous unit. The entire reason I decided to take the chance of conceiving a boy by getting pregnant rather than adopting is that a magical woman from the Compendium bookstore in London said it was easier to allow her child to be his own person *because* he is a boy. She is not tempted to make him a better rendition of herself or to fashion a little one who would avoid all her mistakes. This autonomy with a son appealed to me greatly, since boundary issues have been and still are an issue for me. With the concept of boundaries in mind, I realized that this kid would be a kid, my kid, not my peer. He will never have power over me like a man. He will never be my oppressor because I will always have more power than he. I am his mother. Always. My son cannot take me away from the struggle for women's rights, nor can he force me to take an interest in anything

29

that I don't deem interesting. He cannot be my oppressor because he is my child, and he cannot be a second chance to relive my life because he has his own life. He and I will explore each other's cultures, sharing in what we can and respecting what we can't. He is a magical member of his own culture, and through our love he takes me into his culture, as I bring him into mine. Both of us, respecting each other's sovereignty, can rejoice in our foreignness and celebrate our diversity.

Man Child: A Black Lesbian Feminist's Response (An excerpt)
by Audre Lorde

I have two children: a 15½-year-old daughter, Beth, and a fourteen-year-old son, Jonathan. This is the way it was/is with me and Jonathan, and I leave the theory to another time and person. This is one woman's telling.

I have no golden message about the raising of sons for other lesbian mothers, no secret to transpose your questions into certain light. I have my own ways of rewording those same questions, hoping we will all come to speak those questions and pieces of our lives we need to share. We are women making contact within ourselves and with each other across the restrictions of a printed page, bent upon the use of our own and one another's knowledges.

The truest direction comes from inside. I give the most strength to my children by being willing to look within myself and by being honest with them about what I find there, without expecting a response beyond their years. In this way they begin to learn to look beyond their own fears.

All our children are outriders for a queendom not yet assured.

My adolescent son's growing sexuality is a conscious dynamic between Jonathan and me. It would be presumptuous of me to discuss Jonathan's sexuality here, except to state my belief that whomever he chooses to explore this area with, his choices will be nonoppressive, joyful, and deeply felt from within, places of growth.

One of the difficulties in writing this piece has been temporal; this is the summer when Jonathan is becoming a man, physically. And our sons must become men — such men as we hope our daughters, born and unborn, will be pleased to live among. Our sons will not grow into women. Their way is more difficult than that of our daughters, for they must move away from us, without us. Hopefully, our sons have what they have learned from us and a howness to forge it into their own image.

Our daughters have us, for measure or rebellion or outline or dream; but the sons of lesbians have to make their own definitions of self as men. This is both power and vulnerability. The sons of lesbians have the advantage of our blueprints for survival, but they must take what we know and transpose it into their own maleness. May the goddess be kind to my son, Jonathan.

Recently I have met young black men about whom I am pleased to say that their future and their visions, as well as their concerns within the present, intersect more closely with Jonathan's than do my own. I have shared vision with these men as well as temporal strategies for our survivals, and I appreciate the spaces in which we could sit down together. Some of these men I met at the First Annual Conference of Third World Lesbians and Gays, held in Washington, D.C., in October 1979. I have met others in different places and do not know how they identify themselves sexually. Some of these men are raising families alone. Some have adopted sons. They are Black men who dream and who act and who own their feelings, questioning. It is heartening to know our sons do not step out alone.

When Jonathan makes me angriest, I always say he is bringing out the testosterone in me. What I mean is that he is representing some piece of myself as a woman that I am reluctant to acknowledge or explore. For instance, what does "acting like a man" mean? For me, what I reject? For Jonathan, what he is trying to redefine?

32

Raising black children — female and male — in the mouth of a racist, sexist, suicidal dragon is perilous and chancy. If they cannot love and resist at the same time, they will probably not survive. And in order to survive they must let go. This is what mothers teach — love, survival — that is, self-definition and letting go. For each of these, the ability to feel strongly and to recognize those feelings is central: how to feel love, how to neither discount fear nor be overwhelmed by it, how to enjoy feeling deeply.

I wish to raise a black man who will neither be destroyed by nor settle for those corruptions called *power* by the white fathers who mean his destruction as surely as they mean mine. I wish to raise a black man who will recognize that the legitimate objects of his hostility are not women but the particulars of a structure that programs him to fear and despise women as well as his own black self.

For me, this task begins with teaching my son that I do not exist to do his feeling for him.

Men who are afraid to feel must keep women around to do their feeling for them while dismissing us for the same supposedly "inferior" capacity to feel deeply. But in this way also, men deny themselves their own essential humanity, becoming trapped in dependency and fear.

As a black woman committed to a livable future and as a mother loving and raising a boy who will become a man, I must examine all my possibilities of being within such a destructive system.

Jonathan was three and a half when Frances, my lover, and I met; he was seven when we all began to live together permanently. From the start Frances's and my insistence that there be no secrets in our household about the fact that we were lesbians has been the source of problems and strengths for both children. In the beginning this insistence grew out of the knowledge, on both our parts, that whatever was hidden out of fear could always be used either against the children or ourselves — one imperfect but useful argument for honesty. The knowledge of fear can help make us free.

For survival, black children in America must be raised to be warriors. For survival, they must also be raised to recognize the enemy's many faces. Black children of lesbian couples have an advantage because they learn very early that oppression comes in many different forms, none of which have anything to do with their own worth.

To help give me perspective, I remember that for years, in the name-calling at school, boys shouted at Jonathan not "Your mother's a lesbian" but rather "Your mother's a nigger."

When Jonathan was eight years old and in the third grade, we moved, and he went to a new school where his life was hellish as a new boy on the block. He did not like to play rough games. He did not like to fight. He did not like to stone dogs. And all this marked him early on as an easy target.

When he came in crying one afternoon, I heard from Beth how the corner bullies were making Jonathan wipe their shoes on the way home whenever Beth wasn't there to fight them off. And when I heard that the ringleader was a little boy in Jonathan's class his own size, an interesting and very disturbing thing happened to me.

My fury at my own long-ago impotence and my present pain at his suffering made me start to forget all that I knew about violence and fear, and, blaming the victim, I started to hiss at the weeping child. "The next time you come in here crying..." and I suddenly caught myself in horror.

This is the way we allow the destruction of our sons to begin — in the name of protection and to ease our own pain. My son get beaten up? I was about to demand that he buy that first lesson in the corruption of power, that might makes right. I could hear myself beginning to perpetuate the age-old distortions about what strength and bravery really are.

And, no, Jonathan didn't have to fight if he didn't want to, but somehow he did have to feel better about not fighting. An old horror rolled over me of being the fat kid who ran away, terrified of getting her glasses broken.

About that time a very wise woman said to me, "Have you ever told Jonathan that once you used to be afraid too?"

The idea seemed far-out to me at the time, but the next time he came in crying and sweaty from having run away again, I could see that he felt shamed at having failed me or some image he and I had created in his head of mother/woman. This image of woman being able to handle it all was bolstered by the fact that he lived in a household with three strong women, his lesbian parents and his forthright older sister. At home, for Jonathan, power was clearly female.

And because our society teaches us to think in an either/or mode — kill or be killed, dominate or be dominated — this meant that he must either surpass or be lacking. I could see the implications of this line of thought. Consider the two Western classic myths/models of mother-son relationships: Jocasta/Oedipus, the son who fucks his mother, and Clytemnestra/Orestes, the son who kills his mother.

It all felt connected to me.

I sat down on the hallway steps and took Jonathan on my lap and wiped his tears. "Did I ever tell you about how I used to be afraid when I was your age?"

I will never forget the look on that little boy's face as I told him the tale of my glasses and my after-school fights. It was a look of relief and total disbelief all rolled into one.

It is as hard for our children to believe that we are not omnipotent as it is for us to know it as parents. But that knowledge is necessary as the first step in the reassessment of power as something other than might, age, privilege, or the lack of fear. It is an important step for a boy, whose societal destruction begins when he is forced to believe that he can be strong only if he doesn't feel or if he wins.

I thought about all this one year later when Beth and Jonathan, ten and nine, were asked by an interviewer how they thought they had been affected by being children of a feminist.

Jonathan said that he didn't think there was too much in feminism for boys, although it certainly was good to be able to cry if he

34

felt like it and not to have to play football if he didn't want to. I think of this sometimes now when I see him practicing for his brown belt in tae kwon do.

The strongest lesson I can teach my son is the same lesson I teach my daughter: how to be who he wishes to be for himself. And the best way I can do this is to be who I am and hope that he will learn from this not how to be me, which is not possible, but how to be himself. And this means how to move to that voice from within himself rather than to those raucous, persuasive, or threatening voices from outside, pressuring him to be what the world wants him to be.

And that is hard enough.

Jonathan is learning to find within himself some of the different faces of courage and strength, whatever he chooses to call them. Two years ago, when Jonathan was twelve and in the seventh grade, one of his friends at school who had been to the house persisted in calling Frances "the maid." When Jonathan corrected him, the boy then referred to her as "the cleaning woman." Finally Jonathan said, simply, "Frances is not the cleaning woman. She's my mother's lover." Interestingly enough, it is the teachers at this school who still have not recovered from his openness.

Frances and I were considering attending a lesbian-feminist conference this summer when we were notified that no boys over ten were allowed. This presented logistic as well as philosophical problems for us, and we sent the following letter:

> Sisters:
>
> Ten years as an interracial lesbian couple has taught us both the dangers of an oversimplified approach to the nature and solutions of any oppression as well as the danger inherent in an incomplete vision.
>
> Our thirteen-year-old son represents as much hope for our future world as does our fifteen-year old daughter, and we are not willing to abandon him to the killing streets of New York City while we journey west to help form a lesbian-feminist vision of the future world in which we can all survive and flourish. I hope we can continue this dialogue in the near future, since I feel it is important to our vision and our survival.

The question of separatism is by no means simple. I am thankful that one of my children is male, since that helps to keep me honest. Every line I write shrieks there are no easy solutions.

I grew up in largely female environments, and I know how crucial that has been to my own development. I feel the want and need often for the society of women exclusively. I recognize that our own spaces are essential for developing and recharging.

As a black woman, I find it necessary to withdraw into all-black groups at times for exactly the same reasons — differences in stages of development and differences in levels of interaction. Frequently, when speaking with men and white women, I am reminded of how difficult and time-consuming it is to have to reinvent the pencil every time you want to send a message.

But this does not mean that my responsibility for my son's education stops at age ten any more than it does for my daughter's. However, for each of them, that responsibility does grow less and less as they become more woman and man.

Both Beth and Jonathan need to know what they can share and what they cannot, how they are joined and how they are not. And Frances and I, as grown women and lesbians coming more and more into our power, need to relearn the experience that difference does not have to be threatening.

When I envision the future, I think of the world I crave for my daughters and my sons. It is thinking for survival of the species — thinking for life.

Most likely there will always be women who move with women, women who live with men, men who choose men. I work for a time when women with women, women with men, and men with men all share the work of a world that does not barter bread or self for obedience, beauty, or love. And in that world we will raise our children free to choose how best to fulfill themselves. For we are jointly responsible for the care and raising of the young, since that they be raised is a function, ultimately, of the species.

Within that tripartite pattern of relating and existence, the raising of the young will be the joint responsibility of all adults who choose to be associated with children. Obviously, the children raised within each of these three relationships will be different, lending a special savor to that eternal inquiry into how best can we live our lives.

Jonathan has had the advantage of growing up within a nonsexist relationship, one in which this society's pseudonatural assumptions of ruler and ruled are being challenged. And this is not only because Frances and I are lesbians, for unfortunately there are some lesbians who are still locked in patriarchal patterns of unequal power relationships.

These assumptions of power relationships are being questioned because Frances and I, often painfully and with varying degrees of success, attempt to evaluate and measure over and over again our feelings concerning power, our own and others'. And we explore with care those areas concerning how it is used and expressed between us and between us and the children, openly and otherwise. A good part of our biweekly family meetings is devoted to this exploration.

As parents, Frances and I have given Jonathan our love, our openness, and our dreams to help form his visions. Most important, as the son of lesbians, he has had an invaluable model — not only of a relationship but of relating.

In talking over this paper with Jonathan and asking his permission to share some pieces of his life, I asked him what he felt were the strongest negative and the strongest positive aspects for him in having grown up with lesbian parents.

He said the strongest benefit he felt he had gained was that he knew that he did not have a lot of the hang-ups that some other boys did about men and women.

And the most negative aspect he felt, Jonathan said, was the ridicule he got from some kids with straight parents.

"You mean from your peers?" I said.

"Oh, no," he answered promptly. "My peers know better. I mean other kids."

37

Every Mother's Son
by Robin Morgan

Few subjects so provoke anxiety among feminists as the four-letter word sons.

We've thought and talked about, written and read about, mothers and daughters — as well we should, since whether or not we're mothers, all women are daughters. But with a few notable exceptions, we've averted our eyes from The Other Touchy Subject. Yet that subject goes to the heart of practicing what we claim to believe, that "the personal is political." It goes to the crux of power and of patriarchy — even though it also grazes the living nerves of love.

So we've wrung our hands and hearts about what to do and how to do it. We've compared notes and traded tips in hundreds of quiet conversations. I remember one such talk with a grassroots activists in a Midwest urban slum neighborhood, a courageous African-American woman who confronted drug pushers daily without flinching but confessed that her greatest fear was that by laying down strict rules for her young son in trying to protect him, she would someday taste his bitter accusations that she'd robbed him of his "manhood." I remember another such conversation with a European woman of inherited wealth who had turned her largesse into philanthropy for women's groups but who worried that despite her careful teaching and example, her sons might yet become playboys once they came into their trust funds. And I will never forget the exchange with an advocate for battered women, herself a battery survivor in her late fifties, who wept that years earlier she had been unable to get her son "away from him in time" — and then added, as if in answer to my unasked question, "Every rapist is some mother's son."

Meanwhile, we've watched some women indulge their sons in ways they never would their daughters. We've watched women who sermonize one thing but practice another, who allow (or are unable to stop) husbands whose behavior they know is wrong serve as the model for their sons. We've watched feminists park their politics at the door of the nursery — for instance, inveighing against cultures that practice genital mutilation but then arranging for the baby boy's circumcision. We've watched women refuse to "inflict" the insights of feminism on their sons out of a too-common homophobic ignorance and terror that a male who is gentle will turn out "effeminate" or gay (so what if he did?). We've also watched women boast about their ideal "feminist" sons, creating a future Feminist Prince problem (you know, the guy who gobbles up the latest copy of Ms. *before his wife has time to glance at it and who then maddeningly pontificates about what tactics "you women ought to be using"). And, yes, we've even watched some women crush their sons' spirits in the name of militant politics, strangling themselves and their children in "correct lines."*

This subject was one I'd touched on only lightly over the years, and then mostly in my poetry — the space of intimate and unavoidable truths.

But in late summer of 1993, I succumbed to requests to write an essay for Ms. *on the subject. Once I plunged into it, the essay grew far beyond the space limitations of the magazine and needed to be cut back and simplified. The piece did run, in the short version. The following essay, which is more than twice as long as that article, appears here for the first time.*

You have just spent, say, eighteen hours nonstop doing intensely hard physical work. You have pushed, twisted, squatted, thrashed, hunched, strained, panted, groaned, grunted, gasped, cried, yelled. Your throat is raw, your skin clammy with sweat. Your muscles feel pummeled, your bones feel splintered, and you are more exhausted than you can ever remember being.

Then an utterly vulnerable human wail punctures the air — and your heart — and a voice both nearby and infinitely far away cries, "It's a boy!"

Depending on the culture you live in, your life may now be worth something. Because you are the mother of a son, you will not be shamed, possibly beaten, put aside, or divorced; your husband might not take a second wife; you run less of a chance of multiple pregnancies; you have earned security and might not starve in your old age; you have produced a man-child, a worker for the land, a soldier for the tribe or nation, wealth for the clan, honor for the father, and a future for his family's name. You can exhale relief; you now have (vicarious) power and (reflected) glory. The price for retaining them will be sacrifice and silence.

Depending on the culture you live in, your life is now cast in a stereotype: you are a possessive "Jewish mother" or a castrating "black matriarch"; you are domineering and devouring, manipulative and self-martyring; you are Kali the emasculating Death Mother; you are a seductive Jocasta to an inevitable Oedipus; you provoke both lust and guilt. For centuries misogynistic men worldwide have projected their desires, fears, and failings onto you and have vilified your every act into a cliché; you have been pilloried by Freud, archetyped by Jung, and demonized by Philip Roth. Beyond his infancy you and your son must perforce become alienated, and beyond his puberty become enemies; he must renounce you and embrace the fathers who come to claim him in a thousand rituals. If you do not become enemies, he will be destroyed or you will or both of you will. If you do remain close, you are sick, warped cartoons — Violet and Sebastian in Tennessee Williams's *Suddenly, Last Summer* or even the murderous and murdered mother of Anthony Perkins's character Norman Bates in Hitchcock's *Psycho*. In any event, whatever goes right will be despite your efforts; whatever goes wrong will be your fault.

And, whoever and wherever you are, if you happen to be a feminist, the words "It's a boy" preface one of the greatest challenges you'll ever face.

Blake Morgan, born in 1969 ten days before humans first walked on the moon, is now twenty-four years old. He is an artist I respect, a companion I enjoy, a friend I cherish. He has a sense of humor and a sense of responsibility, a damned good combination. He is a fair, sensible, sensitive, well-balanced person (which permits me to wallow in satisfying retroactive gloat at all those people who were positive that a feminist's son would grow up to be a twitching neurotic). What's more, he makes a great garlic-tomato sauce for his perfectly timed pasta. He is the only man I truly love.

We've been through a quarter century fraught with ambivalence, irony, painful consciousness, difficult choices, hilarity, hard work, delight, fear, pride, love, and joy. I can trace it most honestly in my own poems because they reveal that I knew what I didn't know I knew until I knew it.

In "Monster," written in 1971: "The baby is asleep a room away. White. Male. American. Potentially the most powerful, deadly creature / of the species./His hair, oh pain, curls into fragrant tendrils damp / with the sweat of his summery sleep. Not yet, and on my life / if I can help it never will be 'quite a man.' " And toward the end of the poem, raging at the patriarchy: "Someday you'll take away my baby, / one way or the other."

Yet by 1974, in "The Network of the Imaginary Mother": "I have grieved before my time,...at how you will become / a grown male child, tempted by false gods. / ...But...what I know now is nothing / can abduct you fully from the land where you were born. / ...I say: / you shall be a child of the mother / as of old, and your face will not be turned from me."

Then, in 1988, in "Arbitrary Bread": "My son, grown now, sits making / his music, pressing all the right keys, / his darkening hair tarnished by late summer light. / He is the last man / I will forgive."

Parenting — especially, given the realities, mothering — a child of either sex is a major, exacting job. Society claims hypocritically to revere it, but is supportive very rarely, and then only when the mother is not, for example, a lesbian or employed outside the home or trying to survive on welfare. Meanwhile, we wrestle with internal contradictions: We want our children to be themselves, not extensions of ourselves — and we want them to be the most fulfilled selves they can be. We want them to make their own decisions, to have, to use, and even to expand the definitions of freedom. Yet we also desperately want them to reject the patriarchal status quo. We want to influence them, to mold them toward humane values, but we also want to offer them a wide array of choices and alternatives.

The challenges faced by a feminist rearing a daughter are considerable — so I've noticed, and so friends tell me. But my own experience is as the mother of a son, and I can testify that this relationship is a minefield of complexity for which there are no maps. At least with a daughter (so I've imagined) you can unambivalently tell her, "Go for it! Don't let anyone stop you. Dare to break all the rules, or rewrite them!" With a son you must somehow erode the allure of male entitlement, which means communicating a delicate double message: "Try to fulfill yourself to the utmost as a human being — but try to divest yourself of the male power that routinely accrues to you. Be all you can be as a person — but don't forget that your automatic male privileges are bought at the cost of their denial to female people." If, as in my case, the son is European-American, you also try to communicate a comparable double message about being white in a racist culture.

41

And all this takes place under a barrage of relentless propaganda that undermines your every attempt and reinforces patriarchal images until Schwarzkopf/Schwarzenegger "manhood" values are so pervasive as to seem normal.

It's quite a tightrope you walk as the feminist mother of a son. And there's no safety net, in the women's movement or out of it.

Nor is there, as we know by now, any One Perfect Way. Ultimately, like any woman, I can speak only from my own experience. Which means that some personal context — part of which is specific to my life — is relevant.

I grew up in a house of women, mother and aunts, no men. I have no way of fully estimating the importance of this fact in its impact on how I raised my son (because to me, my childhood, unusual as it might have seemed, felt normal), but I suspect it is not irrelevant. I married the first person I went to bed with — Kenneth Pitchford, a poet and writer. Blake was a wanted — and an only — child (we didn't care about the gender). Both his parents have been fortunate in being able to earn our livelihoods by doing work we chose and love: writing books, augmented by freelance editing. The frequent financial insecurity was a trade-off for the luxury of having time — to do one's own work and to be with Blake. Not everybody has access to such choices. Here the familiar issue of men and child care (*not* just "helping her with the kids") is again important; I wasn't a single mother. Neither our finances nor our principles permitted hired help, so I was again lucky in that Kenneth really parented — and didn't regard fathering as something you do for an hour on Sundays in the backyard with a basketball. We each pulled our own weight; sometimes when I was on the road organizing during the 1970s or in jail or on a writing deadline, Ken did more than his half. And since any child learns more from what is *perceived* than from what is *preached,* it was in retrospect as crucial that Blake grew up watching a man do his share of cooking, cleaning, and other "life maintenance" tasks as a matter of course as it was that he grew up seeing strong women act in nontraditional ways.

Goddess knows, we were nontraditional — with a vengeance. It was that best and worst of times, the 1970s, and though Ken and I resisted communal living or going underground, as many of our friends were doing, we were intense activists. Blake was breast-fed by me or bottle-fed by Ken through endless meetings, was carried in his Snugli to many a picket line and march, and was blessed by

42

the affection of various colleagues of ours, both female and male — a sort of "extended family." We consciously wanted to bring him up in a "revolutionary" way — although with hindsight I think our definition of *revolution* was simplistic, to say the least.

Still, I'm glad that we started early, that when I was pregnant we deliberately chose a genderless name for this being whose sex we didn't yet know, and that we spent hours tie-dying hippie baby clothes in bright purples and reds so as to avoid the omnipresent pink or blue pastels. Every detail *mattered* to us, passionately. And while I might now giggle or even wince at some of the baby pictures (was it really necessary to sew the fisted female symbol on his blanket and teach him the Black Panther salute, for God's sake?), I can understand, laugh at, and forgive most of our excesses; more important, Blake can too. It was a frightening time. Vietnam bled across the TV screen every night, and friends who shared our beliefs and strategies were being sent to prison. We lay awake at night obsessing over whom to name as guardian for Blake in case something should happen to us; the guardian kept changing as feminism gradually transformed our politics.

While there was support from certain friends, there was none from the so-called new left and little from the burgeoning women's movement. A Weatherwoman snarled that I was a bourgeois reactionary to have given birth to a "pig child" (white baby); meanwhile, some radical feminists were experimenting with total separatism and announced that any male — even one whose entire body was twenty-two inches long — was unwelcome at their meetings. (This position grew over the years into an ongoing controversy at some of the major women's music festivals.) I got targeted for being "a living contradiction" — a radical who lived with a man and had compounded the sin by mothering a son.

Meanwhile, we made it up as we went along, with many mistakes but even more love. Blake — whose permission and counsel I sought before deciding to write this essay, since it involved him — remembers some things I'd forgotten. Between us, we've pieced together some of the high (and low) points:

We never lied to him about ourselves, the world, sexuality, the cost of being artists or being political — about anything. This was sometimes very hard, and years later when the marriage ended, it was hardest of all. Some friends worried that a child couldn't handle complicated truths, but if you think back to your own childhood, it was the complicated *lies* that left scars. Blake thinks, and I agree, that this was one of the best and bravest things we did.

We only ever promised what we knew we could actually deliver; this sometimes provoked crankiness, but the end result was genuine trust.

We called each other by our own names to him — never "go to Daddy" or "See what Mommy thinks" — so we kept our identities not as roles but as real, fallible people with feet of clay. It helped empower Blake, and it made the transition easier on all of us as he came to maturity. (When he was about three, Blake decided to experiment with calling us mama and daddy because he heard other kids call their parents that. We said it was up to him, that we'd answer no matter what. After about a week he shrugged and reverted to using our names.)

His earliest bedtime stories were about strong female characters and gentle male characters; we made them up ourselves because there were almost no antisexist children's books then available. Some of our stories were adventures drawn from history: how the witches were really midwives and healers, how the Pankhursts heaved bricks through windows and went to prison for women's suffrage, how Harriet Tubman smuggled slaves north on the Underground Railway. I know some people thought we were "programming" him. But we were trying to throw as much counterweight as possible *against* patriarchal programming, a family-style affirmative action.

Because both his parents were writers who also loved the other arts, Blake grew up in a home where art was regarded as a source of delight, not as a pretension or requirement. That he became an artist is not surprising — although he wisely carved out his own territory (and got his own back at two wordsmith parents) by becoming a musician. A graduate of Berklee College of Music, Blake today is a composer and songwriter; he plays keyboards and is the lead singer for the band Afterimage. He told me recently that the message he got when young — that while being a creative artist required self-discipline, it was nevertheless the best fun there was — had an even more profound effect on him than the legacy of politics. (I think they're connected — and confess that though I'd still love him even if he had become a professional wrestler, I'm hugely relieved he didn't.)

We talked politics with him. He could ask any question, and we'd try (not always successfully) to answer it. Consequently, he was never mystified or patronized about what we are doing or why. Like any child who wants to imitate the grown-ups, he pushed to become involved. (Poor kid, he was the only child I ever knew who had paper cuts on his tongue at age six — from having begged to help lick envelopes during Bella Abzug's campaign mailings). As time went on, applying the principles he'd learned, he radicalized *us,* in turn — about the power relationship between adults and "short people" (children), about kids' rights, and even about children's suffrage. We took his opinions and his criticisms as seriously as we asked him to consider ours. Growing up, he imitated what he'd seen and loved "doing child care" for younger kids who, in turn, liked not being patronized by *him.* The moral: Freedom is contagious.

Nothing was proscribed in terms of reading matter or TV viewing. We were afraid of the "forbidden fruit" syndrome, and we wanted him to see different perspectives. But it's also true that both parents lobbied like hell to persuade him toward values we held dear. (It helped that we were all three avid fans of the *I, Claudius* series and that Blake and I have been for years not-so-closeted [Star] Trekkers; we counted it a personal triumph when the slogan "where no man has gone before" was changed to "no *one.*") Consequently, he could read or watch whatever he liked — but if it turned out to be demeaning to someone's humanity, we'd talk about that.

The same held true for any misbehavior of his; he was never struck and very rarely "punished" in the sense of losing privileges or being sent to his room. Instead we'd talk about it, not with rhetoric but with concrete examples of how speech and actions had consequences, how they could hurt or heal people's feelings, bodies, lives. To this day Blake loves to tease me about these D&M (deep and meaningful) talks. "There were moments," he moans, eyes rolling ceilingward, "when I almost longed to be simply forbidden something or punished for something, like other kids. But no-o-o. Instead, endlessly, we'd Talk About It." Well, okay, so we may have overdone it. But given the less palatable alternatives, I'd do the same thing again. And I've smiled to myself more than once, over the years, when overhearing Blake lobby his peers in the same ways on the same subjects.

We tried to offer alternatives to the patriarchal "norms." We celebrated Wiccan holidays with much pomp, while giving a superficial

45

nod to Christmas and Hanukkah. He was offered — and played with — dolls and tea sets as well as with fire trucks and tractors. Chess he learned at home, but baseball he found on his own; it became a passion (still is) — and in the fifth grade he fought to integrate girls on his team and won. True, war toys were not welcome in the house, but when he began eyeing them at other kids' homes, we tried to think of a substitute. The best we could devise was medieval legend — Arthur, Guinevere, the Round Table. If he played battle, then at least it would be distanced from reality and with archaic weapons; maces and lances were not standard issue in Vietnam. The hope was that he might turn out less accepting of the idea that contemporary weapons are toys and vice versa. (A not-so-bad side effect of this was his growing familiarity with *Le Morte d'Arthur* and other poetry that dealt with the subject.) And, of course, we Talked About It with him. I still consider this Arthurian compromise a bit of a fudge. Nevertheless, Blake turned out to be strongly antiwar, so something must have worked.

We tried to celebrate, not just promulgate, feminism. Blake remembers one of the most successful attempts at this as the Susan B. Anthony birthday party when he turned ten. Since his birthday falls in July, when school was out and his friends were away, we threw him a party on February 15, and he "shared" it with Susan B. Anthony; the presents were only for him, though. Charades were acted out from hints based on her life ("She drove a horse and carriage to distant places to give speeches"); "pin the tail on the donkey" became "pin the ERA star on the state" played with a large map of the United States; and kids were given pencils and scrambled around a homemade huge crossword puzzle on the floor, collaborating to solve such clues as "Susan B. Anthony fought for the right of women to ____." The streamers and cake were in suffrage colors, and everyone got to sing "Happy Birthday" twice, for Susan as well as for Blake. It was a big hit because making the party educative ran second to making the party fun.

Today Blake says he thinks parts of his upbringing at times went "a bit over the top," as he wryly puts it. He notes that it might have been helpful if we'd prepared him better for his classmates' reactions when he denounced Thanksgiving as a holiday insulting to Native Americans, protested classroom Halloween decorations depicting witches as warty-nosed horrors, or proclaimed that babies were *not* delivered by storks, which was why it was important for women to have the right to choose an abortion. He got badly roughed up more than once for objecting to antigay and -lesbian remarks or for refusing to join other boys in a ritual *Playboy* center-fold drool on the school bus.

We ached for him, and we did warn him (tearfully) that taking stands could get you in trouble and could cost you friends, that you had to be tactically selective since no one could fight on every front every minute of the day, and that our approval and love were never contingent on his carrying these banners. But it's also undeniable that we sent a second message: of such pride in his actions (there were quite a few lively visits to the principal's office in his defense) that he also felt challenged to persist in them. If I had it all to do over again, I'd intensify the warnings — but I'd probably be just as unable to contain the pride.

In *Of Woman Born: Motherhood as Experience and Institution,* Adrienne Rich wrote, "What do we want for our sons? Women who have begun to challenge the values of patriarchy are haunted by this question. We want them to remain, in the deepest sense, sons of the mother yet also to...discover new ways of being men even as we are discovering new ways of being women.... If I could have one wish for my own sons, it is that they should have the courage of women." She defines that courage as evident in acts both small and large, private and public, as in daring to think the unthinkable — and as in not settling for "the old male defenses, including that of a fatalistic self-hatred."

With quiet euphoria I've seen glimpses of that courage in Blake. When, around age eleven, he learned that I'd received right-wing death threats and he went through a period of fearing I'd be assas-sinated, he felt free to express that terror — yet when I probed beneath it, he said that I must never stop writing or acting on my beliefs. If at times my radical politics have embarrassed him before his friends, he's felt free to say so — yet to add that he "could deal with it" and that "if they couldn't handle it, that was *their* problem."

But the best part is that he doesn't just parrot or affirm what *I* stand for; he's made his politics *his.* What passed for his "adoles-cent rebellion" — an astonishingly mild version of what I've seen other teenagers, myself included, go through — was about precise-ly this: putting his own "spin" on the values he'd been raised with.

(I recall one fierce argument about the movie *Alien.* He thought it was feminist because of the Sigourney Weaver strong woman character; I thought it was antifemale and also racist because of the depiction of the dark, slimy, fecund evil, "alien" female.) I've even wondered whether we didn't do him a disservice by possibly co-opting his rebellion. He says that a recent exchange about this is typical of our relationship — bizarre, wonderful, and totally hilarious. It went like this:

ME: Do you think we co-opted your rebellion?

HIM: Nope.

ME: Whew.

Why, come to think of it, do we assume that a full-force rebellion against and a rejection of parental values is inevitable? What if, in fact, such rebellion is not a universal process but a symptom of patriarchy? (Animals don't go through it, and in human cultures where a child is parented by the whole tribe, female and male alike, such a concept doesn't exist — nor, by the way, does an Oedipal phase.)

Early on I realized that I could offer Blake consciousness about patriarchy, but I could not force it on him; consciousness can never be forced. Neither could I "give" him the power to be himself. That, only he could discover. Not even a principled member of a powerful group can "give" freedom to those who are powerless; freedom must be not only seized by them but reinvented by them. There is a decided power paradigm in any adult-child relationship, especially when the adult is parent to the child, and it is only recently and tentatively that society has even begun to examine the human rights of children. It's been all very well to sentimentalize children — but their having *rights* is something else: empowering. And threatening. I knew that, as his mother, I had power over Blake and that, however well or ill I chose to use it, not all my best intentions and politics could divest me of it. Nor could I give him his rights. But I *could* give him some tools with which to fight for those rights, even if that might mean his using such tools against me.

When he was about four, I remember, just after I had survived a particularly painful skirmish with my own mother, I told him that if he ever felt I was abusing my parental power or acting in a tyrannical or manipulative manner toward him, he could say, "Rob, you're acting like your own mother," and, like a magic spell, it would freeze me in my tracks. I was afraid he might abuse this tool, but it seemed more important not to pass on certain tics I'd learned from her, which I might be tempted to play out with him. He's wielded this phrase with great restraint — only two or three times in his entire life — and each time it's worked like a charm.

Blake is a grown man now. I don't use the term *feminist man* (women have so few affirmative names for ourselves that at this point in history, I feel possessive about the word *feminist*); I prefer *antisexist man* or *man of conscience,* either of which describes him fairly.

A part of me is vigilant, because I know how clever the patriarchy is. I also know how fatal it is to become lazy or self-congratulatory or to smugly think that one's own man (father, brother, husband, lover, *or* son) is "an exception." No one is. But I *am* proud, not only of what his father and I and a few close friends, together and separately, gave him but also of what Blake himself brought to the equation. I admit to feeling enormously flattered when, for example, as an adult he chose to live near me or when he set a poem of mine to music or when he wrote an unsentimental but stunning song called "Sunrise" about an early-morning beach walk he and I had taken together when he was only seven — the peach-and-silver miracle of his first dawn. So we hold fast — while learning to let go.   **49**

Interestingly, what Blake remembers most keenly from his childhood are the shared moments of spontaneous jubilation about just being alive: finger painting in the nude at age three with his father and making a splendid mess with absolute impunity; splashing umbrella-less at age six through a summer downpour with me, drenched and laughing about it so hard, we could barely catch our breath. These are moments that transcend gender. Which is the point.

Is that what it comes down to, something so simple and so difficult? A minimum of jargon and a maximum everyday *practice of the politics* (which means attention to detail — because children *notice* the details)? Ancient verities such as honesty, hard work, mutual respect? Humor and patience (and impatience) and communication (and humor) and creativity (and humor) and audacity?

Blake is the ultimate expert on his own experience of what it's like to be the son of this feminist mother. I can only relate my experience, not as a model but in the trust that on this subject as on every other, if we break silence and dare speak our truths, failures, and triumphs to one another as women, we all benefit.

Ultimately, of course, it all comes down to love: not a saccharine, Disneyesque brand of love but one fierce enough to demand change — for ourselves, our children, and the planet. *That's* the "mother love" I aspire to.

And they've called me a man hater for it.

Ask my son if I am.

—August 1993

Black. And White. And All the Colors in Between.
By Loree Cook-Daniels

My son, they say, will have to choose. Black. Or white. All the papers he will face will offer only those boxes. All his friends will want to know. To whom do you owe allegiance? Are you black, or are you white? Are you with us or against us?

The answers are both. And neither. More. And less. The boxes, the questions, leave no ground for honoring the Native American great-great-great-grandmother. They leave no space for a Jewish heritage bestowed by a mother who did not also give him DNA. They do not admit the possibility of joining sperm from Northern gene pools with an egg from bloodstreams sourced in many soils. They do not acknowledge that we are all so much more than "race."

They do not acknowledge my son.

Choose, they all tell me. One chorus wants him successful: hard-driving, competitive achiever. One chorus wants him sensitive: privilege-renouncing supporter of women. One chorus wants him a warrior: fearless fighter for his people's rights. What future, they all demand of me, will you prepare this brown-skinned man-child for? Will he be one of us or one of the "other"?

Both, I say, and neither. I will not prepare my son for any war. Dead and wounded crowd our streets already. Someone must start the peace. Someone must stop teaching children the lines, pointing out who belongs on each side. Someone must start the listening, teaching children to hear pain where others see anger. Someone must start showing children that every single one of us belongs. They say I am ignorant. They cannot imagine life without enemies.

They cannot imagine my son.

They will all tell my son to choose silence. Some will tell him his father could not have birthed him into the world. Some will tell him his parents turned traitor. None of them want him saying that men don't always have penises, that little girls don't always grow up to be women. They do not want to hear that his parents refuse to stay within any predefined boundaries. They will tell him he is confused.

I will point out the confusion. I will show him: Some people are afraid of what they do not know. I will tell him: Some people believe different means dangerous and become dangerous in the face of difference. I will teach him not to be what they expect, not to fear or condemn in return. I will teach him to trust his own truths. I will raise him to be all that the universe needs: teacher and student, healer and healed. I will teach him to be who he is.

They will not know what to do with my son.

Lesbian Fathers
by Karen X. Tulchinsky

"He looks just like you," a woman at the park says. I look down at Vincent, my three-year-old nephew. He has brown hair and big brown eyes. His head comes to just above my knees. He is a little short for his age, and stocky. He stands with his feet firmly planted, shoulders back, chest out, both hands thrust in his pants pockets. I look down at myself. I am standing in the exact same position. She is right. He looks like me. He stands like me. Today, like most days, he watches me and copies. I am a male role model for my three-year-old nephew.

Vincent does not realize that he is a boy and I am a girl. He is too young. He has not yet been inundated with society's imposed gender order. He knows, instinctively, only that we are both butches. He knows on a gut level that I am more like his father than like his mother, that I am like him, and that he is like me.

Earlier, when I stopped by his house to pick him up, he stared at my black Doc Martens. He sat on the tiled black-and-white checkerboard kitchen floor. His mother crouched by him to lace up his white running shoes.

"No!" he shouted. "Those ones." He pointed to his black runners. "The ones like Karen's."

She smiled, removed the white shoes, and complied with his request.

As his mother tied his black shoes, he watched carefully, intently, glancing every now and then at my Docs, then back at his own shoes, beaming proudly. "My shoes are like yours," he said, looking up at me, his big brown eyes full of love and trust. "Right, Karen?"

"That's right, pumpkin," I said. "Just like mine."

One day we were walking around our neighborhood — the east end of Vancouver, a working-class residential area with houses, trees, stores, and three-story walk-ups. It was a warm spring day. We could see the top of Grouse Mountain poking above the buildings of the city. The sun was beating down on us as we walked. I took off my blue-jean jacket and tied it around my waist. Vincent was wearing a similar jacket.

"Like you," he said pointing. I removed his jacket and tied it around his waist.

We walked on, hand in hand, Vincent taking big steps with his little legs, following in my footsteps, the arms of our jean jackets silently flapping against the backs of our thighs as we walked.

An older man in his sixties, with gray hair, a gray beard, and a black suit jacket approached from the opposite direction. He laughed when he saw us, smiling as we passed.

"That's nice," he said, pointing. "Like father, like son."

I simply nodded and smiled. What would I have said? *No. You got it wrong. He's not my son. I'm not his father. I'm his aunt.* Or should I have said I'm his uncle? Would it have mattered?

People see what they want to see.

My lover is going to have a child.

"And you will be the father," she announced when we first talked about it.

54   "You mean coparent," I corrected.

"No," she answered. "I mean father. I want you to be the father."

I've been trying to get her pregnant ever since. When I make love to her with my strap-on, I don't use condoms any longer. So far it hasn't worked, although last month we had a false alarm. Her period was late.

We are still trying. We have sex all the time, especially when she is ovulating. (Of course, we know it will never work, that in the end we'll have to find a sperm donor, but you gotta dream, right? We both wish I could get her pregnant. That would be so fine.)

Our friends think we're crazy.

"You can't use that word," they say. " 'Father.' You can't."

"What is a father?" my lover challenges.

"Well...a man," one says.

"A sperm donor," another adds.

"She'll be a better father than our fathers were," my lover says.

She's right, of course. I will be a good father, a role model for our child. Whether she's a boy or a girl. Whether he is femme or butch. He will watch me and learn. I will teach her or him how to tie a tie, how to shine shoes, how to pick out a suit, how to treat a lady. How to be gallant. How to open car doors, fix tires, change the oil, throw a ball, pick out a nice aftershave, stand up to a bully, slick back his hair, wear a tuxedo, smoke a cigar. I will teach him to be honest, kind, loving, brave, sensitive, thoughtful, and true.

After our baby is born, I'm going to start a lesbian fathers group. I am challenging the definition of the word *father.* In the Oxford English Dictionary, the word *father* is defined as: 1. a man in relation to a child or children born from his fertilization of an ovum. 2. a man who has continuous care of a child. 3. a person who deserves special respect.

Lesbians have been reclaiming language for years, using words that were formerly used against us. *Dyke, butch, femme, lezzie, queer.* In the spirit of reclamation, I'd like to add an entry to the dictionary. Lesbian father: 1. a butch in relation to a child or children born to her lover. 2. a butch who has continuous care of a child. 3. a person who deserves special respect.

A few months ago my lover and I were at the birthday party of a three-year-old girl. We sat on a low child-size bench in a corner of the room and watched the kids play. The party was at a day-care center. The large, open room was filled with toys, games, children's books. Mounted high on the walls were bright red, green, and yellow finger paintings, macaroni glued to paper with silver and gold sparkles, store-bought cutouts of Mickey Mouse, Cookie Monster, Bert, and Ernie. I sat on the bench and held my lover's hand, feeling a little nervous.

The birthday girl's parents are a straight couple, friends of my lover. All of the other adults at the party were straight. We were the only dykes there. My lover and I are a visible butch-femme couple. We are in love. Quite naturally we hold hands, sit close, walk arm in arm, express our love and affection. We do this wherever we are. But I was feeling out of place. I didn't really know anyone and was worried that the straight men would be threatened by us, the two lesbians in the corner. By me, the butch.

Sometimes straight men are angry at me. I can see it silently exuding from their eyes. I can feel it. My girlfriend is very beautiful, very femme. I know what straight men are thinking when they see us: They look at us and wonder why she's with me, when maybe she could have been with them.

I worried about this as we sat in the corner of the room, quietly

55

holding hands and watching the kids. They were running around in circles. Some were playing inside a giant dollhouse. Others were jumping up in the air trying to reach the strings of helium balloons that had floated up to the ceiling. A five-year-old girl skipped over, then sat on the floor near our feet. For a while she just sat, listening and watching. Then, looking right at me, she said with a mean edge to her voice, "Are you a boy or a girl?"

The pain of her remark sliced through me. I sat stunned for a moment. I felt the sting of disapproval in my belly, spreading rapidly throughout my whole being, body, heart, and soul. I felt ashamed. A five-year-old girl was capable of hurting me. How was it possible that she could knock me over with what might have been an innocent question? Her homophobia, her hatred of butch women was already formed, tangible, deeply ingrained at the age of five. It wasn't the question itself that was so unsettling. Children are naturally curious and should be. It was the tone of her voice as she asked it. A tone that said, *You are a freak. You are not normal. You are bad. You are a person who does not deserve the most basic respect.* I didn't know what to say. I didn't know how to even begin to answer her question. I sat still, immobilized.

My lover studied my painted face, squeezed my hand, and spoke to the girl. "Well...what do *you* think?"

The child directed her answer at me. "I think you're a girl," she said. And though it sounded like an accusation, her eyes reflected her fear.

I took a deep breath. "How do you know?" I said.

She shrugged. " 'Cause."

I nodded.

"But you have short hair," the child added, confused.

"So? Girls can't have short hair?"

She shrugged. "I guess they can. Yeah." She frowned. She was not yet convinced.

"What's going on?" The little girl's mother demanded as she crossed the room toward us, probably conscious of the intensity of our exchange. The child hunched her shoulders, pulled in on herself. We all turned and looked up at her mother.

"What?" the woman said.

My nephew, Vincent, has known me all his life, from his very first moment. I was at his birth. I held him in my arms in his first hour, and I have held him in my heart ever since. I take care of him once a week. Every Friday afternoon I pick him up, take him out to the park for a walk, to my place. We watch Batman videos, make puzzles, play. He has never not known me. I am a part of his world. His perceptions of the world include me, a very butch dyke.

Vincent has never asked me what I am. He doesn't need to. He already knows. I am his uncle. I am his friend. I am an adult in relation to him. I am a person who takes continuous care of him. I am a person in his life who deserves special respect.

57

The Uncles' Club
by Christina Starr

I think the work and pleasure of child rearing should be a shared responsibility in the gay community, not only among the women but also among the men. We women — even gay women — still do so much of the caretaking in the world, it's high time that gay men, who are often without children of their own, throw a little energy our way.

So a solution occurs to me. I will become an event leader for Out & Out and organize a day at the Royal Ontario Museum for gay men in the company of the children of lesbians. We will do a training weekend first (as is usually offered to those new to certain "sports"), including: the rudiments of first aid, negotiating skills, bathroom and/or diaper management, nap time, places to go, explanations to give, allowable treats, time to say yes, and ways of saying no without saying no. It can become a regular event, like the book club, the bingo night, or the movie outing. We'll charge a fee too, because the economic burden of raising children should be shared and because becoming a child's friend and caregiver is an important and transferable skill that many gay men would not otherwise have the opportunity to gain.

We'll start it out as an afternoon, increase it to a day, and eventually to a whole weekend, so that we lesbian mothers can go off canoeing in the wilderness, secure in the knowledge that our children are well and competently cared for. There can be overnight visits during the week so that we know we have one extra night to ourselves. The lives of gay men will be enriched immeasurably by the relationships they form with children, the children will mature with matter-of-fact acceptance not only of woman-to-woman but of man-to-man relationships, and we lesbian mothers might just be able to have a love life.

Back to the Village
by Grace Woodacre

I look around my child's birthday party and am amazed at the reactions this scene could engender. The right wing would call it heresy, and the radical queers would call it revolution.

I call it getting back to our matriarchal roots.

"Where is this child's father?" the right wing shouts. "Where is his role model?"

Before the nuclear family this would not have been a question. The nuclear family is a new invention, forced upon us just before World War II. Since the 1970s it has been divorcing, disintegrating, falling apart at a surprising rate.

What existed before? The extended family. The community. The belief that "it takes an entire village to raise a child," as the famous African proverb goes. It was a family unit that lasted for more than 4,000 years and was practiced by every single race of people on the earth.

That's 4,000 years for the extended family and thirty years for the nuclear family.

The nuclear family is not a model I am striving to re-create in my household. I am not a new twist or an alternative to the model. I am not a "just as good as them" rendition of the model. My lover and I are not trying to model a mom-and-dad arrangement. I am bringing my child into a much wider arena than that.

In the scenario in which the entire village is involved with the well-being of the children, my child's role models do not have to live in my house or sleep in my bed. My child's role models forge lasting relationships and contribute valuable input because of their connection to my child, because my child has expressed a desire to learn something from them — not because of their gender or because they're in love with me or because of their genetic contribution to my son's physical being.

It took me more than two years to finally understand the nuclear family as an isolationist philosophy. It preaches that everything a family needs it is supposed to find within the confines of two heterosexual adults and a child or two. It bases its experience of manhood solely on the man who is having sex with the mother. This seems very limiting and, frankly, dishonest. If you think of the role models in your life, wasn't it also your debate coach, your football coach, the librarian, your funny uncle Louis, your grandfather, the older kid who lived down the street and let you into the tree house? Your mother didn't sleep with any of them. Her heterosexuality didn't play in any way into your relationship with any of your role models.

I fell prey to the role-model search for a while. In fact, studies have shown that lesbians are more concerned than single heterosexual mothers about providing male input for their children[1] and that the children of lesbians spend more time with their fathers than the children of single heterosexual mothers.[2]

I looked for a few good men, but my son's godfather spends all his time making money and so has spent no independent time with my son — not a single hour. He always brings his own son with him for visits, which makes his son sullen and angry, as if something is being taken from him. I wonder if this entire venture is being positioned as giving to the less fortunate ("Be nice — after all, he has no daddy.") The son feels as if something is being taken from him, not that he is now surrounded by even more friends and the bounty of an expanded family.

My son's namesake couldn't cope with the stress of having to write something meaningful and so sent no card, no gift at the announcement of my son's birth, despite our having been intimate friends for nearly twenty years. When we got together, his wife had bought the present.

Gay men who stop me in the streets expressing a desire to be involved with children finally confess that they are often too irresponsible and self-absorbed to really do it. They are unwilling to commit to the long-term work and self-sacrifice required to raise children. Nor do they seem willing to acknowledge that the mother of the child is the undisputed head of the household and that their involvement is at her direction. They won't be responsible, and they won't play second fiddle.

My failure with these men made me think that I had failed; I needed other men, I was asking too much. Then I realized that, in fact, this is the experience of Western fathering. My son has men in his life who are distant, absorbed elsewhere, and uncommunicative. Is this because I am a lesbian? Not at all.

There is something wrong with fathering in America. Even the right wing agrees with this, but in patriarchal fashion they have identified a problem with men and their tactic is to control women.

In fact, the more I investigate the issue, the more I see that the right wing is up in arms about the role-model issue because learning traditional male activities from women — from butches, from dykes — means that this next generation of boys will not be willing to reinforce the gender stratification that is at the root of sexism and misogyny.

This focus on the male role model is also a smoke screen: In the patriarchal paradigm the man is the center of the family, not the child. Without a man the center of the family becomes something other than the male. In the matriarchal/community paradigm, the child is the center of the family.

In fact, if you believe that it takes an entire village to raise a child, then the role models for our sons are plentiful and readily available. My son's role models are all around him, devoted and loving. None of them happens to be the source of his seed. Our sons will learn to be men from their own innate process; from the kind, gentle, **61** quality men we invite into their lives; from women who share their interests; from members of their families of origin that may or may not be close enough to provide input; from men of their choosing; from men who are drawn to the wondrous spirits of our children; from the male world at large.

1. Kirkpatrick, M., Smith, C., and Roy, R. (1981) Lesbian Mothers and Their Children: A Comparative Survey. *American Journal of Orthopsychiatry, 51,* 545-551.

2. Golombok, S., Spencer, A., and Rutter, M. (1983). Children in Lesbian and Single-Parent Households: Psychosexual and Psychiatric Appraisal. *Journal of Child Psychology & Psychiatry, 24,* 551-572.

Outside the Inside
by Lillian Faderman

In January my partner and I took a weekend trip to Stanford to help our son celebrate his twenty-first birthday. Despite his handsome beard, he still calls me "Ma-y" (his childhood rendition of "Mommy"). My partner (who, while he was in utero, sang lieder to him — her voice directed toward my belly button — to ensure that he would be musical, as she is) he still calls "Mama Phyllis." And he is still our pride and joy. He's always been a star academically. But what makes us proudest is that he's a sensitive, generous, loving, fine human being, a mensch. The woman who gets him will be very lucky.

I knew in my twenties that although I loved being a lesbian, I would always feel there was something painfully missing in my life if I didn't have a child. But I listened passively to the deafening tick of my biological clock until 1974 — when I was in my mid thirties and knew that if I didn't act soon, I would regret my inaction forever. It was the dual proliferation of the pill and donor insemination that finally led me to understand there was no reason I couldn't be both a lesbian and a mother: Women no longer had to get pregnant as a result of having heterosexual intercourse, and women no longer had to have heterosexual intercourse in order to get pregnant.

How, after various outrageous and funny episodes, I found a doctor who would agree to do donor insemination — in Fresno, California, in 1974 — is a tale for another day; as is the story of the transformation of Phyllis's conservative father (our son's "Grandpa Irwin"), who defended me to his friends at church by saying, "But she doesn't want a husband, she wants a child — and that's her right"; as is the account of sizzling phone wires in both straight and gay communities all over California's central valley ("Can you believe...?" "How could she...?" "Impossible!"). But it was possible, and we did it, and motherhood has been the greatest blessing of our lives.

Last weekend our friends Marsha and Marilyn came to brunch. The weekend we were at Stanford, they were in Houston for a professional conference. I did research in the Houston lesbian community years ago, so I was curious about its present state. "We didn't see the lesbian community," Marsha said. "There's this wonderful Baby Superstore in Houston, and that's where we spent all our spare time." They are ecstatic because they are making the final arrangements to adopt a girl baby from China. We talk for a while about the awful treatment of girls in China: "A *small* blessing" the birth of a female is dubbed; apparently Chinese girl babies are left to wither away in orphanages. But it is clearly not humanitarianism or feminism alone that is driving Marsha and Marilyn. "I've wanted to raise kids since I was twelve years old," Marsha said. "Though I never wanted a husband to go with the deal." Marilyn said she "keeps visualizing having this little person around, carrying her on my shoulders. I dream about her all the time."

Marsha and Marilyn said they know of at least a half dozen local lesbian and gay couples who just had or are planning to have — or just adopted or are planning to adopt — a baby. And support groups abound: for lesbian mothers of tots, lesbian mothers of adolescents, play groups for the kids. The baby boom in our community over the past few years is far beyond the most extravagant dreams that Phyllis and I could have conceived of twenty-two years ago, when we dared to think it wasn't crazy to want to bring a little life into our lesbian home.

63

But what does it mean that lesbian and gay parenthood has now become commonplace? What does lesbian motherhood or gay fatherhood have to do with present queer culture — or with its historical icons (imagine Proust and Genet as gay fathers!)? By the conventionality of their desire to parent, are lesbian mothers and gay fathers guilty of (to put it in terms Leo Bersani uses in his book *Homos*) "de-gaying gayness," which will ultimately "accomplish the aims of the homophobes"? Is it that some of us are Queers and some of us are Parents?

The overwhelming yearning we lesbian and gay parents have to love and be responsible for the growth of a little human being does not mean that we share feelings with some heterosexuals that are foreign to many of our queer brothers and sisters. Yet by virtue of our sexual orientation, we remain transgressive, whether or not we see ourselves as queer. We will always be outside the inside.

That position is a fine place from which to parent. It stands to reason that our children are more likely to be tolerant of differences and to eschew bigotry than children from more orthodox families. It came as no surprise to me when Cynthia Martin, Ph.D., reported in 1988 a study that found that "the sons of lesbians were more gentle and concerned with other people's feelings than were other boys" and that the daughters of lesbians had "stronger qualities of leadership and outgoingness than other girls." Our very lives as homosexuals are disruptive of oppressive social orders, and when we become parents we model creative alternatives to those orders. Marsha and Marilyn kept saying, "We feel incredibly lucky that we're going to get this kid." The kid is incredibly lucky she's going to get them.

The Myth of the Male Role Model
by Cheryl Deaner

As a lesbian parent, I want my son to model people who respect the inherent worth and dignity of others. The greatest gift I can give my child is to teach him that there are other points of view than his or that of the dominant culture. I want to encourage his natural sense of empathy at a young age so that he can be more creative and tolerant.

Along with creativity and tolerance, I think boys really benefit from learning negotiation skills instead of using their fists to resolve conflict. In this violent society I believe it is especially important for boys to learn diverse ways of solving conflicts, if for no other reason than that they will be much less likely to die a violent death.

My challenge as a parent is to show Jesse ways of being that are not stereotypical for men. Our society trains boys to be hierarchical and dominant. Many social ills, such as racism, sexism, and classism arise out of the "one up, one down" brand of traditional male thinking.

For example, our family is all white. If I do not educate Jesse to challenge the status quo, I will be raising a racist white boy, because racism is the dominant culture in America — it's a systemic evil like homophobia. In a way I think homophobia is a great teacher. It is easier for my son to understand the idea of oppression because he encounters antigay and -lesbian bias every day at school and in my family of origin. Discrimination is discrimination. I hope his early and frequent exposure to it will give him the impetus to create social change when he grows up.

However, in my work at the All Our Families Coalition, I have also seen how damaging homophobia can be to our sons and daughters when their parents are still unconsciously buying into it. Children listen to what you say — and what you do not say. Talk to your children about being in a family in which at least one of you is a sexual minority. When parents are uncomfortable about their sexuality themselves, it is just that much harder for them to hear that their children are encountering difficulties also. Talk to your kids. Homophobia breeds secrets, and secrets hurt everyone.

I find much misguided concern over the issue of providing "male role models" for our sons. A couple of years ago, there was a nice, liberal father of one of Jesse's friends who started inviting Jesse out with his son frequently. We finally understood that his agenda was to provide Jesse with that "male time" he believed Jesse needed to thrive. He was trying to be helpful, but he was not, and we had a little talk with him and straightened him out. We did not want Jesse soaking up the message that he was less inherently male or lacking some mystical male quality because of his lesbian moms.

We do not consciously look for men to include in his life, but it just so happens that our lives include men. He is with boys and men a lot, anyway — he has lots of boy friends in school, and we have a male roommate in our house. So far the only thing we thought we really needed a man to do was to teach Jesse, at age three, to pee standing up, because he had lousy aim! But once he had that down, that was it. Perhaps there will be more times later, as he grows up, when a man's perspective will aid him. But otherwise he will always be given his parents' perspective on the subject of growing up human.

66 It is a shame that people object to lesbians' raising sons without fathers. Not only do they miss the point of parenting, but they put so much stress on rigid gender roles that you have to wonder how they are damaging their own children.

It is not just men who can have a rigid gender perspective. I am friends with two gay men who have an eight-year-old daughter. When they take the child out together, women give them odd looks and sometimes trail them to make sure they have not stolen the child! When they are alone with her in a public place, strangers tell them they wish their husbands would take their children out more. There are many, many assumptions about us as families based on sex roles, and none of us are free of them totally.

Regarding the issue of active versus nonactive fathers, it's been interesting to investigate whether boys who are donor babies want to know about the paternal side of their biological heritage. Some kids never want to know, and some do. And at different ages, they have different questions.

At the All Our Families Coalition, we do not automatically suggest having a meeting with a child's nonparticipating donor because a child is asking questions. We work with the child's parents first because they know their children and are most likely to know what is best for their child to know and experience at a particular age. In cases where a totally anonymous donor was used and the child is upset, family counseling for the entire family may be in order.

When Jesse was three or four, we told him his father was a nice man who donated his sperm so that his moms could have a child. This satisfied him for a couple of years, although he found it easier, until he reached about the age of six, to just tell his friends that he had a daddy who lived in the basement.

When he turned eight this year, he asked if he could meet his donor. We told him about the arrangement we had made with our sperm bank donor — that Jesse could meet his donor at age eighteen if he still wanted to do so. We also read him some basic information about his father's donor profile. After that he seemed satisfied. We answer his questions, encourage him to be open, and try not to make a big mystery out of it.

When Jesse was five, his parents split up. Although it ended up being for the best, Jesse went through about a year of pain and acting out in kindergarten, and there just was not that much we could do about it other than to try our best to be good, fair, loving, and available to him. The two of us are still his legal parents, and we share custody. We are both now partnered again, so Jesse has four mothers, and the circumstances make us all extended family with one another until he leaves home. However, by that time I doubt that we will be able to *not* be family, even if we wanted to!

Bringing stepparents into a child's life is always a big adjustment, even when the child is accepting of the new parents, as was Jesse. It's all the same things that heterosexuals go through when there is a divorce and remarriage, plus the cultural invisibility of our families. We see a lot of families like ours at the All Our Families Coalition.

I think that my being Jesse's birth mother makes my relationship with him slightly different than his other mothers' relationships with him. He has half of my biological inheritance, and there are some close similarities in outlook and appearance. Since my ex was with him from birth, I think he is more deeply bonded with her than with his two stepmothers. But he loves all of us deeply and passionately, and we love him.

In general, I've observed that lesbians are becoming more accepting and less fearful of boy children. Lesbian society is evolv-

67

ing constantly. When lesbian feminism took root in the 1970s, I think there was a greater need for separatism because before that, few women had experienced an existence without the dominant male culture. I think most lesbians can point to a period in their lives when they needed to learn what it was like to create as nearly a totally woman-centered environment as possible.

I would like to think now that our boy children are welcome in lesbian society, although I know that this is not always true. I also think that being raised by lesbians does not automatically mean our boys are going to be different from other boys. However, as our lesbian community matures, has more herstory and more security in itself, I believe it becomes more able to pass along its heritage to both our daughters *and* our sons.

Growing Up to Be Loving
by Carole Morton

On my forty-ninth birthday, my house was full of guests — mostly lesbians. I'd also invited my son and his girlfriend. They were a little late. Smiling, my son entered the living room and said hello as I introduced him to everyone. How comfortable he was among lesbians! My friends told me, during the next week, how impressed they were with his open, friendly, easygoing manner. I usually explain that he was four years old when I came out (back in New York City in 1970) and my life was completely wrapped up in the lesbian-feminist movement. My son was raised at lesbian organizing meetings, lesbian conferences, lesbian parties, lesbian picnics, lesbian concerts, and even the D.O.B. lesbian bowling team of New Jersey. Lesbians were his mothers, his co-mothers, and his friends. With all the antimale sentiment in the movement at that time, he still came away feeling cared about and nurtured by lesbians and still greets my lesbian friends with a warm smile and an open heart.

So, I ask myself, *how has this upbringing affected his relationships with women?* He'll be twenty-eight next month, and he's involved in his first "real" relationship. Like most children of broken marriages, he was tentative about relationships — especially because after I left his father, I never had an intimate relationship with a man again. The only heterosexual role modeling I supplied him with, therefore, was when he was ages birth to four — and it was by no means positive. Though he never said to me that he was tentative, it was clear he was. So at age twenty-eight he's found someone to be with. I watch them. They're easy together. Affectionate, but not overly so. With a rightful sense to it. It flows between them with a lot of acceptance. At first I thought he might feel funny showing his affection to her around me, but he isn't. I also see that he doesn't take her for granted. It's odd to say, but it seems that, for a first relationship, it's really solid. I'm a counseling therapist, and I work with both gay and straight couples. I see a lot of problems between people, and I've had firsthand experience as well. Was this young man so positively influenced by the lesbian community that he truly knows how to love a woman? Well, I suppose he grew up watching me learn to love myself and other women. Maybe that's how he caught on.

When we moved back to New York City in 1976 (we were in California for a year), he entered a new school for the fifth grade and made three very close friends. One was a Caucasian boy (like my son) without an arm but with a hand protruding from his shoulder (a result of thalidomide); another boy was half African-American, half Puerto Rican; and the third friend was an extremely bright girl who played the violin, modeled, and was very independent from the ways of the other young girls (maybe a budding dyke!). In the sixth grade, back in a new school in California, my son became close with a boy, who, we found out after about four months, was the son of a lesbian. They became best buddies before they discovered their mutual experience. As the semester wore on, more and more of the children at the school became aware of the situation and were pretty brutal. The fact that these two had each other made the school year tolerable. Being the son of a lesbian caused my son to identify with and associate with other "outcasts," even though he had the acceptable look of being male with blond hair and blue eyes. He truly didn't have the easiest time of it, but the results seem to be that he is a very independent being with a wide variety of friends. For several years in his early twenties, he lived with two roommates — a motorcycle-driving straight female and a gay male. He's been sharing a flat for the past several years with an interracial heterosexual couple.

There are studies that say that the children of lesbian and gay parents grow up to become more well-balanced, healthier beings as a result of parenting that respects the child's individuality and differences from the parent. When I was raising my son, I was told by the "good people" that I was being unfair and damaging to him by raising him in the lesbian community. Well, as I look at my son now, I can say without a shadow of a doubt that these "good people" were wrong and that the studies clearly have validity.

Although I am not an advocate of the military, I believe that my son — who grew up without a father or any positive male influence — joined the military to explore his maleness. The result was positive — and surprising, since sexism is rampant in the military. Yet he admired the women who worked hard and achieved rank, and he seems to appreciate the humanness of struggle and achievement whether the person is male or female. His girlfriend is a single mother going to school — just like his mom!

Moms, they say, have a great influence on how sons will treat women. Though my initial role modeling with his father was one of horrifically low self-esteem, he did see me grow strong and proud to be me, and I have supported him to do the same. I was far from being the traditional good mother, but who I was struggling to become seems to be what he has modeled and achieved for himself as well.

71

Marbalo, Lesbian Separatism, and Neutering Male Cats
by Ruthann Robson

Marbalo is Colby's pretend friend and sometimes visits with Colby's pretend father.

Cecile pretends that when Colby reaches the right age — sometime substantially in the future — one of us will be able to explain donor insemination to him in such a spiritually scientific manner that he will have an eternally enlightened attitude toward life or at least not be bitterly confused.

I try to avoid pretending. It's not that I'm an ethicist about it, unless *ethics* is a synonym for *fear.* I'm afraid that I could become addicted to pretending faster than to cocaine. First, I'd start pretending that Colby is a darling daughter, that Marbalo is the twin sister, and that both of these kids have the perfect mixture of creativity and obedience as well as an innate knowledge of sperm banks. Then I'd pretend that Cecile is a lesbian angel who never gets grumpy enough to tell me that I'm irritating her by kissing her on the neck while she's trying to get dressed and who cheerfully cleans up cat puke. I'd pretend that we all live in a two-bedroom cedar A-frame house on eight-foot pilings in the middle of the woods, on the edge of the ocean, or on the crest of a mountain. I'd pretend I have a great job where I work only with the wonderful women of our community, who are consistently loyal, funny, and happy, and everyone appreciates me so much that I have to appear only for morning coffee gossip — and of course I get paid fantastically. If I started pretending, I wouldn't know how to stop. My pretend world would get so perfectly boring that I'd have pretend problems, like finding a preschool co-op for Colby and Marbalo and buying jackets with mittens attached to the sleeves. I prefer my pretend problems to be concrete.

Cecile knows, though, that I can't always avoid pretending. Actually, I pretend a lot. Cecile is always accusing me of being a closet pretender.

"I'm not in the closet about pretending," I tell her, "or anything else, for that matter."

She tells me it's time for me to be in the bathroom giving Colby his bath. The bath is my task. Cecile is the bedtime storyteller.

I wash Colby's reddish curls every night, to which Cecile objects but not enough to hunch over Colby while he splashes her. Cecile thinks that in thirty years, when Colby is in some 21st-century therapy, he won't bemoan his lesbian co-mothers and his nonexistent father but will relive the terrors of a barbaric ritual of nightly hair washing. I like to think Cecile is right.

She just may be right if Colby's screaming tonight is any indication. It seems I've gotten shampoo in Marbalo's eyes.

"But I wasn't even washing Marbalo's hair," I explain in my best patient coparent voice.

"Yes, you were!" Colby cries. It is hard to formulate justifications for pretend transgressions. I try the remorse-and-restitution tactic.

"I'm sorry," I say. "Let's see if we can rinse the shampoo out of Marbalo's eyes."

"Marbalo will drown."

"No, she won't."

More water. More screaming. Some cream rinse, including a dab for Marbalo's tangles.

Colby and Marbalo dry off. Colby and Marbalo brush their teeth with their matching lavender toothbrushes, one of which I use to clean the amethyst ring Cecile gave me on our anniversary. Then Colby and Marbalo stand on the Health o Meter digital scale. Marbalo weighs in at her usual double zero. Colby makes the numbers stop at thirty-four.

It's taken him four years, but he's finally reached the amount of weight I gained when I was pregnant. I guess I actually expected him to be about thirty pounds at birth, which would have allowed me to lose the other four pounds gracefully, in about a week.

It was all Cecile's fault, of course. When I was pregnant she stuffed me with broccoli drowning in cheese sauce and oranges. This combination had some sort of ultimate vitamin factor, at least according to Cecile. I ate it so dutifully, I expected the baby to be green and orange. I also expected a girl. Girls ran in our families and in our politics. We didn't even have a boy's name picked out. So while the incredibly heterosexual midwife was pretending it was business as usual, Cecile was rummaging through the refrigerator, thinking quickly. She came back with the name Colby.

73

"At least the cheese in the refrigerator wasn't Muenster," she'd say later. Sometimes Cecile thinks she is funnier than she is.

When the midwife left, packing her fetascope, her aspirators, her blue cohosh, and the vital-statistics certificate with the empty space under NAME OF THE FATHER (to be filed in the same building as the Division of Motor Vehicles), we looked at Colby and cried.

What were two dykes going to do with this miniature emissary from the patriarchy who had invaded our lives? One of us would be the one to give him a bath every night. The other one would be telling bedtime stories.

I can hear Cecile from the hallway: "Once upon a time, in an Amazon land, far, far away, lived a bunch of strong, wonderful women who were always loyal, funny, and happy. They made beautiful weavings from cat hair. One little boy, named Cheddar, lived with them..."

Lesbian separatism is an ethical/moral/political/social/theoretical lifestyle in which lesbians devote their considerable energies, in so far as it is possible, exclusively to other lesbians or, in some cases, exclusively to other women.

74 In my postpartum paranoia I became convinced that Cecile would leave me. Even if it had been a joint decision, even if I had become the "natural" mother because I'd gotten pregnant first, I somehow had the ultimate responsibility for the misunderstanding that resulted in this male child. I kept thinking of all the concerts from which we'd be excluded, all the radical conferences at which we wouldn't be welcome, all the women's land on which we could never live.

Until Colby, Cecile and I had been loyal lesbian separatists. However, the fact that my breasts were filled with milk to feed a ravenous baby boy wasn't the only indication that Cecile had always been a little more loyal. I've always thought it was easier for Cecile to be more separatist because she'd been married — only for six months, when she was seventeen, but married is married. Now she works with a lesbian collective, facilitating cultural exchange between North American and Latin American lesbian artists. She says it's exciting work. The pay is pure puke.

The pay is much, much better at the Dade County Division of Motor Vehicles, where I work. So far the highlight of my career — apart from winning the administrative hearing to get maternity benefits even though I was unmarried — is one man's license plate: He wanted to pay the extra fifty-dollar fee so that his Florida tag could read COCAINE. My male supervisor originally rejected this request, but I convinced him to authorize it by pointing out that if someone was stupid enough to advertise his tastes to law-enforcement officials, the county should not intervene.

My supervisor laughed, called me a pragmatist, and approved the request. Later I found a white envelope with my name typed on the outside and a hundred-dollar bill folded on the inside. I think I used that money to buy sperm.

Cecile did not leave me. In fact, she said the thought never entered her mind. In fact, she said she thought that I might leave her.

Instead our friends left us. Even our most loyal friends.

Inez said she could no longer come to meetings at our house because our rooms exuded maleness.

Raquel told us she couldn't believe we simply didn't give up the "male child" for adoption when "the bourgeois" were starving for healthy white baby boys and it would be so easy for us to start over.

Anna gave speeches about lesbian strength being dissipated, about lesbian separatist ethics, about lesbian obligations to the future, about the inviolability of gender.

A woman with whom I'd refused to sleep on a camping trip to Key West the summer before stood up at the Coconut Grove Lesbian Dance, Meeting, and Pot Luck and proposed a rule that would bar all "lesbians in any way participating in male-energized households" from the group.

That was when Cecile walked up to the microphone. She was smiling somewhat sexily. It's one of the features of our monogamy that I realize Cecile is angry when she smiles that way at anyone other than me.

Before Cecile said a single syllable, Inez attacked: "You are a traitor to your species."

"Oh, come off it, Inez," Cecile shot back. "Don't give me that shit. What about Isherwood? What about Orpheus? What about — goddess save us — Samson?"

"They're cats!" Inez screamed, squinting as if she had shampoo in her eyes.

"Not just cats. *Male* cats."

Sure, it was ridiculous. Even so, we later heard that Inez had given all her "nonwoman" cats away. Cecile and I became more and more separatist, separating ourselves even from other lesbian separatists.

Neutering male cats can alleviate such problems as obnoxious odors, howling, fighting, and staying out all night, and if cats are castrated at an early enough age, these undesirable traits will never develop.

Cecile and I are discussing Bob over our compulsively routine breakfast of grapefruit and eggs scrambled with cheese and half-and-half. Although Cecile is the one who suggested the procedure, she is the one who has the most reservations. I know she's written some letters about the involuntary sterilization of dissident women in Central America. She's also just more generally thoughtful than I am about these kinds of things. After all, she was the one to make the impulsive decision not to get Colby circumcised. She has a theory that such infant barbarism is responsible for males' being hateful.

Colby (and Marbalo, I suppose) found Bob — a little kitten with weird markings, especially on his stomach — in the front yard a few months ago. Cecile showed me an article in the newspaper about some rare Himalayan cat that had stripes and spots, just like Bob, selling for $700. I doubt we could get a dollar for Bob, even if we believed animals were property that could be sold.

Bob does look a lot like a bobcat, though, which is why Cecile and I named him Bob. Bob is not named after any actor or writer or artist or visionary or famously flaming male homosexual. Our dog is Stella. Cecile and I are hopelessly compatible: We'd never have a cat named Colette or a dog called Dionysus. It does make us wonder about the origins of Marbalo, though.

"Okay. Let's get Bob's balls whacked off." Cecile can be very decisive when she wants to.

"I'll call the vet," I offer.

"Why not the spay and neuter clinic? It's cheaper."

"I don't trust them," I say, abandoning all claims to pragmatism.

"You just have a crush on the dyke vet, old Mary what's-her-name."

"Don't be stupid."

In fact, I've always secretly suspected that the vet had a crush on Cecile. I figured that the vet would not disparage Cecile the way she does unless she were trying to placate me. Besides, when Colby was born the vet was less than sympathetic. I heard she said that more scientifically sophisticated women could prevent the conception of a male. Of course, another woman said something similar about spiritual enlightenment, the phases of the moon, and the failure to birth a girl.

When I take Bob to the Feminist Animal Hospital, I do have to admit that one of the vets there, Maria Lourdes, is kind of cute. She's got these great bushy eyebrows that grow together so that her forehead looks like a hawk with a terrific wingspan. Still, no one's eyebrows could ever match Cecile's — all wispy and wild and defiantly vulnerable. Once, long before Bob or Marbalo or Colby, when Cecile was on a crying jag about some crisis we've both long forgotten, she screamed at me, "I don't know why you love me!"

"It's your eyebrows," I said.

She smiled as if she thought I were kidding.

Maria, the only lesbian separatist veterinarian I've ever known, is being sweet. "I know you'll worry," she says. "I'll call you at work after the operation is over."

I get a telephone call from Dr. Lourdes at the Division of Motor Vehicles. "Everything's fine," she says. Then she starts expressing sympathy about the hard life I have, working with men in a male bureaucratic system. "Cecile," she adds, "doesn't have to do that."

I can hear Maria smiling.

When I get to the Feminist Animal Hospital, Maria is still smiling. She asks me to have dinner while Bob recuperates a little bit longer from his surgery. She tells me she's heard Cecile is terrible in the kitchen and that I deserve a good meal after Bob's ordeal.

I sort of smile myself, in a half-sexy way.

It's one of the features of my monogamy that whenever I smile my special Cecile smile at anyone other than Cecile, I'm actually approaching anger.

I pretend to be flattered by Maria's request. I pretend to be gracious as I decline. I pretend I don't even consider vomiting. I pretend I am not pretending, for I'm afraid if I start pretending, I won't be able to stop.

Maria coaxes. "Well, then, won't you at least join me for wine and cheese? We really do have a lot to talk about. It seems we haven't spoken for years. Is Cecile still not letting you out to play?"

At our compulsively routine dinner of egg noodles, asparagus, and cheddar cheese, I resist telling Cecile what's wrong. She'd be sympathetic, but she'd also tease me.

"Let's leave Miami," I say. "Let's move to Minnesota." I crave a problem I can solve, like keeping mittens attached to sleeves.

"Can Marbalo come too?" Colby asks.

"We'll see," we say.

77

Piercing Times
by Cindy T. Rizzo

My son is constructing his image. Pieces of this image are being revealed to my lover and me one at a time. First, at age six, he asked that his ponytail be thinned out and braided. He called this a "rat's tail." Since that time, this rat's tail has grown down the length of his back so thin that it's held in place by the smallest of rubber bands, wound four or five times around.

Then he asked us to buy him a leather jacket. A black one, tight in the sleeves, with lots of zippers, snaps, and other shiny metal decorations. We refused. Where would he keep such an expensive item at school? Certainly not out in the open on the cubby hooks that line the hallways. No, the leather jacket would wait until seventh grade, when the demands of adolescence warrant kids the issuance of a school locker.

Nonetheless, the summer of our son's seventh birthday, we gave in a little and went browsing through the many leather stores that line Commercial Street in Provincetown, Massachusetts. No harm in just trying one on.

To our chagrin, he looked great. His small, wiry torso gained some needed bulk, and his already-forming muscular chest and shoulders were complemented by the snug leather. Still, we stuck to our decision and put off the purchase.

His most recent image enhancement was an earring. He lobbied, pleaded, begged, cajoled, and whined about getting his ear pierced. We demurred. "We'll discuss it," we told him.

The earring was number one on his list for his eighth birthday. So my lover and I discussed it and discussed it and discussed it. It wasn't long before we realized that these earring chats were really conversations about what it means for two lesbians to raise a son.

What would it mean for our son to wear an earring? Would people think we had pushed this on him as some sort of statement? Would they think we wanted him to be more feminine? Would they think he was gay, or worse yet, that we were encouraging him to be gay? Once your mind goes down this road, it's hard to get off. So we proceeded to our ultimate dead-end destination. Wouldn't we be irresponsible as parents if we let this happen? After all, we're sending him out into the world alone, with nothing but a skinny, long braid and an earring.

We agonized, we delayed, and we hoped that his passionate wish would disappear or become transformed in the same way that Ninja Turtles had become Power Rangers. The thing is, our son is not a kid who wants a lot of things. He is careful, almost parsimonious, in his desires. But when he really wants something, the longing just doesn't go away.

His relentlessness forced us to confront our worst fear (and perhaps the worst fear of many lesbian mothers of sons): We really don't know how to raise a boy. After all, how can we prepare a boy for the competitive, winner-takes-all world of men? Are we doing our son a disservice when we refuse to buy him one of those high-powered water guns that look like Uzis? What do we say when he comes home drenched because the neighbor's kid pulled the trigger and all my kid had in his hand was a water balloon? And what happens next time he goes to the neighbor's and he's wearing an earring? Isn't it better for the boy if we just revert to traditional notions of child rearing and encourage more—"gender appropriate" activities, including those that teach him to be a little heterosexual in training?

I would be lying if I said that in this instance my lover and I successfully rose above all these fears and said, "To hell with what other people think." Instead we made the decision to let our son pierce his ear, because he needed to know that we support his most persistent desires to be the person he is. He was also nagging us to death, and we didn't have a strong argument to offer in opposition. As far as society goes, we decided to just hope for the best.

But as soon as we gave in, we got stuck again. Now we asked ourselves, *Which ear should he pierce?* What we really wanted to know was, Which is the "gay ear"? If he chose the wrong one, would he get teased? Maybe we could avert impending disasters by making the correct ear choice. I asked a gay male friend who informed me that you can always remember that gay men pierce the right ear by thinking, *Gay rights.* Great. But do we tell our son this? And what does it mean if we give in to this kind of thinking?

79

Thankfully, our son ended our neurotic indecision. Out of pure personal preference, he wanted his right ear pierced. We got hold of our senses and skipped the gay/straight ear discussion.

So on my son's eighth birthday, we took another walk down Commercial Street. This time our destination was a jewelry store where we knew he would receive a quick and painless ear piercing. In an instant the deed was done. We even took a picture to record the moment forever.

Our son was faithful in his nightly alcohol swabbing and earring turning. He waited impatiently for the day when he could replace the small gold ball with an earring of his choosing. Then he asked us for dangly earrings. Again we demurred, telling him that long earrings wouldn't be safe since they might get caught on his shirt. Okay, it was a cop-out.

I decided that my lover and I could use some support on this issue. But we didn't know any other parents with young sons who wanted earrings. So when I actually met a straight father with an earringed, long-braided eight-year-old son, I thought I had found a kindred spirit. Here at last was another parent who could share his angst, his concerns, and his decisions with me. I was beside myself with joy!

Casually I asked the father how long his son had had his earring. "Oh, I don't know," he said rather spacily. "Let's ask him."

Before I could interrupt and explain that what I really wanted was to share our own pain and our own doubts, parent to parent, he had called his son over and I was speaking directly to him. He'd had the earring since he was six. No big deal. Any other questions? No, no. I'll just stand here like a fool wondering why I've been so crazed by all this.

I'll tell you why. Groovy straight dads don't contend with the same assumptions and prejudices as your average lesbian mom. They don't feel the need to be as worried about or protective of their kids' gender or sexual identities.

Nonetheless, despite all our protectiveness, the inevitable did happen. A kid in my son's karate class came up to him, looked at his new earring, and said, "People will think you're gay because you have an earring."

Well, there it was: The worst of our fears had come true. Our son was left completely defenseless. And it was all our fault. We had not adequately prepared him for this. We hadn't explained that there was this gay–earring link. He had not been coached for this moment.

But as it turns out, maybe he had. Maybe our discussions about sexism and prejudice against gays and blacks and Jews had added up to something. Maybe our attempts to build a secure family life and provide support by encouraging close friendships with other kids of lesbians had paid off.

Because when that kid made that remark, when the most loaded of childhood insults was hurled at my child and someone actually said, "People will think you're gay because you have an earring," my son turned around, looked at the kid, and calmly replied, "So?"

This retort silenced that kid. It also finally made me realize that I cannot always be there at the exact moment when the thing I fear most will happen. But on the other hand, I and all other lesbian mothers are not totally powerless against external dangers or against the evil that lurks within ourselves. We just don't always realize that the values we live by and communicate to our kids often end up as our best protection. Sometimes all it takes to remind us is one earring and one perfectly chosen word.

Making a Family

How We Ended Up With Four Sons and Only One Daughter, and What Happened Then
by Merril Mushroom

"*You* had a *choice!*" My separatist friend is furious. After all these years she's telling me what she thinks. "It's bad enough that lesbians are having babies to begin with — and even worse, so many of them are boys — but *you* had a choice, and you *chose* boys." She waits. I assume she's ready to counter any impending justification of my own, any excuse or rationale that I might offer about children — even boys — needing to be adopted, about raising gentle men who respect women, etc.

I don't offer any excuses, don't rationalize, do not even explain to her that, in fact, I did *not* have a choice; that I truly believed any child, even a boy, who appeared before me as the result of an adoption application was my "meant to be" child, my karmic match, my karmic obligation. Of course I would have preferred girls, but if a child who was meant to be adopted by me turned out to be a boy, I'd expect to go with it. But I must say, in retrospect, that I never expected to end up with *four* boys. It happened like this:

Back in the '60s my dear fairy friend Gabby and I decided to coparent adopted children. We were queer hippies and felt that our paths were taking us toward moving out of the city and onto the land to do community. We intended to adopt children who might not otherwise have an easy time getting out of the system. To facilitate this we married, which was the queer hippie event of the decade.

We filed our first application to adopt with a public agency. We didn't specify gender but said we would consider any child who was labeled "hard to place" because of ethnicity, age, or disability. We were approved and shortly after that were called in to the agency to meet a mixed-race foundling infant — an abandoned baby with no available history. We took him home with us that very day.

The second time we applied to adopt, we'd moved to another state. Again we applied through the state's protective-services agency. This time the caseworker had just found out that a white-looking baby boy whose mother had placed him at birth was really a black baby boy,

85

which caused him suddenly to become "hard to place" (another issue altogether). Within a year he came to live with us.

The third time we applied, we specifically requested a girl child and no babies — we'd had enough of diapers and crying and teaching of the very basic skills for living. We looked through a copy of the state's "used children" catalog and found six specific older girl children who all were "hard to place" for various reasons, any of whom we thought might fit in with our family. We gave the list to our caseworker. After much time went by, she finally called to ask if we would like to meet a normal baby girl whose very young mother was not able to raise her. Figuring that getting one out of our two requests — a girl, but a baby — was good enough, we agreed, and she came to live with us.

When our daughter turned three, we again applied to adopt. We were obliquely informed that the agency considered us to be "atypical but highly desirable" as an adoptive home. We wanted only a girl, preferably one close to our daughter's age. We told our caseworker, "Do not ask if we want to see a boy. Do not tell us about any boys. We do not want any more boys. *No boys!*"

One day the caseworker said, "*Hmph,* too bad you won't consider boys. Your family photo fell out of your file onto the floor, and another worker grabbed it up and said, 'Oh, this would be the perfect family for Ricky! He has to be moved from his foster placement, and he has some emotional problems, and I want it to be a permanent adoptive home this time.' Of course, I told her to forget it, that you wouldn't even consider another boy."

The goddesses work in wondrous ways to circumvent our personal plans and intentions.

After Ricky came to live with us, we didn't apply to adopt any more for a while. We dearly wanted two more girls, but the Appalachian shack we lived in was very tiny, and we were in the process of building a bigger house. When it was finished we'd apply to adopt again. Girls only. Meanwhile, we took children in foster care for short, usually emergency, stays.

Then we got a call from the infamous caseworker: "I know you are a short-stay home, but please, please would you consider taking a child in long-term foster care? This is an emergency. This little boy is so wild from being abused that he's already been through four other foster homes in the past two weeks. You're the only folks who might be able to do something with him. Just keep him long enough to improve his behavior so someone would want to adopt him. He's a cute little five-year-old white boy. We just can't keep bouncing him around like this."

So the boy came to live with us, but with the understanding that it would be only for as long as it took him to get a grip on himself so that someone else would want to adopt him. Life with him was very difficult for a while, and then he began to calm down a little. We invested a great deal of energy in him. He was as endearing as he was disturbed. We became attached to him, but always we were open and forthcoming about the fact that he would be going on to an adoptive placement someday. Then one day he came to me. "Mom," he said, "if you send me somewhere else to be adopted, I'm gonna be *so* bad..."

I suppose you can guess what happened next. Need I say more? There we were, with four sons and only one daughter.

We had longed for two more girls, but dealing with the last two boys with their intense emotional and social needs strained our resources to the end of the line. The other children also had developmental disabilities, and we could not divide our energy among any more children. Even so, boy children continued to come our way for brief periods of time — children of friends who needed temporary assistance or respite for a few days, weeks, months; foster kids; runaways; and lost souls. Sometimes I don't know how they found us. Often I have wondered about just what is my karma as a lesbian with all this male energy.

87

We live in a very rural area with a large population of various kinds of counterculture folks as well as straight rural Christians. The children understand that there are many different kinds of family configurations and that what's important is respect and treating one another well. They know I am a lesbian and have girlfriends. They know their dad is a fairy and has boyfriends. They did not think this was at all unusual and did not understand the ramifications of this until they reached their teens.

The children were schooled within a community free home-education collective until they were old enough to want to attend public school. They went to lesbian and gay events. They attended heterosexual hippie get-togethers and environmentalist happenings. They went to adoptive and foster-family events. They spent time with different families and individuals. They did not usually go to church or other places of conventional worship but did attend occasional festivals and spiritual rituals.

Always, in the process of child rearing, we've called their attention to the realities of racism, sexism, anti-Semitism, homophobia, ageism, ableism, and other ways that people keep other people down. We believe that the children need to understand oppression so they don't do it themselves to others and also for their own survival as poor, black (and one redneck) children who have developmental disabilities and white, gay, Jewish parents. However, in real life all this talk seems to work much the same way that the adoptions themselves worked — we get part of what we hoped for but not all of it. The children were always very much themselves, but peer values and group behavior come home with them as well, sometimes rearing their ugly heads in my face.

A friend is cleaning out her belongings. She is ready to toss a box of costume jewelry. "Oh," says my nine-year-old son, "could I have that for my dad? He's a fairy, and he just loves jewelry."

My fourteen-year-old son comes home from his first day in public school. "Mom," he says, "I just don't understand these boys, I mean the way they act toward the girls. They think it's funny to do stuff like walk up behind a girl and snap her bra." He makes a face. "That's so disrespectful! I would never even dream of treating a girl that way. Why do they do it?" We have a discussion of sexuality, self-concept, sexism, confusion, media, communication. I am pleased.

A few weeks later I hear loud rap coming from the tape deck in his room. It's awful. I listen, barely making out the words, but what I understand is sickening. It's the 2 Live Crew. I try to get past my rage and disappointment and call my son to me, giving him the violence-against-women rap of my own. He nods his head, looks serious, understands. A couple of days later, I hear it again. Now I have to think about what I am going to do this time. I could forbid him to play the tape, which would make it all that much more attractive and almost guarantee that he'd play it even more, probably when I wasn't around, because teenagers do that. I could make him get rid of the tape, which he probably would pretend to do, and it would be even more precious then. Finally I tell him, "Do me a favor — from now on, every time you listen to that disgusting, violent, woman-hating rap tape, think that it's me and your sister they're talking about, that it's your sister and I being fucked and beaten and degraded. Get the picture?" His eyes get wide, and a look of horror twists his face. He nods. I think maybe he gets it.

The next time I hear the tape, I steal it when he's not home and throw it out. He looks all over for it, questions his siblings as to its whereabouts. I don't say a word.

Someone asks my fifteen-year-old son how it is for him to have queer parents, especially ones who are so obvious about it. "Well, at first it didn't mean anything to me," he explains. "But then I learned how people put down lesbians and gay men, and I got embarrassed because my mom and dad were like that. But then I thought to myself that they're my mom and dad, and I love them. And I'm proud of them; and I stopped being embarrassed and got mad at people who put down lesbians and gay men."

My seventeen-year-old son comes home from school. "I'm so disgusted," he tells us. "Today in history class they were talking about the ban on gays in the military, and I was the only one who thought the ban was stupid. Even the teacher was just repeating nonsense. I tried to talk sense, but no one would listen. I really wanted to stand up on my desk and holler, 'Listen, you all don't know what you're talking about. My dad is gay, and my mom's a lesbian, and they are perfectly wonderful people. The only reason they shouldn't serve in the military is because they don't believe in violence.' But of course I never could do that, because it would be too dangerous."

I find my fourteen-year-old son's stash of cunt photo magazines. He is terrified. I find it easy to remain rational. We discuss curiosity, sexism, coercion, economics, intimidation, humiliation. Then I tell him, "Just imagine someone taking photos of you with your legs flung wide, displaying every angle of your dick and balls and asshole *and* your face, in a magazine for everyone to look at."
He rolls his eyes. "Got it, Mom," he says.

Puberty roars through my house like a tornado, a tidal wave, a volcanic eruption. My house reeks of testosterone. Hormones are crashing together in the very air. Myself menopausal, I join the party. The emotionally disturbed thirteen-year-old is bouncing off the walls. Suddenly my lesbianism has become an issue for him. His verbal abusiveness takes on new dimensions, adds a new twist — sexual insults toward me and my lover. I know that he is questioning, protesting, expressing, and all of those important signals, but

89

he is leaning on every one of my buttons, and I cannot deal with him in any kind of healthy, straightforward manner. My intellect and my emotions have never been at such odds, and I am unable to sustain controlled dialogue. The best I can manage is to remove myself physically from these verbal assaults, to close the door and plug my ears, when what I really want to do is split his face with an ax.

My daughter came to us with a strong personality: extremely assertive, bossy, demanding. Many people have said stuff like, "I suppose she had to develop that way to keep up with all those boys." No, I explain, she was always like that. The fact that she has brothers has nothing to do with it. I hate when people say shit like that. I have little patience with this kind of stereotyping. The fact that she is the strongest of the children has to do with who she is, not with anyone's gender, hers or theirs. She will forever be angry with me because she doesn't have sisters. We both long for more girls in the family.

Although I avoided the issue with my separatist friend, I really did, from deep in my gut, have hopes, have dreams of raising gentle boys who would grow into men who'd help make the world a kinder place. I thought that with care and awareness we could avoid all the things that boys get into in our society that are hurtful to women and also to one another. I have mixed feelings about results. I love my sons dearly and respect each for who he is, and basically they *are* gentle men who respect women. But the power of society, peer pressure, testosterone, and bombardment by the media are very strong. Even my lover's son, who's one of the most politically aware, sensitive, feminist men I know will bring home a video that's "yeah — racist, sexist, violent, Mom."

I love my sons dearly. Although they tend to go along with the crowd, they aren't afraid of who they are. They'll wash dishes and change diapers. They hang out with Southern rednecks and blacknecks. They drink beer. They drive too fast. They get into fights. They are struggling into adulthood, learning what their abilities and limitations are, at ease about having queer parents. For better or for worse, they are my children, and I love them.

The Circle of Love: A Letter to Mikey
By Karen Bellavance-Grace

A warm, sunny Sunday in May, our first full day together. Your blond hair is shiny, the long curls bouncing and falling over the back of your overalls as you run headlong down the grassy hill. You stop halfway to examine another tiny miracle: a small purple flower cupped in your hands. As you bring your face down to meet its soft petals, I can hear you exhale, an imitation of our smelling the lilacs at the top of the hill. When you lift your head, I am stunned by the bright pure light in your blue eyes. Tears well up at the sight of your smile. And then you are off again, chasing after the dog to the worn dirt path at the foot of the hill. I watch the way your body moves with such freedom and joy. I can see now the overalls you wear are just a bit too small, the cuffs falling somewhere between knee and ankle, and the sneakers are probably a tad too big. Like everything else in our lives now, it is a question of trial and error; we will keep on, and ultimately we will get it right.

91

Our decision to become foster parents was largely a compromise. We had talked about the possibility of having children in our lives, although our views were still widely divergent. Lynn always knew she wanted to be a parent. The issue for her was clear-cut: not *if* but *when.*

I had never felt those maternal longings. In fact, I still remember the day I realized that getting pregnant and having children was not something that just happened to you the same way that at a certain age menstruation just happened to you. When I finally understood that there was some measure of volition involved, I was overjoyed. If pregnancy was not, in fact, obligatory, then I would certainly not participate. I had, I thought, all the maternal instincts of a turnip. The so-called miracle of childbirth seemed to me a rather gory and masochistic experience, and I have never had a high tolerance for either blood or pain. Then there is infancy — long months of fussing, crying babies who can't even tell you what's wrong. Cats, it seemed to me, were a much more reasonable proposition.

Years later, it is strange to find myself with the love of my life, the mate of my soul, the plum of my pudding, who has a primal, undeniable urge to be a parent. With each progressive compromise we reached, I found myself warming up to the idea of having children and feeling more confident about my strengths as a potential coparent. The first level of compromise involved the purchase of countless plants and shrubs and the subsequent planting of a garden. Lots of fuzzy green growing things to nurture. When the magic of horticulture began to fade, we agreed to try the puppy thing, something sweet and cuddly that would actually return affection. But nothing totally sated Lynn's maternal longings. After much discussion we finally decided that foster parenting would be a good way to have children in our lives and also have more time for ourselves when the children were returned to their families of origin. We could see firsthand what kind of parents we would be, away from the textbooks and theories, down and dirty in the ditches of runny noses and messy diapers. As I was beginning to get used to the idea, I could even imagine how nice it would be to have a little girl, to someday raise a daughter with love, strength, and confidence in a world that doesn't value women.

Of course, things never really work out the way you plan.

We are walking now, and you have run ahead to hide behind a boulder, preparing to pop out and surprise us. It is the day after your second birthday, and hiding behind the boulder with you is Giant Bunny, the favorite gift from last night's festivities. The big gift this year was a molded plastic mountain surrounded by train tracks with a road bisecting and a helicopter landing pad on top. A transportation dreamscape, replete with trucks, trains, helicopters, and airplanes. But it was this stuffed animal that grabbed you. From the moment it was unwrapped, Giant Bunny has stayed at your side, sitting beside you to share birthday cake, perched on the sink to oversee your bath.

There was hardly room for both you and Giant Bunny in the crib that still served as your bed. Later, as I watched you sleep, Giant Bunny was still clutched to your chest, and I was half afraid it would suffocate you during the night. I wonder whether I will always fear the people and things that are closest to you, those things that I cannot share.

I woke several more times that night and returned to check for the sound of your breath.

Two years after that Sunday in the park, we are still in the process of adopting Mikey. It has been a long and exasperating administrative process. On a personal, experiential level, however, it has been an extraordinary series of lessons. I see things in Mikey that I had hoped to encourage in my hypothetical daughter: self-reliance, independence, and a strong will. I worry that these qualities in a boy will translate into arrogance and self-involvement once he becomes a man. I am beginning to understand that I cannot raise a child to be free of our culture's often paralyzing gender stereotypes. Rather, I walk a thin line daily between such an ideal upbringing and the reality of contextual parenting. It is an ongoing struggle to impress upon Mikey the values of gender equity when he sees and hears evidence to the contrary at school and on the playground. At school they talk about policemen, and at home we talk about police officers, although all the police officers our family knows happen to be men. Still, we must hold open that semantic possibility and impress upon him that it matters. He can identify clothes and toys and even food that is "girls' stuff," and that lesson is reinforced in books, in schoolyards, on television 93 (yes, even PBS). We explain over and over that toys are meant for children, not just boys or just girls, but many times that possibility exists only in our commitment to it. It is all we can do to provide him with an environment that will, like a photographic negative, illuminate the shadows and cast a pallor on the overbearing and pervasive norm.

I find myself questioning and second-guessing my actions. If Mikey were a daughter and not a son, I am sure she would have received the transportation mountain set, but would we buy her stuffed animals? I would certainly dress her in sensible overalls, but would I delight in the flow of her long blond curls? Would I encourage her to help in the kitchen or do laundry with me, as I do with my son? Would I let her take dance lessons? Would I urge her to play football?

Of course, there are no right answers, although the process of articulating the questions is invaluable. I must continually strive to know this incredible, unique little person as the individual that he is and not as a representative of his gender. I must learn to respect his very personal interests and needs without projecting onto his choices the unwelcome baggage of sexist expectations.

"I'm gonna getcha! Because, you know, I am Batman, because I have pointy ears and angry eyes and I fly without my cape on, and now I've got you! Pchoo! Pchoo!*" and with a flourish of your cape, you leap off the sofa.*

You had never seen or even heard of Batman before last Halloween, when your friend Jason showed up in his now-infamous costume. And you have known since the beginning of forever that guns and weapons are not allowed in our house. As you stand here before me with your angry eyes and point your finger menacingly, I wonder what happened to that sweet child who hugged trees, animals, people, flowers; who embraced life and love and joy. Is this Batman a foreshadowing of the angry young man you may become? For the present, I remind you that Batman never actually used guns.

"Yes, he does," you answer definitively.

"No, sweetie, Batman saves people by using his brain and his words." I know he never used firearms, even if I am censoring out some of his "pow" and "zowie" and "bam."

"Well, this is not a gun," you say, looking thoughtfully down at your extended forefinger and thumb.

"Really? Well, you were holding it like a gun and making gun noises with it."

"No, it's not a gun. It's a...brummerfohnger." You say it with such conviction that I have to believe you, even though a rose by any other name can be as deadly. It is a small reminder of how different our perceptions of reality can be. For now, I must determine how I can play with this batman and keep my principles intact.

There seems to be no limit to the number of responses to the War Toy Dilemma. It appears to be a nearly universal phenomenon among boys of a certain age. Whether or not there are cartoons in the house (there are not) or older siblings (none) or school-age friends with superhero action figures (nope), one day it just happens. Once innocent toys, sticks, bananas, and fingers suddenly become loaded. The only way I can understand it is in terms of a child's status in the world. It is one of the few ways a child can feel in control of his environment. But this does not explain why similarly powerless girls only rarely exhibit such a fascination with weaponry.

We have tried, like my fictional Batman, to use words and minds to overcome the violence society foists on its children. We do not allow him to watch *Mighty Morphin Power Rangers*, for example, though we cannot pretend they don't exist, since not all parents agree that it is an inappropriate program for three-year-olds to watch. Rather, we explain to him why we do not like programs that model violence as a good way to solve problems. He knows that we will not play weapon games with him and that he may not have guns or swords in our home, but we certainly cannot control his play at day care or when he gets to the schoolyard. The most we can do is to control the activities within our domestic circle, and as he grows up and his level of understanding deepens, we hope he will respect our decision to keep our home violence-free in a disturbed and random world. We hope that on some level he will recognize in this episode a model of how to live with integrity in a world of hard choices.

I remember the time — you were almost two then — when Lynn found a dead mouse in the garage. It had surprised her quite badly. She was shaken and crying and she held tightly onto you while I disposed of the mouse. Then I met you in the driveway and tried to put my arms around you both. You pushed your arm out violently and told me, "No! Get away!"

It was at that point that we began to understand how your past worked in your present. We seemed to be playing out a rehearsed dynamic here: One parent hurts the other; that parent then holds on to you closely in her search for security. We would later learn the details that bear out this theory only too well. At the same time, you had already taken a step toward healing. You said no, perhaps for the first time.

95

We explained why Lynn was crying and that I had not hurt her, that I only wanted to help her feel better, and ultimately the three of us embraced together. I trace the seeds of our current family dynamic to this incident. Lynn has been cast as the archetypal vulnerable one, in need of protection, and my motives, it seems, are always suspect. We have been pressed into the model of parenthood you have known although the fit is as uncomfortable as the proverbial square peg. Gradually your understanding changes along with your sense of security, and you can articulate and experience our relationship on its own terms.

In thinking again about his growing fascination with guns and arrows, I wonder whether we are overly sensitive to the war toy–violence connection, given this child's personal history. He spent the first year and a half of his life in an environment in which force and violence were used regularly as a means of both interpersonal control and conflict management. We fear that as a child who has witnessed domestic violence, even at so young an age, Mikey may quite easily fall into a pattern of using force to get his way. After all, this is the very first model he had for interpersonal relations, particularly those between men and women. On some subconscious level I know that it will always be with him. This is what I fear most when he is playing "Gotcha" or "Bad Guys." This is why it is so critical that we acknowledge the violence around us — after all, he knows about it firsthand. Yet we must be able to offer alternatives that will feel powerful to him and also respectful of others involved. It is a thin line to tread.

Story time is over, and our nightly ritual continues. "I love you in our house," you say. "And I love Lynn at our house. But I don't love you at Mathew and Noelle's house. I love Mathew and Noelle and Lynn at Mathew and Noelle's house. But I don't love you, and I don't love Noelle. Only sometimes I do."

"Well, I love you everywhere in the whole world every day, and I'm so happy to be one of your parents," I answer, putting away the storybooks and turning on the night-lights.

"Well, today I love you," you say. "But you should go away now. Tell Lynn I need him."

I remind you that Lynn is a "her" and not a "him," then I bend to kiss you good-night and try to turn away before you wipe it from your cheek. Going into the kitchen where she has been preparing your lunch for the next day, I tell Lynn, "Tag, you're it." Already you are yelling from your room, "Mommy, I need you!"

After an hour I will go back to your room to wake Lynn, who has fallen asleep, as have you, nose to nose, your arm draped casually around her neck.

It's odd, the way Mikey figures his algebra of love. It seems there is not enough love to go around and that it must be carefully rationed. There is one place where both Lynn and I can be loved simultaneously at our home. There, apparently, he cannot love his grandparents, Mathew and Noelle. But he can love them at their house, along with Lynn, but not me. Unless it's a month with an r. The thing is, it makes sense to him, and it seems to have to do with his being in control of his own emotions, if not of his environment. Consistently, I will answer that I love him everywhere and always. I am confident that as his sense of safety grows, he will understand the possibility of love without conditions. In the end the algebra of love will prove that love multiplies as it is divided and shared.

"You forgot to kiss him!" you shriek.

I was about to commit the ultimate heresy of getting out of the car without kissing Lynn good-bye. Never mind that we are in the middle of a busy intersection and the light is about to turn green; we have our rituals, and they are important.

"First a hug," you orchestrate from the backseat. "Now a kiss." I remind you (again) that Lynn and I are both "hers." I don't know why you call everyone "him," though I am not overly concerned about your sense of gender identity. We have just come from our friend Diane's house, whose three-year-old daughter Tabitha calls everyone "her." It seems to be a three-year-old thing.

In fact, you seem to be just beginning to discover gender at all. Last week in the park, as I walked with you and Tabitha to the nearest rest room, you asked, "Do you have a penis?"

"No, sweetie, but you do."

97

"Does he have a penis?" you said, "he" being, of course, Tabitha.

"No, she doesn't." Now, you have asked this before, primarily during bath time, when I have been able to explain that boys and men have penises and girls and women have vaginas. That way, we each have something and neither of us is defined by our lack of anything. But here on a crowded public playground, I can't quite bring myself to say "vagina" out loud, so I compromise. "Mommy and Tabitha are girls, and only boys and men have penises."

"Daddies have a penis."

"Yes, that's true."

"But mommies don't."

"You're right," I say, trying to hurry past the busy swing set.

"Well," you announce when we finally arrive at the bathroom door. "When I'm a grown-up, I'm gonna have big boobies!"

Great, I think as I explain again how only girls and women have boobies when they grow up. Three years old, and already size matters!

There are several daily rituals to which we must adhere. There must be three bedtime stories at night. You must have your juice first thing in the morning. Most important, there must be a hug first, then a kiss whenever one of us leaves the others — anywhere, anytime. I am told there will be a time when you will feel "too big" for good-bye kisses, but I am hopeful that we will be able to achieve some form of compromise whereby we can give our good-bye hugs at home before we get out in public. I can't believe you will ever be "too big" for me to hug. There is a part of me also that fears each time we say good-bye will be our last, so tenuous is this "preadoptive" status, and I am determined that you will know how much I love you every day. Just in case. And so I treat each parting as though it were the last. Not letting you know how you are loved will not be one of the things I will grow to regret.

In the process of identifying us as Mikey's permanent family, the question arose as to how two lesbians could raise a boy. In the privacy of our home, Lynn confessed, "I haven't a clue...but don't tell them that!" It is an impossible question to ask of anyone. If there were a right way to raise boys, there certainly would not be so many men, grown-up sons, abandoning or abusing their families, sending their own children into state-sponsored foster care. Nonetheless, much of our interview revolved around the assertion that Mikey would have male role models. The social worker even took the unusual step of traveling out of state to meet with Lynn's mother and stepfather, a normal or, rather, heterosexual couple who were and would continue to be active in Mikey's life. It seemed to assuage her fears a bit. Additionally, our dear family friend Jonathon spends one day a week with Mikey, and the social worker came one day to meet him and observe the two interacting together. She never asked (and we never offered) whether Jonathon was gay. The fact of his maleness seemed to satisfy her that Mikey would not be the lone testosterone raft awash in a sea of estrogen.

I expect we will come across this attitude many times over as Mikey enters the larger world. It is amusing on some level, since the task of raising children has traditionally been considered women's work, and here we are, two women with but a single purpose. I think there is the fear that we will raise him to be self-hating, although that is precisely how most girls are raised in this country. I truly believe Mikey's life will be richer for his experience of growing up in our family, one that embraces a larger and more eclectic extended family. I am not afraid that the absence of a "father figure" will turn him into a "sissy." I am confident that we will be able to help him understand what it is to be human. I do not need a penis to do this. Nor do I to teach him so-called male values of responsibility and commitment. We can leave him with an understanding of family in its truest sense and trust that that will carry him successfully into his own experience of parenthood.

Lynn and I were attending a three-week reading group on the book *The Courage to Raise Good Men.* We were exhilarated after the first session to hear the experiences and hopes and fears of other parents of boys of all ages. When we returned home, the baby-sitter said how wonderful Mikey had been that night and told us this story:

> It was time for bed, and Mikey was explaining how he had to have three bedtime stories because his parents always let him have three. "You know," he said, "I love my parents."
> "They love you too."
> "Yes, and you know, these are Lynn's books," he declared with a sweeping theatrical gesture to the right. "And these are Karen's," he continued, indicating the shelf to the left. Bringing both arms around before him, he drew an imaginary circle around himself, saying, "And I am part of the circle of love in our family."

99

I do not have the slightest idea how lesbians can possibly raise sons. But I'm sure Mikey will show me all I need to know.

Snakes and Snails
By Ellen Grabiner

Next to my father, who bought me my first and only pair of boxing gloves, Harry Belafonte was the man who most influenced my developing feminism. I think my mother had the hots for him, and along with *Scheherazade,* Frank Sinatra, and *My Fair Lady,* his music was a staple in our home. When Harry sang, "It was clear as mud, but it covered the ground," he spoke to me. I loved his raspy voice, his ease, his commitment even way back then to multiculturalism.

"That's right the woman is, uh, smarter," Harry convinced me. I believed I could do anything I set my mind or body to do. I wasn't crazy, and I didn't think I could fly like Superman, but within reason, the fact that I was a girl wouldn't keep me from achieving my goals. I believed that inside, where it counted, men and women were potentially the same. If raised in an ideal culture that valued both, men and women would not develop along stereotypical lines. I thought it was reactionary and heretical to think otherwise.

But that was before I had a son. Having a son didn't lessen my commitment to changing our society, to fighting sexism in all its forms, to ensuring equal opportunities and education for our young girls, to exploding the stereotypes of our culture. But I now believe that if one could create a nonbiased culture, even a peaceful culture, in which boys and girls were raised evenly, without distinctions based on chromosomal composition, the boys would still come out shooting.

It has been ten years since my lover, Susan, and I became parents. As I look back, it is only too clear that our current lives hardly resemble our so-called lesbian lifestyle pre-Alex.

In some ways we are like those folks we know who got stuck in the '60s, only we got stuck in the early '80s. Our lesbian music collection is full of Meg's and Holly's and Chris's early albums, and we even have Ferron's first. We of course know who Kate Clinton is, but we are ashamed to admit that we have never seen her perform. The last women's music festival we attended was in 1983, the year before I got pregnant. We haven't been to a women's concert since

I can't remember when, and we rarely see women's theater or films. This year we didn't even make it to the gay pride march.

In 1983 almost all of our friends, with few exceptions, were lesbians. Now almost none of our closest friends are lesbians. This happened in stages and for a variety of reasons. Some of our closest lesbian friends went through difficult and prolonged breakups that affected all of our lives. Some of our closest lesbian friends moved away. Some of our closest lesbian friends are no longer lesbians. And some of them couldn't deal with the fact that we had a child and gradually drifted away. We look around and notice that now the people we spend the most time with are people with children Alex's age.

One striking difference is that there are many more men in our lives. Susan and I had fantasized that there would be men who would take an interest in Alex, who would function as a surrogate dad or uncle. Unfortunately, this has not happened. Instead we have made friends with men, straight and gay, who are in our lives not just for Alex but for all of us. Having a son forced us to look at the ways we had generalized to all men the most heinous traits of the worst men. Loving Alex forced us to come more into balance in our lives. It forced us to reintegrate a part of our lives that we had cut out. **101**

At a series of junctures leading to parenthood, Susan and I were forced to examine our feelings about being lesbians mothering a boy child: when we began the process of inseminating, when we were interviewing our obstetrician, when we saw the first ultrasound of Alex's tiny penis, when our friends asked, "Won't it be hard to raise a boy?"

We considered the difficulties we thought we would encounter. What would we do about women-only events? Would we attend and leave Alex at home? Would we boycott? Would we bring our male infant with us? Truthfully, we were not all that worried. At least, not at first. Baby girl or baby boy, a baby is a baby. The procedure is the same, with some small variations.

We knew, for example, that we would have a bris. After all, we had gone to the trouble of procuring and using Jewish sperm, so we decided to go all the way. I called a *mohel* (this is someone trained in ritual circumcision) who was recommended to us. Over the phone he explained that he needed some information, such as the child's Hebrew name, the father's Hebrew... Oops! I couldn't imagine explaining to this seventy-year-old Jewish man, this variation on the theme of grandfather, why there was no father. But he was hip, he was cool. No problem, he assured me. Nowadays anything goes. My stepfather, Jack, was given the honors, the horrifying honors, of holding down Alex's tiny thighs while the *mohel* did the deed.

The bris, attended by our family and friends, lesbian and straight, was a nightmare. Until forced to part with his foreskin, Alex had let out no more than a whimper. That day he learned to bellow. I already knew I wouldn't be able to watch, so I was grateful when I was handed a prayer book and told to read. I kept my eyes on the words as they swam before me. My knuckles turned white as the *mohel* held Alex up for everyone to see what a clean, neat job he had done (to his credit, Alex's penis healed handsomely), and it was all I could do not to snatch the poor traumatized child right out of his arms.

Soon enough I put him to my breast, sneaking in drips of infant Tylenol until he conked, whether from exhaustion or agony, we'll never know. Susan and I bundled him up and got out the brand-new Aprica stroller and went for a walk.

We survived the bris and it's aftermath, cleaning the wound. (I say *we,* but really it was Susan's job to change the gauze and apply the ointment.) We imagined how it must have stung when he peed, and we settled into the joys of parenting. Alex was kvetchy and uncomfortable for the first four months of his life and then underwent an amazing transformation. He began to laugh and smile and giggle and crawl and for the most part has been an easy, happy kid ever since. It was when he began to speak, though, that Susan and I had our first inkling that boys were innately different from girls.

Our first clue was when he and Emily, his good friend and playmate, were learning the sign-language gesture for *more.* Emily's parents both worked with deaf children and signed often as they spoke. They taught Alex and Emily the sign for *more,* which looks something like this: You place your thumbs up against your fingertips as if you were going to pick up something very tiny, a hair perhaps. Then you bring the fingertips of both hands together and tap them to each other a couple of times. When Emily did the sign, she used only the thumb and first finger of each hand, as if to pick up a tiny bead, letting her other fingers trail elegantly like a ballerina's hand. When Alex signed *more,* he banged his tightly closed little fists together. You tell me. Two children, both raised by lesbian parents in homes with similar values, showed exactly the same sign taught by the same person at the same time and voilà: chromosomes.

One of our first official acts as parents was to declare a gun-free household. We had decided that it was in keeping with our feminist ideology. By the time Alex turned two, we realized we would have to become a block-free, Lego-free, pencil-free, and carrot-free household, and even that would not ensure that Alex wouldn't find something — an oblong pillow, a bar of soap, a mascara brush, for god's sake — that would become, in his pudgy little hands, a weapon. We did, pardon the cliché, stick to our guns, however, and we purchased no weapons for our son.

That is, until that fateful night the circus came to town. Susan and I had always hated the circus, but we felt we couldn't deprive our son of a cultural experience just because of our personal biases. So when the three-ring Ringling Bros. and Barnum & Bailey Circus came to the Boston Garden, we were there.

The lights dimmed, and we thought the show was about to begin. We were wrong. Apparently a tradition had sprung up in the thirty years since we had each been to the circus: Now the lights go down, and the brandishing of the light sabers begins. Whether this evolved post–Stars Wars or not, I don't know. But what I do know is that of the thousand or so children in the arena that night, 999 of them had plastic swords that now, lit up, were swirling in the dark with their dancing blades. **103**

In the past Alex tried to reassure us that even if we didn't know the difference between a toy and the real thing, he did. For him, a toy gun was just that — a toy. Still, we stood our ground. That night Alex — sweet, wiser than his years, and perhaps more manipulative than we will ever know — didn't beg, didn't cry, didn't even ask if he could have a light saber. Instead he sat quietly, looking into his lap. It was more than we could stand. I sent Susan off to fetch him a light sword of his very own that he could flourish among the best of them. Wasn't it enough that he had to have weird parents? Couldn't we at least let him feel normal once in a while? Alex's gratitude was evident. That night and for the next several months, along with his blankie and stuffed animals, he took his sword to bed with him and held it close to his heart.

That, however, was just the beginning. Then came the gift from Marsha and Vida in California. (This was before they adopted David. Now we'll see how *they* like it.) They sent Alex a dart gun, of all things, with a bull's-eye target to hang on the wall, and somehow that was okay because you shot it at the wall. And then water pistols were okay because they just shot water and that was fun and harmless. And then there was the authentic pirate pistol that we just *had* to buy at Pirates of the Caribbean — well, after all, it *was* Alex's birthday trip to Disney World.

The arsenal of weapons Alex has accumulated could arm the entire neighborhood. We drew the line at automatic weapons, the ones that made "lifelike" sounds of rounds of bullets being fired. But I was the softy when it came to space weapons: I loved the toys that mimicked the sounds on *Star Trek.*

Even the devotion to *Next Generation* episodes we share breaks down along sex-stereotyped lines. At the beginning of each episode (and we've seen them all at least twice), Alex will announce whether this is one that I will like — meaning it's romantic — or one that he will like: a shoot-'em-up one with lots of chase scenes.

Yet there is a part of me that believes it has been easier to raise a boy than it would have been with a girl. I worry about my own internalized misogyny. I suspect that if I had had a daughter who refused to wear jeans, who wanted ribbons in her hair, who didn't like to get her hands dirty, who was fastidious, who preened, who deferred to the little boys around her, I would have gone apeshit. I would have wanted her to be a feminist, maybe even a lesbian. I would have been judgmental as all get out. I would have overidentified, I would have been in her face, I would have been critical, sarcastic, unrelenting, dogmatic — I would have been a nightmare of a mother. Just like my mother was.

Yet sometimes I find myself missing the very girlie things I abhor. For my sister's wedding I decided that I wanted to get a braid, the kind the kids all have, wrapped colors of embroidery thread surrounding a thin strand of hair. May, the daughter of Alex's fourth-grade teacher, was a pro. I was invited to her friends' house, to sit on the bed in the young girls' bedroom while May wound the brightly colored string through my white hair. I looked around me. There were no weapons of any kind, no pictures of Geordi and Data, no spaceships, no Legos. In the room of these adolescent girls were ruffles, pillows, bedspreads, dolls, doll furniture — even a doll canopy bed. There were ribbons and cloth remnants, posters of young men that I assumed were movie stars and rock-and-roll heroes. I recognized none of them. There was a little mirrored dressing table cluttered with perfumes and makeup. The only thing this room had in common with Alex's was the piles of clothes scattered across the floor and the unmade bed.

As May braided, I was privileged to eavesdrop on their conversation, three of them watching May work, talking about Joey, the boy they had a crush on; about Marla, the girlfriend with whom they had just broken off relations; and about what they would wear the following day. Not a word was said about shooting, killing, fighting, or blowing up an entire galaxy. I understood their lives and yet felt as if I were visiting a foreign country. I wished then that once in a while Alex could bring the same intensity to examining a relationship that he does to recounting the minutest details of the most recent suspense thriller he has just seen.

When I observe Alex's girl friends and girl cousins and see how easily they spread cream cheese on a bagel and get themselves something to drink, I worry about the way we have raised him. I wonder if he is just lazy, if it's genetic, or if it is our fault that he acts as if he is a little prince waiting to be served.

I decided that it was time for him to learn to cook. After all, I started cooking when I was ten. The problem is that when I was a child, we ate "real" meals. Sit-down-at-the-table meals. On Monday, meat loaf and mashed potatoes. Tuesday was fried chicken, dipped in cornflake batter. Wednesday I sautéed pork chops in Wishbone salad dressing, cooked rice in Lipton soup. On Thursday, tuna noodle casserole (my favorite) made with Campbell's cream of mushroom soup. You get the picture.

105

But our lives are so crazed that most of our meals are now heat and eat. So it is that Alex has learned to make himself both macaroni and cheese and rice pilaf (from a box), chicken dogs (he pops those in the toaster oven), and bacon. We have started to enforce little rules: Hang up your towel after your bath, put your clothes away after the laundry is done, clear your plate after you eat, put it in the dishwasher. I would insist that he set the table for dinner if we ever all three of us sat down to a meal together. He cleans his room, helps with bringing in and sometimes even unpacking the groceries, helps take out the garbage and the recycling. But it is all a struggle. He seems to have no interest in becoming self- sufficient, takes little pride in these, his household accomplishments. Yet when he was finally able to figure out how to program the HyperCard game he was animating so that the ball would drop when he clicked on the mouse, that he was proud of. So what's wrong with that?

The other day Alex told me that the girls in his group at camp weren't interested in the same things that the boys were interested in. He thought it would be a good idea if girls got a chance to practice taking care of kids so that they would learn how to make good mothers. Furious, I barked at his idea: "Don't boys have to learn that too?"

Yes, he replied wisely, but it really is mostly the women who take care of the kids. I wanted it to be different, but Alex was telling me it wasn't.

"It's just that girls like taking care of children more than boys do," he tried to explain.

"But you like being with little kids, don't you?" I have watched him with Anika, a little girl we baby-sit for. He was gentle and patient with her.

"Yeah," he replied, "but only for a little while."

For all of our politically correct intentions, all of our agonizing, we had to face the quintessential truth of parenthood, lesbian or otherwise: Ultimately you have no control. We can't block out the world, and we can't block the relentless flow of testosterone. We can offer only the example of our lives and the love in which we wrap our son and share the delight he brings to us. And hope that this will be enough.

My biggest fear as a lesbian mother was that somehow my choice to love a woman would be interpreted implicitly by Alex as a rejection of his very essence. It seems unfounded. If there is one true thing I can say about Alex, it is that he knows he is loved. He is secure in his family, in his sense of self, in his ability to move in the world. It's true that he is just ten, in the so-called latency stage. The stage in which his mother is the best mom in the whole world and his "Pipi, the best Peep." We have not hit adolescence yet. We have not had to deal with wet dreams, masturbation, sex, drugs, and rock and roll. We have not yet had to stay up nights worrying because he is out with the car, because he got some girl pregnant, because he is gay and is he having only safe sex? We have not yet had to deal with the rebellion, the rejection that is sure to come. We have not had to deal with his shame or his embarrassment or his wishing we would not say that we are lesbians. Yet. We are not so foolish as to believe that things will always be as rosy as they are now. But for now my complaints are few and lightweight compared to what they could be. And there's something to be said for the child that soars down the fast-paced, techno-driven information highway and who also knows where the "uh" goes when his mother sings Harry Belafonte. That's my boy.

Your Mom Looks Like Superman
by Ilsa Jule

My [step]son, who isn't my [step]son, is named Jacob. He is four years old. He's my girlfriend's son, but saying "my girlfriend's son" doesn't roll off the tongue with ease and also implies that I'm not directly involved in the parenting process. "My girlfriend's son" imposes a sense of separateness, that I watch her raise him, mutely. Whereas, in reality, I often feed him, assume the role of lifeguard during bath time, take him to the park to play, watch cartoons with him, entertain him, and care for him. I do not consider these activities to be chores; I enjoy his company, and we get along great.

He also can't be my [step]son because women are not allowed to marry one another, and even if we could, I'm not sure that we would. I have often thought about what it would be like to legally marry my girlfriend, but I quickly experience that unoriginal feeling that many before me have, of being confined and constricted in a legal institution that has sought to enslave women for centuries. Our version of a marriage includes compassion, consideration, and communication, so why bother with the law? Aside from not being able to place each other on respective health plans and file taxes jointly — privileges reserved for straight married couples — we'll manage.

I certainly can't call him my son; eyebrows would furrow in any conversation in which I introduced him as such. People would be greatly puzzled at the thought of my bearing children. Believe me when I say that the idea that I might conceive is inconceivable.

I've sought to be a parent for my [step]son, but I have had awful role models, and being with him sometimes causes me pain. I've been a step-mother for less than a year, but many times he has pushed me to the end of my patience. After a grueling day at work, I require a ten-minute nap, and every time I'm just about asleep he comes over, hits me, and asks, "Are you asleep?" And as much as I'd like to put him out with the recyclables or yell at him, I can't and I don't.

In fact, when I am nice to him, I remember how categorically abusive my parents were in raising me, and on some days when I am feeling fragile, it takes a lot of energy to not have a small emotional breakdown. ("Why are you so upset?" the doctor might ask. "Because I was being nice to my [step]son" I would reply. "How odd," the doctor would respond. "Most people get upset when they are mean to their children.") He's just a kid, and the next time I might need a nap and he wants to show me his latest coloring-book masterpieces, I won't get angry, I'll gladly look at them. Besides, he's not going to let me sleep.

In order to get straight answers from children, one has to ask straight questions. (It's true that queers are sometimes in search of straight answers.) My wife and I have been raised in a culture that has recently seen some states sign into law gay civil rights measures, which by and large have not been able to erase all the prejudices so many people have lived by. These prejudices can appear at a young age, and in a predominantly heterosexual culture, it is not uncommon to hear antilesbian slurs.

Although Jake might not know what lesbians are, he could certainly develop a hatred toward them. And being that I am the first person whom my wife has lived with since her separation from her husband and possibly the first lesbian he has had extensive contact with, I often wonder how he feels about my being with his mom.

Most nights before falling asleep, my wife and I talk about all the bits that you save up to tell your mate. Most times she tells me about conversations she and Jake had during the day. When I place the two of them together talking, I always picture them riding the bus. I look forward to hearing these bus anecdotes. As she and I snuggle, searching for that comfortable place amid a tangle of arms and legs to fall asleep in, she reports on these exchanges.

"I asked Jake if he liked having you live here."

"And?" I ask.

"He said he *loves* it."

I smile at this. She then relates the following dialogue:

JAKE: Mom, do you love Ilsa?

MOM [*laughing*]: Yes.

JAKE: Do you want to marry her?

MOM [*laughing*]: Yes.

JAKE [*smiling*]: That's funny — two dresses.

The other night when I came home from work, Jake was sitting on the sofa watching cartoons. I greeted him as the door slammed shut and proceeded to walk into the kitchen to give my wife a kiss. My trip was interrupted. "Want to see my writing?" he asked. I stopped, turned left, and sat on the sofa next to him. He opened his newly purchased Mighty Morphin Power Rangers notebook, purchased with his first weekly allowance, and on the page was a random assortment of letters, in his hand, and then three words: ILSA JULE OUT. (I had no idea he was so politically aware.) "That's excellent," I said. "I didn't know you could write." He is continually making a fuss over things he claims he can't do that I know he can do, like put on his shoes and tie them. I understand his wanting to fake people out so that they will perform these tasks for him. He turned the page and revealed some more letters and the word BATMAN. He then lost interest in me and the notebook and turned his attention once again toward the television set. I then stood up and moved into the kitchen.

Lately when I look at him, he seems small. In fact, each time I see him, he appears smaller than the last time. But his clothes are getting tighter, not baggier. I suppose I am finally getting used to him, understanding what it means to be with a child for whom I am partly responsible. I am no longer overwhelmed by the idea of him and by him physically. I have grown accustomed, and he fits comfortably into my life.

109

I've been thinking of myself as a parent. Not really a mother — my breasts have never lactated for anyone — and not a father. I like *parent* — it's not gender-specific. I'm not gender-specific. I can change a flat tire, bake, do the wash, program the VCR, play ball, and hug when needed.

My thoughts, when thinking of the family, often turn to the law, about title and authority, about courts separating mothers from their children, about Newt Gingrich wanting to end welfare, thereby criminalizing single mothers. (What about the fathers? The laws pertaining to abandonment, which is criminalized, ought to be enforced and penalized. Why should mothers bear the burden alone? Only a man would think that forcing mothers into prisons and children into orphanages is a solution for what ails the modern family.

In the midst of being a parent and having done my best to act like one — although I had come to the realization that I can probably only really be a friend to my [step]son — Jake just started calling me "Mom" and kissing me on the face. He would sometimes kiss my hand if we were walking down the street, but his displays of affection became grandiose: Kissing me on the subway, kissing me on the neck, hands, face. I was usually in a state of joyous surprise and wasn't able to accurately gauge the responses of the other passengers as Jake exclaimed "Mom" to someone who clearly looks like "Dad." Perhaps they thought it was some sort of private joke. I figure some parents must be bored by such a display, since kids generally refer to their parents in such a fashion, but for me, in an instant I became a mom. There can only be one mother, and "Mom" suits me just fine.

Being a [step]mom is a fearful experience for me. I am a worrier by nature. I believe my imagination, when not properly occupied, thrives on creating narratives, darkly hued stories of mishaps and accidents. Most of the time my worrying proves to be an activity with purely abstract roots. There are real dangers, however, present dangers. Not the least of which includes Jake being left with his father. Once he fell off a tabletop at the launderette and hit his head — no real damage done. Another time, however, he got up in the middle of the night, fell down a flight of stairs, and broke his arm. Children are not mindful of their own safety (as cute as they are, they are possibly the clumsiest beings), so taking your eyes off anyone under the age of five is life-endangering.

Strangely, when Jake and I go to the playground, I am not the doting type. I tend to worry only when he is out of sight. He is a shy person, and he ignores the other children. Sometimes I chase him around and watch as other mothers sit in groups and gossip. Even if I were to sit with them, I would not be included in any of these hen circles — I don't look the part.

I usually end up putting the kids, whose mothers are gossiping, into the swings or helping them climb the jungle gym. I watch as tragedy brushes a gentle hand across playground antics. Most of the time the children avoid its touch, and in New York City a thick, squishy black rubber matting lines all the critical areas of the playground so that scraped knees have almost been done away with.

I have tried to help Jake make the transition from playing with me to playing with other kids. Sometimes it works, often it does not. After he broke his arm, having a cast drew a lot of attention, and kids would come up and ask, "What happened to your arm?" He wouldn't reply, and I'd say to Jake, "That kid is asking you a question." Jake would remain frozen, and then I might say, "He broke it." They knew he broke it, but they wanted details. Some would launch into their own tales of broken limbs.

One day as we were playing on the slide, a couple of kids asked him about his arm and I told them he had broken it. A few minutes later one of the kids came over to Jake and said, "Your mom looks like Superman." Jake looked at me and said, "They're talking about you, Ilsa." I chuckled. *What a wonderful sentence!* I thought.

Maybe they had seen me catch that milk truck, the one Lex Luthor had flung into Tompkins Square Park that was on its way to crashing down on their heads. The one their mothers were too busy gabbing to one another to notice. Moms can be heroes, and I'd rather be Superman than Wonder Woman, anyway.

Jacob has taken to calling me "the baby-sitter." This almost pisses me off, but I am curious to know why. It was a few months ago that he shocked me by calling me "Mom" (for me, this was like winning an Oscar). During the months that preceded this exclamation, I had been thinking *I am a parent* but stressing that I was his friend. 111 It was also during these early months that I realized how poorly my parents rated at having been able to provide for me. It occurred to me that you don't have to give your children much to give them a lot. By this I mean giving in the sense of not diminishing your child's status as a person, supporting and loving so that he or she may flourish. I do not mean giving in terms of toys or money.

I am almost more upset about being called the baby-sitter, thinking that it might be the inverted homophobia of a five-year-old. I am not even sure he knows that I am his mother's lover. He has talked about the fact that she and I want to marry each other, but I don't think he is sure about the sex part. I wonder whether kids at school have been pestering him about my not being his mother or his father and whether they think I am his father because I look like a guy.

Many times as I sat in the hall waiting for school to let out, other children walking around would approach me and ask questions. After a few weeks it was a known fact that I was there to pick up Jake. Other first graders would walk up to me, and the following exchange would take place:

FIRST GRADER: Are you here to pick up Jake?

ME: Yes.

FIRST GRADER: Are you his dad?

ME: No.

FIRST GRADER: Are you his baby-sitter?

ME: In a way.

Then they would walk off, their minds already on another topic of interest.

I am amazed at the complexity of the social pressure I have witnessed at the kindergarten level. I feel that these early relationships are as intensely convoluted as any I have had as an adult. I have heard him use the word "faggot" once without knowing what the hell he was talking about. (My brother and I once received a long lecture in our early years about the words "hooker" and "faggot" because we were running around the house referring to each other in these terms.) It's hard to talk to children about bigotry. It's such a complex topic, and making explanations to them about fundamental aspects of life is difficult, let alone dissecting the intricacies of hatred.

I fear for him and for myself because he will at some point have to face people who are unable to deal with his mother and I as a lesbian couple. I am hoping that by that time he and I will be good friends and that he won't question the values that our family is based on. I fear his fear, because young people need to be accepted. He has often seemed insecure about himself, and I don't want to add to his burden.

I have my own burden to tote. When I was younger I really thought part of my identity as a lesbian was to make sure that I was out. Not that I felt compelled to announce my status, but if anyone asked, I just said, "Yes." As a lesbian who is helping her lover raise a son, I feel I deserve some respect as a parent. Sure, I wasn't around at the moment of conception, I didn't endure waking at all hours of the night during his infancy to feed him, I didn't change his diapers, and I didn't teach him how to walk, but now I am part of his family, and I want to ensure that he is allowed to be exactly who he is. (Fighting with children who are creating their identities is a losing battle, so why waste any time trying?) I indulge many of his whims, and the ones I don't are either harmful or just plain impossible. I have offered encouragement and support.

It is frustrating to hear from his mother that his teacher has uttered words of praise: "He did a great job reading/dancing/clean-ing up," etc. Whenever his teacher sees me, she assumes I am a baby-sitter, and I don't want to sound like a lunatic as I start shriek-ing, "I'm one of his parents! Tell me about something wonderful that he did. I'm part of his learning process, his family — include me too!"

I believe I suffer from the propaganda that wants to marginalize families that are not based in biology. It may be written in law, but it was never written in nature that heterosexuality is a tenet upon which families are based. I think that being a woman, whether I am butch or not, causes me to think that I am supposed to have given birth. The culture stresses this. This is a tactic used to discrimi-nate. If two men want to have a child, they have to adopt it. Too many states have laws against such practices, yet it is interesting to note that during the periods when it is permissible, many lesbian and gay couples do adopt. The fact that these families are a minor-ity is not by choice but constructed by the law. The law and the cul-ture want to diminish the status of such families, as if they are pre-tend families. This is unfair to lesbians, because in a lesbian rela-tionship (assuming both women didn't give birth) one of the moth-ers is left to feel like an impostor. I'm not even attempting to claim 113 the status of mother; I am seeking to be a mom.

Jake and I went to withdraw some money from an automated teller, and he asked me what I was doing.

I said, "Getting money."

"What do you mean?" he asked.

I said, "You know, dollars."

He asked, "What about quarters?"

"You can get them inside the bank," I said. "Dimes and nickels, they all come from a mint."

He said, "You mean like how pennies come from the sidewalk?"

Sometimes I really don't know why I am helping my lover raise her kid. I suppose it has to do with the fact that I love both of them. I knew I liked Jake the instant I met him. I had watched him eat lunch from one of the floors that overlooks the playground at our college, not knowing he was hers. I like to watch the kids run around and scream. I used to sit in a particular spot at school to watch her go and pick him up from day care. I was trying to be casual, like I just happened to be there. She invited me to walk over and meet him. He was sort of shy with me, but something passed between us. It was almost as if he'd said, "You look like a lot of fun," and I had replied, "I am," and we agreed to be friends. He was so cute. I fell in love with his mother for having made such a beautiful child. Our future together was uncertain, but my feelings for both of them were not: It had been love at first sight.

I have an irrational fear that Jake will sue me when he's forty years old. His father is a lawyer, and in this particular nightmare he turns into a personal-injury loss shyster and after a series of bad investments convinces Jacob to sue me so that he can make a real-estate investment with the award. The grounds on which the case is tried are those that I caused Jake irreparable emotional damage by having turned his mother into a lesbian and forced him to live in a degrading household. The Supreme Court rules in his favor. I become the example, a *Guinness Book*–size scapegoat. A message goes out to all those who reside in the closet, to those who are afraid, who seek excuses to do nothing to fight homophobia. They are reassured that their choice was correct, to never chance being out, because if they did as I did, they too would be ridiculed by society, punished for being lesbian, criminalized for raising children in an unholy way. I often feel it's a case of damned if I do, damned if I don't.

The nightmare turns to fantasy. In this scenario he grows up to be a fairly well-adjusted guy who treats women as his equal, who appreciates having had two moms, and who, when he hears people bashing gays and lesbians, passionately and articulately argues that having been brought up by two lesbians never did him any harm. His audience is left slack-jawed. People who never would have guessed are impressed that such a nice guy came out of a "deviant" household in which two women who were in love with each other did not neglect to give him the love, affection, and support he needed.

I prefer the second scenario over the first, and perhaps someday he will have developed a satisfactory narrative of his own that is somewhere in between.

Being that I am a [step]mom, there are certain duties that I am not expected to perform, such as the age-old custom of reading the bedtime story — this is a time reserved for mothers.

If Sarah is not going to be around to read Jake a story, he usually goes without one. This is not because I do not want to read him one; it's just that, like all kids, he has an innate sense of wanting to break the rules when his mother is not around. So if I'm the one who is putting him to bed, he ends up falling asleep on the sofa watching TV with me.

I am continually criticized for not doing things Mom's way. "That's not how Mom makes pizza." I purposefully do things my way because I think it's silly for people and children to expect everyone to behave in a uniform fashion. I understand a child's wanting things to be familiar, but as long as no one is being harmed, it's never too early to appreciate a variety of perspectives on life.

The only time I ever read him a story, he and I assumed the correct positions: He was sort of in my arms as I held the book outstretched. I leaned back on a pillow resting against the headboard. It was a classic tale of colonialism, oppression, and indoctrination: *Curious George Takes a Job*.

Sarah had never coached me on the finer points of bedtime-story reading, although I should have guessed that any child under the age of six living in the United States knows that George is "always very curious." I also should have guessed that Jake had memorized the book. And this is a fascinating thing about children: They can listen to the same song and watch the same TV show over and over without getting bored. In fact, sometimes they seem to *prefer* things they already know. When they find something they enjoy, they stick with it.

When we reached the crucial "He was always very curious" line, Jake shouted this out. I was jarred from the brink of sleep. I had fallen under the story's spell while Jake had been waiting for his cue.

I have often had to go into Jake's room to wake Sarah up from putting Jake to bed. I never understood why she was falling asleep, but it is a relaxing time, and if done properly, it is *supposed* to put you to sleep. Bedtime stories are about intimacy, sharing a physical space, creating an event, and listening to your mother's voice as she reads to you.

I am a little bit envious that Jake gets a bedtime story. Part of the problem is that I can't sit in on his because there is this feeling of "When is she going to leave so we can read the story?" Not that this is meant to be offensive; it's just the way it goes. I remember my mother as being a wonderful storyteller and how I enjoyed the times when she read out of a book as much as when she just seemed to make up stories.

Stepmother — a hateful epithet, perhaps one of the most doomed words in the English language. A word that almost achieves the status of an insult.

I know that it has taken ten years for me to be able to have a civil conversation with my stepmother. In the early days I loathed her, and now I can tolerate her. I think it could just be a conflict of personalities, but then that wouldn't account for the fact that most kids don't get along with their stepmothers.

The aspect I detested most was the authoritarian attitude she adopted. My parents couldn't manage me, so why did this woman think *she* could? The fact that I was barred from attending my father's second marriage because I wanted to wear a man's suit didn't help matters much. If she was the "friend" my father claimed she was, then she should have done something, made some gesture, fought for me to be able to dress however I felt most comfortable. The adage "if you can't beat 'em, join 'em" has gained no mileage with me or my biological or stepparents.

116　There are families within families, and I have managed to be the outcast of all the families I've ever had.

Now it's my turn to be called stepmother, dreaded name of all names. Stepmonster. I have not achieved the status of stepmonster, although I have caught myself doing the things that annoyed me most as a stepchild. I have been in the position where I have had to be the one to say no. A little while back when I had a particularly stressful and demanding schedule, my usual lack of patience was diminished even further and it seemed like every time I opened my mouth, I was telling Jake not to do something. One morning I was grumpy enough that my explosive comments caused Jake to leave the room, avoid me, and ask Sarah if I still liked him.

I'd been searching for the definitive family experience. I wanted an event to take place that would crystallize my idea of family and make it real — not just for me but also for my wife and for Jake.

We got it over Fourth of July weekend. The family vacation: part myth ("We'll relax and enjoy ourselves"), part nightmare ("Trains are delayed, leaving hundreds of people stranded on hot, overcrowded platforms), and part reality ("A cool dip in the ocean"). We had the proper elements; it was merely a question of whether they would coalesce to form a holiday or struggle with one another, pulling us apart and sending us in different directions.

The weekend started with Jake sobbing because he wouldn't get to spend the usual days with his father. He really likes being with his father and started to complain immediately. I should have suspected that a holiday weekend would amplify our family dynamic, forcing us to face ourselves separately and as a group. The edginess at the start might have been dispelled, but instead the tensions escalated.

I can always rely on Jake to be blunt: "Your breath stinks," "I'm hungry," "How much hair is in your armpit?" etc. When situations become emotionally complex, he stops talking and starts acting out, throwing things, saying things like "You're stupid" and ignoring me when I'm speaking to him.

Lunchtime on the second day ended with my wife crying over the fact that Jake and I antagonize each other. We don't take it as seriously as she does. She became frustrated, wanting us to be the best of friends all the time. In fact, we are — the antagonizing is just a way for us to establish boundaries. She kept repeating the phrase "We're on our vacation." I believe she meant it as an incantation, one that would break the spell of misery and restore peace. **117**

Jake started acting funny a little later. He grew completely agitated over not getting an ice-cream bar at exactly the moment he demanded it, and this climaxed in a crying fit, the magnitude of which left him winded. In between sobs he exclaimed, "You never listen to me!" I was puzzled by this, as was his mother. But I believed that he meant it. I remember feeling frustrated at not being able to articulate feelings when I was young.

In a renewed fit of frustration, Sarah rushed to the house to pack up all our belongings so that "we" could catch a train back to the city. *They* could go wherever they wanted; *I* went to the beach, not about to budge. The last place I wanted to be on the Fourth of July was in a sweltering, stinky, noisy, crowded, city.

As I lay on the beach, sunning myself and eavesdropping on the breeders that overpopulated the beach (no pun intended), I looked out across the ocean, felt the cool breeze, ran my fingers through the sand, and found myself dozing in the intense heat. I was awakened by my wife saying, "Jake has something he wants to tell you." I looked up at him, his brown eyes red-rimmed from tears. Wife walked off, leaving [step]son and [step]mom together.

"What's on your mind, Jake?" I asked.

"Nothing," he said, turning his small, tanned back on me.

I called Sarah back over, saying, "He has nothing to say."

She looked at him with one of those mother looks, a slight alteration of her features indicating, *Do not mess with me, mister.* He asked, "Why are you looking at me?" She just kept looking at him. He finally relented. "Okay." She walked off.

He has this way of launching serious conversations by saying, "I have one last question." In this case his last question was, "Why do you live with Mom?" In this moment many things became clear. Instead of answering that question, I answered the question "Why don't my parents live together?" I provided a somewhat muddled explanation about friendships that don't last, that his parents didn't get along anymore but that they loved him as much as when they were together.

He seemed satisfied with this and told me he had something to show me. We walked to a tide pool and looked at mussels ranging from fingernail size to "steam me and lay me alongside a plate of pasta" size. I told him that we hadn't reached a conclusion, and he said, "Yes, we have."

118   "What?" I asked.

"Friends!" he shouted.

After dinner, while we all played Boggle, Jake wanted to be on my team. Wife ended up losing in the long run but came up with an impressive word in one of the early rounds. It was every man for himself during crazy eights. I could feel that the tension had eased greatly. I was happy to be with both of them.

The next evening, as we headed back to the city, while we were sitting on the train, I overheard some women across the aisle discussing us. The phrase "nontraditional family" crossed their lips. I watched the reflection in the window as one woman kept looking at me, trying to figure me out.

I was pleased and distraught. In my mind we're just "family," and our vacation had been about as traditional as any I had been on in my "traditional" family experience. In fact, the nontraditional family experience hadn't included any hitting of or yelling at children. Wife, [step]son, and [step]mom had all attempted to talk when things got unbearable. Other than that, it had been the mundane — hot dogs, Good Humor bars, a town parade, fireworks, an overcrowded beach, a wonderfully cool ocean.

I am not partial to politically correct terminology. In some instances, such as when the language is used to discriminate on the basis of gender, I appreciate the new words. I prefer the terms *flight attendant, postal worker,* etc. Not that the workforce has been revolutionized switching from gender-based terms to gender-neutral ones, but at least the new words are inclusive. I feel the term *non-traditional family* would apply. But under the current circumstances, *family* is still appropriate and correct.

119

Having Something in Common
by Laura Davis

One of my favorite things about becoming a mother is that I have something in common with 98 percent of humanity. My fears and hopes and fierce love for my kids is the same as it is for a mother in New York City, a father in Nepal, and parents in Taiwan and Mozambique. The fact that I happen to be a lesbian pales in the face of the parental bond.

Aside from some basic inequities — like Karyn and I having to jump through a million hoops so she could adopt her own son — it's been hard for me to come up with much that's different, negative, or challenging about being a lesbian mother. In that, I know I am fortunate — and privileged. I've never been in a custody battle or struggled with hostile relatives, and neither of my boys has ever faced institutionalized homophobia at school.

Here in Santa Cruz, California, Eli was not the first child of lesbians in his day-care center. (In fact, his afternoon caregiver was a lesbian.) Other kids with parents like us have preceded him in the Scouts, at the Boys and Girls Club, in school. So far, for us, it has only been advantageous to be lesbians — Eli got bounced to the top of the waiting list at his preschool because we were lesbians and they wanted more diversity. We are not breaking any new ground here.

For me, one of the best parts of being a parent has been opening up to the bigger world and stepping out of the insular lesbian one I lived in for so many years. Because of Eli I've made friends with men, dads who are straight men, and I've thoroughly enjoyed it.

Roxie's dad, John, was the first. When I first met John, my impression of him was that he talked too much. The first time his wife, Kathy, invited me over to their house, four years ago, there was John: tall and forty-something with a ponytail and an earnest face. He still had a little Alabama in his voice and could lapse into more whenever he cared to. John loved to jaw. Later, after we'd shared some quiet times, I learned that all those words were his way of covering over his nervousness. John was basically shy around new people.

John had been a truck driver and a union rep and had held a host of other jobs, but after a back injury he was now the chief cook and bottle washer in their house. Once Roxie was born and Kathy went back to work, he took care of their daughter, did the shopping, and put dinner on the table. There was no doubt John adored both the women in his family. He was forty-five when Roxie was born; he and Kathy had been married fifteen years. As John once told me, "I never really wanted a child, but then my big-bellied wife changed all that."

Kathy and I met in a prenatal yoga class when we were both four months pregnant. We spent much of our remaining pregnancy going for leisurely walks, finding all the outdoor bathrooms in Santa Cruz (and squatting in the bushes when we couldn't), talking, napping on each other's couches, and eating together. We discussed on giving birth and admired our round bellies. We became fast friends, and our kids have visited, grabbed toys from each other, and played together ever since. Kathy and John and Karyn and I have taken the kids camping, gone to Kathy and John's wonderful old creaky summer house on the Russian River, and shared all kinds of dinners **121** and crises, large and small. Just recently I asked John to give Eli peeing lessons, and he happily obliged. I'm glad Eli has a man like John in his life.

Young children are a great leveler. Regularly I find that I have more in common with my straight friends than I do with lesbians who don't have kids. In fact, the only negative responses I've ever gotten about being a mother have come from lesbians — not from my family, not from straight folks, not from heterosexual parents.

This is something I learned long before I had kids of my own. The first and last women's music festival I went to was one of the early ones at Yosemite. It was the early days of "womyn-only space," and lesbians with "boy children" were an outcast minority.

During an afternoon concert on the first or second day, I sat near a little boy of maybe six or seven years old who was playing Frisbee in a field. His Frisbee got away from him and accidentally hit a woman who was sitting there, drinking beer and listening to the music. She snatched the disc, stamped over to the boy, and grabbed him by the shirt. "*You stupid little prick!*" she screamed into his upturned face. "You're just going to grow up to be a rapist anyway! Men are all alike!" She kept shaking and berating him. He struggled to stand, her angry hand bunching his small white T-shirt in her fist. She towered over him, continuing to scream. Her eyes were wide and unseeing, and she spit as she talked. The boy's mother was nowhere in sight. Some people ignored what was happening; some noticed, but no one did anything.

Finally I stood up, ran over, and grabbed the boy away, holding him to my breast while his small chest heaved uncontrollably. I looked at her and yelled, "He's just a child! It was an accident." The boy clung to me silently, his face snotty, his eyes wide and terrified, his body quivering.

The woman's white puffy face loomed large. She continued her tirade: "It's never an accident! They're all a bunch of violent pricks! Why do they let little rapists come here anyway?" I tried to whisper soothing words in the boy's ear as I quickly hustled him away. Her sharp, angry words continued to pelt us as we crossed the endless field of naked women dancing to the music with their sun hats on.

Later, after I found the boy's mother and returned him to her, I hiked over to the child-care area. A group of us compared notes about what was going on with boys on the site, and none of us liked what we saw. The incident I'd observed had been the most violent, but boys weren't being treated well anywhere. A mother of two boys said her two- and four-year-old sons were begging to keep their clothes on because they didn't want anyone to know they had penises. Mothers of older sons had been warned to keep them at home, and those who brought sons said their kids were being subjected to ridicule and objectification or were simply being treated as if they were invisible. "People look right through them," one mother complained. "It's as if they didn't exist."

As we stood talking, deciding what to do, I said, "If you want boys to grow up hating women, just treat them the way boys are getting treated here!"

Later that evening, some of us went up on the stage and during the announcements read a statement about the rights of all children. At the time, I remember thinking, *If this is what lesbians are like, I don't want to be one.* I swore that if I ever had kids of my own, I'd never subject them to such a gathering. And I never have.

That was fifteen years ago. Now there are lesbian play groups, lesbian moms' groups, lesbian moms' (and gay dads') on-line support, sperm and egg mixers (so gay men and lesbians who both want kids can "mingle"), and a very different social climate. But I still find that I have more in common with parents — be they straight or gay — than I do with lesbians who don't have kids. There are some notable exceptions among our family's friends — lesbians who want children, love children, and, most important, love our children.

But I still find myself spending a lot of afternoons happily jawing with John and Kathy in the backyard, comparing notes on house paint, temper tantrums, and good sources of vitamin D. When it comes right down to it, our immediate concerns as the parents of verbal, lively three-year-olds supersedes whatever differences we have. It's just one of the ways being a mom has made my world a larger — and better — place.

123

To Raise a Future Man
by Sara Michele Crusade

When at age twenty-one I came out to myself and the world as a lesbian, I stored away all previous desires to become a mother. Motherhood seemed contradictory to a lesbian lifestyle, as I viewed it. I didn't see any lesbian moms around, mentoring young politicized dykes in parenting. Lesbianism seemed to me to be a world of independence: free to play, study, and be political.

As I closed in on thirty, however, I found the maternal instinct running up on me. I was in a relationship at the time, and my significant other (who was a mother), supported my desire to have a child. We looked into a couple of different sperm banks, and I became pregnant after my second try with the help of a fertility doctor.

My son, Dare, was born in the spring of 1992. But even before he was born, he began to change my life and alter my perceptions around raising male children. To begin with, I thought I would be having a daughter. Having a female child seemed like it would be safe; after all, I am also a female. Gaia, the Earth mother, didn't want me to have it too easy, however. Where's the challenge? So the ultrasound in my third trimester revealed a healthy baby boy, flaunting his maleness with a prenatal erection.

I had loved this child, growing inside me, for so long that it didn't matter to me that he was a "he." I'd already had a name picked out, just in case. My significant other, however, was terribly displeased and withdrew much of her support at the news. From that point on I felt like this was my child, not ours. I would be making the decisions and providing the support for him. Suddenly I found myself with a set of questions I didn't have answers for: Should the child be circumcised? What color clothes should I dress him in that will be boyish enough without being stereotypically male? How do I raise him to be strong in society and still be compassionate, nurturing, and intuitive? How do I protect this future man from patriarchal brainwashing?

My midwife recommended a book on circumcision, and after reading it I felt sure about making a decision against the procedure.

My significant other tried to convince me otherwise, but I stood firm in my conviction that my son should be as he was created. It seemed senseless to me, also, to have a home birth and attempt to create tranquillity for Dare's entrance into this world, only to turn around and allow someone to surgically amputate part of his penis.

The penis. As a lesbian with very little experience with males, I pondered how I would teach my son about his sexuality. How will he learn to use a urinal? What are the boundaries for his self-exploration?

It turned out that a lot of my son's clothes were blue, not because blue is a male color but because his eyes are blue and it's a very becoming color on him. Dare also wore a lot of yellow and red as a baby, and some pink. Most of his T-shirts were about saving the animals and the planet, and I refused to dress him in "manly" shirts with construction trucks, weapons, or race cars on them. I felt then, as I do now, that Dare's clothes should reflect the fact that he's a member of the human race first and the male of the species second. Every day is a lesson in teaching Dare that philosophy. Even though I've allowed no war toys in our home, Dare still knows how to fight and is quite proficient at make-believe sword dueling. He can be killing off a monster one minute and cradling one of his dolls the next.

125

It is very important to me that Dare understands that "humanness" is paramount and that he feels comfortable expressing the full spectrum of emotions and feelings that are part of being human. Because if I can give him little else besides love, I can at least give him a holistic perspective on life. Not very many sons have lesbian moms; however, many lesbian moms have sons. It's as if nature is trying to shift the balance away from patriarchy by having future men raised in an atmosphere that teaches tolerance, compassion, and nurturance as basic elements of life.

The idea of caring for oneself is also important to me, so I teach Dare how to cook, clean, and fold his clothes. Dare loves to help wash the dishes and is often interested in watching me prepare food. I want Dare to grow up being self-sufficient, not needing a wife to re-mother him. One of my duties, among many, is to teach Dare to challenge society's roles for men and women.

I want Dare to regard himself and others as people first, not men (and all the connotations that go with that) and not women (with all the connotations) — not "them" and "us." And yet I know that one day Dare will be a man, and Dare knows it too. Sometimes I lie in bed, holding my son, and wonder what kind of man he'll grow to be. I believe he'll be loving, nurturing, intuitive, and kind as well as creative, strong, and articulate. Those are all things I have tried to model for him and open him up to. Unlike a lot of preschoolers his age, Dare still likes to climb on my lap and be rocked in the rocking chair. He still likes to climb in my bed and sleep with me. And why shouldn't he? There's no one around our home to tell him otherwise. Yet Dare still picks up society's messages about maleness.

One day, after I picked him up from child care, Dare told me it's not okay for boys and men to cry. I explained that it's human to cry and that it's okay for men and boys to cry when they're sad or hurt or even happy. But I realize that one explanation will not be enough and that as Dare grows older he'll face even more conflict from his peers and society. Simply having a lesbian mom is difference enough to isolate Dare. So I try to make our family situation and my sexual orientation commonplace. I share my feelings openly about loving women; point out openly lesbians, gay, and bisexual people on television and in the movies; take Dare to gay pride parades; create extended family with friends who are supportive; and encourage him to ask questions and explore his feelings as they arise.

And in the long run I pray that Dare will have the tools he needs as he grows up to feel comfortable with how he has been raised, to love and accept himself as he is, and to be aware that it's a strength to be different — when the difference is reached in a healthy way and it's a healthy difference. Having a son has meant thinking of healthier ways to raise him than the average way male children are raised in this society. And being a lesbian mom has given me an outlook and philosophy about raising a son that I probably wouldn't have had otherwise.

Raising Cain?
by Margaret Bradstock

I have an older son (as well as two daughters) by an early marriage, and two younger sons, who are the biological children of my lesbian partner of twenty-one years, conceived by "self"-insemination (with a little bit of help from her friend!). The older boy is not an issue here — he is twenty-nine years old, has a good job, a house, and a "spouse" and has long ago conquered all feelings of homophobia occasioned by my "changing horses in midstream" during his early teens. The question I wish to consider is that of raising two boys in a lesbian household and whether it is a disadvantage for them in a world that regards their upbringing as abnormal.

First, as I trip over AFX car sets and discuss with the four-year-old his current fascination with penises, let me stress that this could not be described as an all-female environment. At the moment the power center is female, but that will continue to evolve as the boys move toward adulthood.

The constant concern of heterosexuals is that such children have no male role model and may become...what? Castrati? Girlish boys? Bent? Disturbed? The first answer to this is that the boys know and admire their donor father and that, through visits with my older son, sons-in-law, and male friends both gay and straight, they have access to the male world. Okay, they don't have a resident daddy, and I'd have to admit that this disturbed them sometimes during their early years, but they've learned to cope and to accept family differences. J.J., aged four, loves singing "We Are Family" (the catch cry of Mardi Gras), and I and the dog are always featured in his kindergarten drawings of his family.

Among other things, I've always been annoyed by the arrogance of heterosexuals who assume that they, in themselves, are necessary and sufficient role models. I don't expect any of my children to be just like me. I expect them to look at us, at our friends and relations, female as well as male, and decide for themselves, ultimately, the qualities to emulate and those to avoid. The more role models they have access to, the more likely they are to be able to assess accurately.

The boys know that there are many men and male values in this world that we *don't* like but can rest assured that the men we mix closely with have our seal of approval. We hope to impress upon them the need to become the sort of males women can live with and like. There's no sexist division of labor in our household. It's hard going at times, and often it's easier to pick up the dirty socks and underwear and throw them in the laundry basket myself, but they know what's acceptable and what isn't. Above all, they don't see girls and women as inferior. BeBop's best friend (who has, sadly, gone back to South Africa) is a girl. Her heterosexual parents have often commented on how unique he is, how different from other boys — he never put her down or behaved in a prurient way; in short, he treated her like another human being.

They're no angels (in fact, BeBop qualifies as house devil, street angel) but any rudeness or defiance we experience is directed at us not because we're women or lesbians but because we're the power system in our household and necessarily threaten their autonomy. And there is, fortunately, a great need to work their way back into our good graces.

128

What about sexuality? BeBop is nearly eleven and beginning to undergo physical and emotional changes. We've always talked openly with the boys and are able to discuss — without embarrassment — these things and what they can expect. BeBop is fully aware of the circumstances of his conception and is able to have a good laugh about some of the more amusing details. (He calls himself a "jar baby.") He understands what's involved in both heterosexual and homosexual sex and has no hang-ups about one or the other. "Do you two still do that?" he said to us with a grin one morning. "I thought you'd given it up!" He knows that, for him, the choice of sexual partners is his own and that he won't be pressured except in regard to safety and considerateness. My bet is that both boys will be heterosexual, though — they both relate so well to women and have also seen the hurt society can inflict on those perceived as "different."

The one area we've all agreed to lead a double life is in regard to school and kindergarten. There's a sense of solidarity in this. We tried the "BeBop has two mums" approach early on and found it resulted only in constant questions and an inability to place him in a known context. (Single mums and even single dads, by comparison, are apparently easy to pigeonhole and comprehend.) All children of lesbians suffer this discrimination, but for boys the problem is slightly exacerbated, with the illogical assumption that they must be effeminate, if not "queer" as well. BeBop's acceptance at his first school was a very hard-won and tenuous affair. We've had many offers to appear on TV together or in magazines and newspapers, but we've made the decision not to inflict that notoriety on the boys. You end up not educating the community but becoming, as BeBop says, "like the Elephant Man." At his new school (in a class for gifted and talented children) I've agreed to be known as "auntie," though as he comes bursting out of school to meet me shouting, "Guess what, Mum!" I wonder how long that will last. I have the status of guardian at both school and kindergarten, and letters and invitations to parents usually do me the courtesy of inclusion.

J.J. used to call us both "Mum" until his kindergarten teachers informed him that I'm not his mother and that he should call me Margaret. He's a very fair boy. He retaliated by calling us both by our Christian names, though the kindergarten didn't like that either. He's now developed the same instinctive solution as BeBop — when we're all together he uses Christian names.

129

When just one mother is present, she's "Mum" — and the boys don't mind who attends their functions, so long as one of us does.

How do I feel about raising sons? The early attitude of lesbian and feminist households was to make boys feel inadequate, but in a coalitionist world those days have largely gone. (I still recall a militant woman in an IWD march chanting, "Boys will be boys. Kill, kill, kill!") Most of our lesbian friends are tolerant of the boys, and some genuinely enjoy their company and include them in social activities. With the current lesbian baby boom, there's a great deal of interest in the phenomenon, though daughters are, perhaps, still regarded as more of a status symbol and a badge of correctness.

For myself, most of the time I gain a great deal of satisfaction from parenting sons. I was always something of a boy myself and actively prefer choosing boys' clothes and toys. Not that we're sexist about toys — they're not supposed to have guns (a few have crept in under the guise of water pistols), and my more enlightened self couldn't condone anyone, boys or girls, having a Barbie doll these days. (My daughters did but finally took delight in blowing up the Barbie camper as a resounding statement on those values.)

Both boys were given dolls and prams when they were little but phased these out fairly quickly. No doubt societal expectations contributed to this, but basically I'm glad BeBop takes his new basketball sneakers to bed instead of a doll! It makes life easier, though if he preferred the latter, we'd have to go with it. Overall, their toys are educational rather than gender-based.

In Australian schools sports are very important, especially for boys. BeBop doesn't play football — he's never been introduced to it and has never missed it — and he can't run to save his life. I've written my share of notes excusing him from cross-country running on various grounds (just as I did for my younger daughter, now a doctor — I wish someone had done that for me). BeBop's main interests are writing, acting, and swimming, and it's this last activity that gains him peer-group respect. He has a swag of medals and trophies, can swim more than two kilometers effortlessly, and has already had the pleasure of competing in the pool designated for the 2000 Olympics. It's been important that he develop skills such as this to counter the smugness of footballers and other athletes. He enjoys tennis and bowling as well. J.J. can swim too now (with some trepidation). As I am the mother in charge of swimming, it's an activity I share with them (dare I say as role model?), and swimming three kilometers a week myself is an added benefit. J.J. shows a greater interest in running and kicking a ball around, and if he ends up asking to play soccer then that will have to be fitted into our scheme of things. Above all, we want the boys to have self-esteem so that they'll treat others well.

BeBop has gone on radio as saying that it's not a problem having lesbian parents ("It's just that you have two of one sex instead of one of each," he said). Likewise, my expectations of sons are no different from that of daughters. They'll grow into men, of course, but hopefully into tolerant and considerate *people,* and we believe our lesbian household is fostering this. Many of our values are filtering through, and the opportunity of parenting sons has become both a unique challenge and a largely rewarding experience (though rainy Sundays can be *hell*). When my partner and I have differences, we realize we have to try harder, because these boys and I couldn't cope with a separation. We are family!

Lesbian Divorce
by Sara Michele Crusade

I am the lesbian mother of a four-year-old boy named Dare. He was conceived through alternative insemination while I was in a long-term relationship with another woman, Elizabeth (a pseudonym) — who is also the biological mother of an adolescent boy, Ken (also a pseudonym). Dare was born into this family unit believing that both Elizabeth and I were his parents and that Elizabeth's son was his brother. Although Elizabeth and I had problems in our relationship, we attempted to maintain homeostasis in our family unit. However, when Dare was two and a half years old, Elizabeth and I separated and she and her son left the state. Our separation was hard on Dare, who missed Elizabeth and Ken, but frequent phone contact maintained a sense of connectedness for Dare. Not long after Dare turned three years old, however, Elizabeth made the decision to sever all contact with Dare and me, leaving my son feeling scared, betrayed, and abandoned.

I was left picking up the pieces of Dare's shattered family unit and having to cope with the grief Dare began to express through acting-out behavior. I know from studying psychology that acting out is common for children of divorce. Dare became aggressive, hitting, kicking, and talking back to me inappropriately. I knew it was important to acknowledge my son's loss by talking about the situation with him and validating his feelings. I also knew it was important to share my own sense of loss over Elizabeth's absence so Dare would feel comforted by knowing that I was also affected and that he was not alone in his grief.

I asked a wonderful child-therapy instructor how I could help my son work through his anger and pain and how I could create a safe place for Dare to express his feelings. She suggested giving him a doll to vent with. So I encouraged Dare to work through his anger with a doll given to him by Elizabeth prior to her leaving. Dare would take a toy hammer and beat on the doll's feet while yelling at the doll (using Elizabeth's name) that he was mad at her for leaving. He was expressing that he felt she walked away from him. Dare would tell the doll that his heart was broken, and then he would smash her feet some more. While he was processing his grief, I would acknowledge Dare's feelings by telling him that I could see he was very angry and by repeating back to him the words he used to describe how he felt. In this way I was able to redirect any violent acting-out behavior.

The child-therapy instructor also taught me that play is another way of helping a child deal with the loss of a parent. I found playing with Dare to be very therapeutic for him as well as for me. I let him lead our play sessions, and I took on the role of supporter and observer. During one play session Dare brought out a wooden train set and engaged me in play. The engine represented Elizabeth, one of the cars represented Ken, a third car was symbolic of me, and the littlest car was Dare. Dare gave the littlest car to me to play with while he played with the others. In his play scenario the engine left the other parts of the train. Speaking for the Dare car, I would say things I knew to be true about how Dare was feeling: "I'm scared. Don't leave me. I need you." Occasionally the Ken car would leave also. Again, I would give voice to how the Dare car might feel: "Mommy, where are you? I'm scared." Dare would then act out the mother car, expressing how he felt about her ability to be present with him and care for him during this tumultuous experience.

The play session not only helped Dare give voice to his frustration and bewilderment, but it also helped me see, through his eyes, my strengths and weaknesses as a support source for my son.

What I felt when left as sole head of the household was that my world had been turned upside down. It was very stressful finding myself parenting alone as a lesbian mom with none of the support that I might have had as a newly divorced heterosexual mom. I always tried to remember, however, that Dare was also deeply affected by the change. I was honest with him about the impact the separation was having on us both and stuck to what I believe about communication as the key to opening up to the healing process.

Or Not
by Leslie Lawrence

Tired from being schlepped, the boys
stretch out on a floor smudged with ashes
and discuss the big question.
"Anyone can die," says Sam, three.
"Everyone does," says his older cousin.
(Above them: chandeliers, fluorescents, halogen floods...
Around them: clip-ons, goosenecks, itty-bitty
bed lamps designed to save one's marriage...
So many lights! As if here
in that district of the Lower East Side
seeing were really valued,
people still read *War and Peace*.)
"No!" Sam arches, kicks.
I'm surprised. Just weeks ago death wasn't that bad.
Of the bird on the pavement: "Dead.
Let's take it to the doctor."
Of the dog who died when he was a baby:
"When am I going to see Corky again?"

We lunch at Katz's. (SEND A SALAMI
TO YOUR BOY IN THE ARMY!)
Sam is cranky — won't eat.
But more cheerful in SoHo, aloft my shoulders:
"So, Mom,
am I gonna die or not?"
I clutch his spongy calves.
Stride past pushcarts —
Santa socks, peacock feathers, kid gloves...
"Hey, look!" I point:
troops of boxer shorts emblazoned with the mouse.
"Mickey!" Sam squeals.
The bloodshot eyes of a man catch mine.

"A quarter for the homeless? A quarter for the —"
My mother's eyes upon me, I turn from him.
Thirty years before I begged her not to kill a spider;
she said, "*Someday* you'll understand."
Now she chides, "You must be looking too compassionate."

The next day, a bug in the toilet.
"Dead!" Sam declares.
Fear and compassion don't mix.
He aims his pee, flushes it down,
his someday already here.

Balancing
by Tara Prince-Hughes

For the Seattle gay pride parade this year, my son, Aris, decided to wear makeup. He spent the evening before experimenting with eye-shadow colors, applying and reapplying lipstick, and strutting in front of the mirror, declaring, "You can *never* have *too* much lipstick!" On the sidelines the next morning, we cheered for the Dykes on Bikes; the gay Native, Asian-, and African-American coalitions; and the drag-queen floats. At one point Aris squealed, pointed out the drag queens to my partner, Dawn, and yelled, "We're the boys who like to wear makeup!" When PFLAG came by, Aris and I joined Dawn and her family in marching. Aris, decked out in his makeup, baseball cap, and bright plastic beads, waved to spectators from his bike and grinned as people waved back and cheered. I felt as if, for a few moments, my life as a mother and my life as a lesbian were coming together.

Mothering my son has felt challenging from the beginning. Before Aris was three months old, I was reading Adrienne Rich's *Of Woman Born* and scouring bookstore shelves for information on mothers and sons. Having had no brothers and few male friends when I was young, I needed to know how my son's life might differ from mine — what social, biological, and spiritual forces would he face that I did not? How could I, as a woman, develop a meaningful relationship with him? I found a lot of material on mothers and daughters but, outside of Rich, little on mothers and sons.

In addition to raising these questions, Aris's birth launched me into an unexpected series of revelations; at twenty-five, isolated at home with no one but a baby to talk to, I began to grapple with years of low self-esteem and self-alienation and to look at my world from a new perspective. Although it had never seriously occurred to me that I might be lesbian, I suddenly found myself powerfully attracted to a woman. I underwent what felt like a ruthless series of changes.

When Aris was two and a half, his father and I separated and Aris began spending part of his weeks with each of us. When he was three I began living as an out lesbian. Since I have considered myself gay for only a few years, my identity as a lesbian has been shaped within the context of my relationship with my son, and my practices as a mother have, in turn, been shaped by my experience as a lesbian. At the heart of both experiences is my need to reclaim the concepts of "male" and "female" from reductionist Western thinking and to construct for myself a gay identity that balances those concepts, both within myself and in my relations with the world.

During the summer of my divorce, I experimented with a lesbian identity, associating almost exclusively with lesbians and attending my first women's music festival. I heard through friends that the festival didn't allow male children, and although that wasn't a practical problem for me, I felt funny about it. What about all the mothers of boys who couldn't — or didn't want to — leave their children with a caregiver? It was my first experience with lesbian separatism and my first indication that my relationship with my son and my participation in the lesbian community might conflict.

I found my misgivings reflected in Susan J. Wolfe's essay "Jewish Lesbian Mother" in the anthology *Nice Jewish Girls.* Wolfe cites the

Michigan Women's Music Festival's announcement that boys over six years old would be placed in a camp miles from the festival, a policy that not only ignores the lasting impact of the Holocaust on Jewish women but also trivializes women's bonds with their male children. Forced to choose between the festival and spending time with her son, Wolfe chose her son. In my first year as a lesbian, I found myself contemplating a similar conflict between protecting my emotional ties with Aris, his father, and other men and building a primary community with other lesbians.

Since that summer, at feminist reading groups, gay gatherings, and lesbian parties, I've heard men vilified, made objects of sexist jokes and comments, stereotyped, smashed in the form of clay figures, and generally treated with disrespect. On one level I understand where these behaviors come from. Based on my own experience and my relations with women of various ethnic and economic backgrounds, I am acutely aware of the subtle and blatant ways in which women around the world suffer at the hands of men and male institutions. I have at times felt anger, frustration, and helplessness at the cruelty of women's lives. For women to heal it's crucial that we laugh at our perpetrators; there is a sense of communal bonding and support when women can vent in a safe place, and I acknowledge a spiritual component to women's gatherings that is different from what I encounter in mixed-gender groups.

But even when I vent my frustrations with women, I can't forget that I am the mother of a son. My connection with him is one of the most primal of all bonds, rife with protective instincts and inextinguishable love. He will be a man someday, and I will be one of the biggest influences on how he matures. And, ironic as it might seem to many women, I worry about the impact of lesbian sexism on his self-esteem. Not only is he exposed to antimale banter and invective at women's gatherings, but even my own thoughtlessness can cause problems.

Recently Dawn and I were driving in Seattle with Aris, now five, in the backseat. A red sports car shot around us and, without thinking, Dawn and I simultaneously shouted, "Penis car!" We derided the driver for his (her?) recklessness and laughed at the aptness of our own joke. A few moments later Aris, puzzled, asked, "Mama? What's a penis car?"

Dawn and I looked at each other as if to say, *Oh, shit.* We lamely explained that the joke had nothing to do with real penises but that since men often drive those kinds of power cars and men have penises, we call them penis cars.

As I watched him in the rearview mirror, Aris looked thoughtful, nodded, and solemnly said, "Oh."

A week or two later, Aris's other stepmother delicately brought up the topic with Dawn and me; Aris had been using the phrase at his dad's house, and she was worried he might think there was something wrong with his body. Until I learned that my comment had stuck in his mind, I don't think I understood the power my own language has over my son. The implications frighten me. It is such insidious sexist slurs, disguised as jokes, that erode the self-esteem of women in this culture, and I should know it. This incident solidified my growing conviction that in order to teach my son respect for women and for himself, I could not afford to indulge in sexism or exclude men from my own life.

My decision to live in connection with men has not, however, led me to accept contemporary European-American definitions of what it means to be male or female. At the same time that I've awakened to my responsibilities as a lesbian mother of a son, I have also, over the past two years, launched a search for an identity and a sense

137

of community that I would describe as tribal. The influences on my development have been many: my participation in Native American ceremonies; Dawn, who maintains a primary, intimate spiritual connection to her ancient European ancestors; lesbian friends who live in accordance with Native, pagan European, and Wiccan traditions; and historians of gay tribal history, such as Judy Grahn, Paula Gunn Allen, and Will Roscoe. As a result of my shifting perspective, I have felt slabs of my old Westernized identity fracture and fall away like fragments from an iceberg. And although I am sometimes terrified to the point of paralysis at having to let go of the paradigms that have structured my life, I am reconstructing a way of being that recognizes the need for balance between women and men, emphasizes human connectedness to spirit and to the rest of the natural world, and honors gay people as valuable community members.

In thinking of the terms *male* and *female* in a tribal sense, I must distinguish them from their Western associations with such dichotomies as active/passive, strong/weak, dominant/submissive, private/public, as well as from reductionist views of anatomical difference. For tens of thousands of years, women and men in tribal communities have worked together to acquire food, raise children, and hold rituals and ceremonies. Their work is different, but, in contrast to Western cultures, their roles usually respect the physical, emotional, and spiritual contributions of both sexes. At the root of many tribal belief systems is the conviction that harmony between women and men is necessary for the harmony of the world.

138

Recovering this sense of harmony has been crucial to my developing lesbian identity and to my view of my parental role. As a child, I felt whole. I knew what I thought, was curious about anthropology, evolution, astronomy, and geology, and felt a close kinship with animals and the land. As I underwent social conditioning in my teens, though, I lost faith in myself. I became externally focused and fear-driven, setting goals to win social approval rather than to meet my needs. Unlike some of my lesbian friends, I have, as an adult, identified as feminine, but the messages I have internalized about what femininity means have left me feeling inadequate and afraid of making decisions.

Part of this fragmentation is due, I think, to the repression of parts of me that I would call male in a rich, tribal sense of the word. In many tribal cultures worldwide, people who in English would be called "gay" have been thought to combine the spirits of a man and a woman within one person; among the Zuni people, for example, such individuals traditionally did the work of the opposite sex — and sometimes of both sexes — and performed vital spiritual, economic, and social functions. Because of their dual nature, they were honored as intermediaries between women and men and between the human and spirit worlds, and "gay" beings still figure prominently in tribal mythology. In contrast to Western notions of *homosexual* and *sexual deviant,* terms coined by nineteenth-century psychotherapists and physicians, the tribal notion of an internal, spiritual balance between male and female offers an image that acknowledges my unique perspective as a gay person. Claiming the strengths of both sexes allows me to honor feminine traits — my desire for interconnection, my nurturing ability, my empathy, and my intuition — that Western tradition dismisses as immature and weak. Now I am reclaiming the spiritual power that connected my female ancestors to the earth and moon, to birth, blood, and death, thousands of years before Rome colonized tribal Europe and Europe colonized the Americas. At the same time, I am learning courage, responsibility, and respect for my individual needs — traits that, when expressed in a community context, represent a masculinity free of the romantic Western myth of alienated individualism. By nurturing my female and my male parts, I feel more whole, more aware of my own goals, and more connected to the world around me.

As I strive to redefine myself, I return again and again to my son's developing identity. Regardless of whether he is gay or straight, I want Aris to experience himself as a whole being. I want him to be able to honor desires that his culture derides as "feminine," and I want him to take responsibility for aspects of "masculinity" that his culture aggrandizes — aggressiveness, physical strength, and sexuality.

Given that Aris will grow up in a culture that values competition over community, money over planetary health, humans over other animals, and men over women, I realize that the task of helping him find internal balance will be an ongoing struggle. While he's young, Dawn and I are trying to foster his respect for nature, spirit, and other people and to encourage him to explore different ways of expressing himself. We've begun to answer his questions about sex, teaching him about both gay and straight relations, and modeling respect for all sexualities.

I don't know what I would be like if I didn't have a son. His birth and life have been a crucible in which much of my own changes have occurred. As he grows, he causes me to remember myself as a child, my early sense of connection and wholeness. His maleness, in all its innocence and possibility, rounds me out. Mothering Aris has given me a doorway into a connection that predates contemporary sexual definitions and politics and enables me to honor both the male and the female in my life and myself.

Here Comes the Groom
by Pearlie McNeill

England 1990. It was the scene outside the church that bothered me the most. I lay awake worrying about it, night after night. Who would line up alongside Catherine and Chris when the photographer called for the happy couple's parents? Would my ex-husband and his wife (my ex–best friend) dare to take center stage despite not having had anything to do with Chris for almost nine years? How would Catherine's family and friends respond when I stepped forward, flanked by my partner, Meg, and my ex-lover Marie? I was uncompromising in my expectations. I wanted Meg and Marie to stand alongside me, to be accepted for who they are.

Back in 1978 Marie and I had begun a relationship. Chris had been eleven years old then, and Trystan, thirteen. We became a family of five when Marie gave birth to Susannah in 1981. I had no doubts whatsoever that Marie had earned the right to be acknowledged as Chris's parent. Meg too had contributed a great deal. She had been (and still is) my partner since 1986, and though *all* our lives continued to change in various ways around that time, the commitment to young people continued and even widened to include four children from Lancaster whom Meg had known and helped care for since their early childhood.

In my late-night fantasy, Catherine and Chris walked out of the church into dappled sunshine (fingers crossed about the weather), obligingly and self-consciously smiling for the cameras. But my mind came to a whizbang halt just when the crucial moment arrived. I simply couldn't move the scene along, couldn't envisage how we three women would handle the situation. I didn't realize at first how stunned I really was. I felt trapped, stuck in a tiny groove, going over the same things again and again. It was all so unexpected. The thought that one of my sons might choose to marry had never occurred to me. Any wedding would have been a challenge, but to attend this one under these circumstances, as mother of the groom?

I kept replaying a conversation Chris and I had had late in December 1989, days before I left for a four-month working holiday in Australia. He'd talked briefly about his relationship with Catherine, insisting there was no suggestion of their living together. Besides, Catherine was only eighteen, he'd added, and neither of them was ready for such a big step.

We had a deal, he and I. As long as the commitment between him and Catherine was low-key and mostly social, I'd accept his decision *not* to reveal that his mother was a lesbian. If their relationship deepened, became more permanent, he'd be expected to keep his promise to tell all to Catherine and to her parents at the earliest, most opportune moment.

In February a letter arrived at Trystan's Sydney address. We'd set up this arrangement because I was moving around a lot. Excited and impatient, I asked Trystan to read it over the phone.

"If only I could tell you this face-to-face instead of in a letter..."

Trystan struggled to read the letter, and I began to cry.

Catherine was pregnant. They'd both assumed that when the doctor had prescribed the contraceptive pill, to help regulate Catherine's periods, it would also work as a contraceptive. The baby 142 was due late August. Catherine's parents were not in favor of abortion. The wedding was planned for June, soon after my arrival back in England.

From the moment that letter arrived, I was in turmoil. The phone calls I had with Chris over the next few days were strained and almost unbearable. His replies to my questions were constantly interrupted and overshadowed by comments from Catherine's mother. At the end of each five-minute call, Agnes would take over, conveying updated information about a long list of arrangements and winding up with a plea that I simply relax and enjoy myself "over there" and come back full of anticipation for a wonderful wedding day. Agnes assured me she would see to everything.

My trip to Australia had been planned for a long time. There were four of us traveling together: Marie, Susannah, Meg, and I. I would not have flown back to England even if I could have afforded the fare. I had commitments and wouldn't have chosen otherwise, but I was sorely aware that Chris and Catherine had no one, apart from her family, to talk to. The next letter made clear that Chris had explained *everything* to Catherine and had also told her parents and brother, Clive. He made no comment as to how this news was received.

Chris's decision to keep others from knowing too soon about my lesbianism had not developed, as you might think, from a tendency to homophobia on his part but was linked directly to his own experience of discrimination because of other people's homophobic responses to me.

When the boys started school in the early 1970s, I was married and living in the western suburbs. I had a fear then that public high school education, particularly in the west, would be more like entering a factory than a school. As parents, Peter and I felt we were thinking ahead when we chose to send the boys to a nearby Catholic school. It was small, class numbers were low, and we felt these benefits more than justified the effort needed to pay the fees each term.

When my marriage broke up, I moved to an inner-city area, renting a flat in a large house. The house was owned by a feminist and occupied by women. The boys were able to transfer to a Catholic school in Lewisham. In his last year of primary school a year later, Chris mentioned to his lay teacher that his mother's partner was a woman. I guessed this information had been passed around a bit, yet no one seemed bothered. One male teacher, newly arrived from the bush in 1980, visited the boys at home, met Marie and me, and came back several times. Had we given him half a chance, I have no doubt he would happily have moved in as an honorary third son. **143**

Things continued on much as before — that is, until Brother John took over as school principal and decided that Trystan was unruly and disruptive. It is true that Trystan had been ticked off by a prefect for carving entwined initials, his and a girlfriend's, into the back of a bus-stop seat. Further incriminating evidence came when one of the senior brothers spotted him in a shopping center late one Thursday afternoon wearing a jeans jacket with the sleeves cut out. Then came a weekend when he left his school shoes behind at his father's place. I insisted Monday morning that sneakers were a better option than taking a day off. During assembly Brother John noted the offending footwear. Trystan was immediately escorted into his office by two prefects. After giving Trystan a lengthy dressing-down about unacceptable behavior, Brother John then expressed his views about lesbians, making it plain to Trystan that his mother was despicable, disgraceful, disgusting, and "a sinful, immoral woman both in the eyes of God and in the eyes of man."

The boys' Catholic school education ended that day. I quickly understood, after several distressing phone calls, that I couldn't take on the Catholic Church, unwilling as I was to allow further insult to my sons and with no promise of a positive outcome. I cannot say, though, even now, that I regret sending them to a Catholic school. We know, don't we, that prejudice and bigotry exist across a broad spectrum. The conclusions that arose from our experience centered only around Brother John.

Trystan and Chris were soon enrolled at the local high school, and everything was done to help them make the adjustment as smoothly as possible. Unexpectedly, Peter called by the next week to announce he was seeking a divorce. His plan was to marry Rita as soon as he was free. Only a few days earlier, I learned they'd been seeing each other for several months. She hadn't chosen to tell me, but he had. Perhaps she would have felt uncomfortable? Embarrassed? Not Peter; he'd been in a mood to boast. Since leaving the marriage, I'd avoided the subject of divorce, fearing, with some justification, that he would make an issue of my lifestyle in court. He'd threatened to insist on sole custody, and I had been reluctant to take on a battle I could so easily lose. Ironically, his tactics changed overnight, a convenient adjustment to his new situation. The threat to me was dropped, replaced by the intention to 144 abandon his children. And here he stood, heavy with pronouncements. I would not have minded that so much had he not insisted that Trystan and Chris hear every single word. He had given up too many years already for the sake of the boys, he declared; it was time he had a life of his own. In the future he wanted only occasional contact with his sons. They were almost grown up now. They simply had to understand that he'd had enough. Handing me a sheaf of papers, he headed for the door.

This rejection, following so soon after the episode with Brother John, was to have a devastating effect on both Trystan and Chris, though nothing they said or did that night gave any clue as to what lay ahead.

The sequence of events over the next six months remains hazy in my mind. Was Marie pregnant when the boys left St. Thomas's? When did the letter arrive informing us that Trystan was not attending school? Was that before or after we heard that Chris had slipped from being a cheerful boy near the top of his class to a depressed youngster in need of remedial reading lessons?

I clearly remember my seesawing responses to Trystan's imploding fury. It was a bitter blow when he left home, not yet sixteen, only weeks before Susannah was born, and promptly set about blaming my lesbianism for everything untoward that had ever happened to him. It was the school counselor who found him a place in a young person's refuge at Paddington. In town one day, Trystan approached me. I drew back, wondering how the hell this stranger knew my name. The much-admired auburn hair had been dyed, matching perfectly the unfamiliar clothes — black jeans, shirt, leather waistcoat, and skinny pointed boots that looked at least three sizes too big. If he hadn't spoken, I would have passed him by. He did come home to see the baby, but it was to be another five years before we could have a peaceful conversation again.

Meanwhile, Chris's self-confidence was waning, and he began describing himself as stupid. He was still communicative, but it was obvious he was confused and unhappy. He cheered up the night Susannah was born, expressing excitement and responsible concern when the midwife gave him small tasks to do, making a point of repeating her instructions to be sure he understood. He loved Susannah from the very first moment and was keen to be involved with caring for her. Susannah has always been a cherished, much-wanted baby, but the continuous swirl of emotions was inevitably exhausting and affected each of us in different ways.

145

The divorce case went through without too much hassle, and Peter and Rita were married in due course. Trystan and Chris heard all about the wedding several months later. They never did ask why they hadn't been invited. For a long time I walked around with this odd feeling that someone close to me had died. Rita had been my friend from the very day we'd moved to the same street. We had planned the birth of two of our children to coincide and almost succeeded. Chris is three months younger than Rita's third child, also a boy. Abandoned by her own husband, she had been so scathing about mine. *What had changed her mind?* I wondered. No way was I going to ask — better simply to withdraw. Chris was also hurting. I could tell he felt replaced in his father's affections by Rita's younger son.

My anger was persistent and purposeful. Okay, I'd lost one son, but damned if I was going to give the other one up without a fight. I had to do something, but what?

The small business Marie and I had set up in 1979 involved the publication of a few titles, running a bookshop, and making infrequent selling trips in a camper van up and down the east coast between Brisbane and Melbourne. Things were not going well. The bookshop was not in a good position, and we were beginning to lose money hand over fist. Reluctantly we agreed it was time to quit. We came up with the idea of selling the house, buying a cheaper one, and traveling overseas with the surplus from the sale. We planned to be away from Australia for a year. This decision proved to be a good one for Chris. Removed from the situation with his father, he flourished in rural Devon. This time we kept our lifestyle strictly private for the sake of the children. Chris's attitude toward schoolwork improved only slightly, but he did take a keen interest in sport. In his last year he won the school's Citizenship Award, which was no mean feat for a colonial boy in an English school. The following year Marie decided to study homeopathy, a four-year course, and I settled down to write and to teach creative writing. Susannah, always a happy child, took to water like a duck, proving herself to be a good swimmer quite early on. Our twelve-month stay stretched, remarkably, to thirteen years.

But in the hectic weeks before we left for England, a grim struggle ensued between us and a tabloid newspaper. In recent years I had written a few pieces for *Forum (Australia)* during the time Bettina Arndt was editor. At my suggestion Marie wrote an article about alternative conception, intending to make the information and what we'd learned from the experience accessible to other women. Not only did Bettina Arndt like the article, she wanted to use it for the launch issue of a new magazine. We were "out" lesbians, so Marie used her own name. When the magazine hit the streets, Marie's article was picked up by the Sunday newspaper and we suddenly found ourselves at the center of an explosive situation. In negotiations with the editor, my intention was to keep our names out of the limelight. He had already made it quite clear the story was going to run whether we liked it or not. It seemed our names *could* be kept out of it if, in return, we would agree to hand over the photograph I'd taken to accompany the article. This photograph showed mother and baby in profile, foreheads touching. It could have been almost *any* mother and baby, and I doubted whether anyone would have recognized Marie or Susannah, so I agreed, relieved to have got off so lightly.

The story appeared the Sunday before we left in November 1981. Not satisfied with the snapshot as it was, the newspaper decided to whip up a more scandalous image and ran it on the front page,

146

with two oblong blacked-out sections over the eyes (including Susannah's) and a caption alongside that read: LESBIAN MUM'S AMAZING CONFESSION...SEE PAGE 2.

Page two made no reference to Marie's article or the new magazine and gave the impression that the reporter had unearthed this depraved couple and their fearful secret all on his own. The Rev. Fred Nile was quoted as saying we were an "abomination and a grievous sin." We did manage to laugh about that one and could never quite work out which of us was which.

Susannah was now five months old. Chris was fourteen. Trystan had recently turned sixteen. At the airport he told us not to worry, he would be all right. We'd asked him repeatedly to come, but he had other plans. As I hugged him good-bye, I felt both concern and relief. Perhaps he shared my ambivalence? Days later he helped burgle a flat. Too scared to do much, he acted as lookout while two of his mates did the business inside. The next day, when the two went back for a second go, the police just happened to be dusting the place for fingerprints. Trystan was picked up within the hour. He was placed on probation for eighteen months but was so scared at being in trouble with the law, you could almost say it was a good thing. In 1985 he was badly burned in an accident, and I flew back to Australia in a mad panic. For the second time I failed to recognize my son. This time his hair was a different kind of black, standing up in tufts at the back, singed to mere stubble in front. His skin was blackened too, shaped in ugly ridges, more a grotesque mask than a human face.

"No," I said firmly to the nurse, "that's not my son." I heard the sob as I moved away. Peering closer, I noticed a tear leaking out of one eye. "Trystan?" I asked, trying to contain my horror.

It was a slow and painful recovery for Trystan, and he still bears traces of the scars on his face and both arms, but it was the start of a new dialogue between us. Of course, Trystan couldn't talk at first, but he did manage to scrawl a few words onto a paper pad. The last time I saw him at the hospital, he was well enough to be wheeled around in a special chair. He'd undergone two operations to graft skin from his thighs onto both arms and was optimistic he'd be playing his guitar in another few months. His life had lacked direction these past four years. Would the accident effect a change in how he faced the future? We agreed he'd had a lucky escape and that something as traumatic as this required him to think carefully

147

about what was happening in his life. As time has passed, it is evident that the accident marked a turning point in Trystan's understanding of himself, of his childhood, and of the people in his life.

Now, almost five years to the day since Trystan's accident, Chris was getting married. There were so many things to think about, to worry about, but despite my feelings I would, in the end, accept the choice Chris was making, even if, as I suspected, the choice had not been made actively by either him or Catherine. Rediscovering my sense of humor, I concentrated on practical things: How to get around the parochial thinking of a small Devon village? What exactly are mothers-in-law supposed to wear for such occasions? It soon became a joke among my friends, and some of the suggestions were hilarious.

Back in England a Danish lesbian friend offered to make me a three-piece suit, in a shade of blue acceptable, we thought, for a nonfrilly female to choose for a wedding. The Danish touch was an imported method for using material with a special adhesive to create picture patterns. I chose satin, the same blue as the suit. The back of the jacket featured a tree with outstretched branches. Here and there small birds nestled among the leaves in various groupings. Machined embroidery held the whole thing in place. We intended the design to work like a code for those in the know and managed to include a triangle on the waistcoat. The trousers were comfortable and wrinkle-free, and I had previously bought a cream silk shirt that would go quite well. Shoes were the biggest challenge. Reluctantly, I bought white sling backs with a small heel, beseeching Sappho (and anyone else I could think of) to allow me this one small concession. The hat was a riot. I was sure it had to be fate when I saw it in a department store. The blue was perfect, and I loved the solitary feather sticking out at a jaunty angle. By the time I got to wear it, I was convinced I looked like Marjorie Maine in one of those old films about Ma and Pa Kettle down on the farm.

When the day finally arrived, I was spoiling for a fight. Agnes was proving hard to pin down when it came to information about how the head table was to be arranged. Rita and Peter had arrived the night before and were staying in a bed-and-breakfast establishment down the road. I had a nasty suspicion that Agnes was deliberately avoiding me, hoping that by the time I arrived at the reception venue, I'd agree, rather than cause a scene, to sit where I was told. Did she intend to shove me off to the side in favor of Rita and Peter?

The groom was resplendent in his hired morning suit. We three women and the best man, an old friend from Chris's school days, walked with him down to the church, cracking jokes, pretending not to notice how nervous he was.

Down the aisle came the bridesmaids in long, lolly pink dresses, all four of them resembling steps and stairs versions of Little Bo Peep. Susannah's upward swept hairdo, caught on top with fake flowers and tulle trim, was a bit sophisticated for a ten-year-old, but her sparkling eyes and happy grin softened the impact. She gave a little wave as she walked by. Catherine swept by in a cleverly styled white dress that fitted firmly at the bustline but became loose and flowing the nearer it got to the floor. What a relief it was to watch the antics of the youngest bridesmaid, a chubby two-year-old whose laughter and giggles made such a welcome contrast to the thunder-and-brimstone sentiments of the vicar. Four bell ringers pulled and heaved on thick jute ropes as we all piled out of the church. The photographer, a local man, had to be reminded the groom had a family at all.

The reception venue was within walking distance, down the bottom of a steep hill. Catherine and Chris were already positioned at the door, greeting guests, when we arrived. Agnes and Bill could be seen hurrying from table to table, saying their hullos and showing people where to sit. Meg and I made a beeline for the head table, and, sure enough, there was my name on a place card, positioned to one side of the head table. We looked in vain for Meg's name. Before I had time to check where Rita and Peter were to sit, I glanced up and saw Agnes advancing toward me. If I were going to do something, it had to be now. I plopped myself down in the nearest seat. Was I next to the groom or was it the bride? Did it matter? Did I care? The main thing was that I'd scored my seat of honor, and that was that. Seconds before Agnes reached me, I spotted her handbag. It was navy blue and looked like a large envelope. It had been placed between the knife and fork directly in front of me. Then I saw her name. I hadn't planned this, but here I was, sitting in the very place Agnes had chosen for herself.

I looked up in time to catch the uncertainty in her eyes. Smiling at me as though we were the closest of friends, she indicated my allotted place at the end of the table. I didn't hear her words but knew instantly she was going to pretend I had mistakenly sat in the wrong place. I looked her full in the face before opening my mouth.

"I have a right to be here, Agnes, and this is where I'm staying."

149

I kept my voice low, but there was no doubt I meant every word I said. What she didn't know was how badly my legs were shaking and how grateful I was to have Meg standing nearby. Agnes stood stock still, unsure what to do next. I held her handbag in my grasp, waiting for her to take it. She snatched it away and walked hurriedly to the far side of the table, where her son, Clive, was standing with his girlfriend. It didn't require much imagination to guess what was being said. I watched and waited. When Clive looked over and shot me a filthy look, I deliberately misinterpreted him. Picking up a glass of wine I raised it in his direction as though making a toast.

And so it was that Agnes sat at the side table on her daughter's wedding day while I sat next to the groom. Bill was master of ceremonies, so it was fitting that he sit next to Catherine. Peter was given the seat I'd rejected, and Rita got to sit with Meg and Marie at the long table nearby. I doubt that anyone but those involved realized there'd been a showdown at high noon. I've often wondered if even Chris and Catherine ever knew what really happened.

Standing up to Agnes was not simply an act of assertion. Attitudes are slow to change, and those of us who live our lives in alternative ways, who rear our children in alternative ways, have to fight persistently and with vigor for recognition and respect from the wider world, and there'll be times when we feel equal to that struggle and many times when we won't. Our gains are not usually measured in great triumphs but in brief moments that we learn to hug tight against us for solace and encouragement when times are bad. One such moment for me came that June morning when over the breakfast table Chris said that one of the good things to have come out of all the anguish and distress he'd felt these past few months was a clear recognition that he no longer cared who knew about my lifestyle. It was a fact of life he no longer felt troubled about.

When he made his speech, he thanked his father and Rita for making the long haul to be present and then went on to say how much he had appreciated Marie, Meg, and his mother for having been so supportive, given that he and Catherine had decided to wed in such a hurry (here he paused for the expected laughter), and that he was pleased, very pleased, to have been brought up by these three women who'd looked after him so well.

This was written with the approval and support of Marie McShea and Meg Coulson. All other names used are fictitious.

150

Facing Losses

Declared Not Fit
by Minnie Bruce Pratt

In this month of grief I am crying for my lover.
Suddenly my children appear under my closed eyelids
inside my grief, as if in a pitch-dark room,
vision: apparitions heavy with distance, absence.

I think: This is how you see your past just
before you die.

My eyes were the rearview mirror
years ago. The boys were small and round, waving
good-bye. Their eyes were the young eyes of children
looking at their mother, that she will explain.

What were the reasons? Power of a man over
a woman, his children: his hand on power he lacked,
that my womb had made children as the eye makes a look.

What were the reasons? Terror of a man left alone,
the terror at a gesture: my hand sliding from her
soft pulse neck, to jawbone, chin, mouth met,
mouth of sharp salt. We walked the barrier island,
us, the two boys, the skittering orange crabs,
public deserted beach. In front of the children.

The danger: eyes taught not to cringe away,
the power of their eyes drawn to our joined hands.

Filthy, unfit, not to touch:
                                those from my womb,
red birthslime, come by my cry of agony and pleasure.

Hands smeared often enough with their shit, vomit,
blackness of dirt and new blood, but water from my hands,
and in them, weight of their new bodies come back to rest.

When behind the closed eyelid of a door, in the heavy bed,
sweaty, salty, frantic and calling out sublimely
another woman's name, hands unclenched, I brought down
a cry of joy, then my mouth, mind, hands became
not fit to touch.

                    The work is the same.

What are the reasons? I told them these.
They were young, they did not understand.
Nor do I. Words heard in the ear, hollow room.
The eye waits, sad, unsatisfied,
to embrace the particular loved shape.
Eyes, empty   hands, empty   waiting.

custody
by Shelley Adler

my sons decided
their father needed them
wanted them
would give them
more
than I

(who never told them he did not and)
who anyway had their sisters;

because soon
they would be, should be
men together,
my sons decided
they could not
stay with me;

and I, who would not have let
anything harmful
or even just wrong
happen to them,
let them, had to let them
go;

sometimes I cry or
let things get to me,
but I do not
let my daughters see

Children in Lesbian and Gay Families: Theories and Evidence
by Susan Golombok and Fiona Tasker

L esbian families first became a focus of public attention in the 1970s when previously married lesbians began to fight for custody of their children at the time of divorce. Unlike custody disputes between heterosexual parents, in which the care and control of children is generally awarded to the mother, lesbian mothers were almost always unsuccessful in their attempts to keep their children. Although the likelihood of a lesbian mother's retaining custody may be slightly higher in the 1990s than it was in the 1970s (Rivera, 1991), it remains the case that many lesbian mothers who go to court are denied care and control of their own biological children. Even fewer gay fathers live with their children (Wyers, 1987). With the odds stacked against them because of their gender as well as their sexual orientation, most gay fathers do not even attempt to gain custody of their children following divorce. Custody is generally refused to lesbian mothers and gay fathers on the grounds that they would not be effective parents, that the children would experience difficulties in peer relationships and would develop behavioral and emotional problems as a result, and that the children would show atypical gender development (editors of the *Harvard Law Review,* 1990; Green, 1992; Kleber et al., 1986).

Researchers of the psychological development of children raised in homosexual families and of the quality of parenting of lesbian mothers and gay fathers have attempted to determine whether there is any empirical support for these assumptions. There are clearly important practical implications of this research — for example, in informing courts of law and social policy makers concerned with issues such as adoption and fostering. There are also theoretical implications that arise from an understanding of the psychological development of children raised in lesbian and gay families. Comparisons between children in homosexual and heterosexual families allow questions, such as the importance for children of having a parent of each sex or of simply having two parents irrespective of their sex, to be addressed.

In studies of lesbian families, researchers have generally compared children in lesbian households with children in households headed by a single heterosexual mother (e.g., Golombok et al., 1983; Green et al., 1986; Hoeffer, 1981; Huggins, 1989; Kilpatrick et al., 1981; for reviews see Falk, 1989; Patterson, 1992; Tasker and Golombok, 1991). These two types of family are alike in that the children are being raised by women without the presence of a father but differ in the sexual orientation of the mother. Most of the children in these investigations have been born into a heterosexual marriage, so the children in the two types of family also share the experience of parental separation or divorce. Limited research has been addressed to the issue of how children fare when their father is gay. The two in-depth studies lack comparison groups of heterosexual fathers (Bozett, 1987a, 1987b; Miller, 1979), and the controlled studies, such as that of Harris and Turner (1986), are restricted by their small sample size. Although much of the data on children with gay fathers are provided by the fathers only, many of whom have little contact with their children, a few investigators have obtained data from the children directly (Bailey et al., in press; Bozett, 1987a; Miller, 1979).

Researchers of children with lesbian mothers and gay fathers **159** have tended to examine the areas of child development that have been the focus of concern in custody cases — gender development, emotional and social development, and the parenting ability of the mothers and fathers themselves.

Children's Gender Development

Background
In all that has been said and written about lesbian and gay families, greatest attention has been paid to the consequences of being raised by a homosexual parent for children's gender development. Whether or not children of lesbian mothers and gay fathers will differ from children brought up by heterosexual single mothers will depend on the extent to which it is possible for parents to influence the gender development of their children. Insofar as gender development is biologically determined, the way in which parents raise their children should make little difference, and for this reason biological explanations will not be discussed here. The three major psychological theories — psychoanalytic, social learning, and cognitive

developmental — vary according to the psychological processes that are believed to be operative and also in the role ascribed to parents. Each of these theories will be examined in terms of their explanations of the processes involved in gender development, particularly with respect to what they tell us about the mechanisms, if any, through which parents may play a role.

In investigations of gender development, a distinction is generally made between gender identity, gender role, and sexual orientation; *gender identity* is a person's concept of himself or herself as male or female, *gender role* includes the behaviors and attitudes considered appropriate for males and females in a particular culture, and *sexual orientation* refers to a person's sexual attraction toward people of the opposite sex (heterosexual sexual orientation) or of the same sex (homosexual sexual orientation).

Psychoanalytic theorists believe that relationships with parents early in childhood are central to the development of gender identity, gender role, and sexual orientation in adult life. According to traditional psychoanalytic theory, gender development is rooted in the phallic stage of psychosexual development, which occurs at about five years of age (Freud, 1905/1953, 1920/1955, 1933; Socarides, 1978). It is in order to resolve the Oedipal conflict (i.e., the conflict between his sexual desire for his mother and his fear of castration by his father) that boys are believed to shift their identification from the mother to the father and take on his male characteristics. The mechanisms involved in female identification are rather different and less clearly described. The resolution of the Oedipal conflict in girls is believed to be driven by penis envy and involves transferring identification from the father back to the mother and adopting a female role.

For psychoanalytic theorists, the acquisition of nontraditional gender roles and the development of a lesbian or gay sexual orientation are viewed as negative outcomes resulting from the unsuccessful resolution of the Oedipal conflict. It is believed that boys who fail to identify with their father and girls who fail to identify with their mother at the completion of the Oedipal period are more likely to identify as gay or lesbian, respectively, when they grow up. The quality of children's relationships with their heterosexual parents is considered to be an important determinant of children's passage through the Oedipal phase. The combination of a domineering mother and a weak father for boys is thought to lead to a gay sexual ori-

160

entation. A lesbian sexual orientation is believed to result from a girl's hostile and fearful relationship with her mother.

Although psychoanalytically oriented theorists hold the view that homosexuality arises from disturbed relationships with parents, empirical studies of the influence of parent-child relationships on the development of gay or lesbian identity have produced inconclusive results. In an early study of psychoanalysts' reports of the family relationships of their male homosexual patients, the fathers of homosexual men were described as hostile and/or distant and the mothers as close-binding, intimate, and dominant (Bieber et al., 1962). With a nonpatient sample Evans (1969) also showed a similar pattern of a close mother and a detached father. Rather different findings, however, were reported by Bene (1965b), who found no evidence that homosexual men who were not in therapy were more likely to have been overprotected by, overindulged by, or strongly attached to their mother than heterosexual men, and in a well-controlled large-scale study by Siegelman (1974), no differences were identified in parental background between homosexual and heterosexual men who were low on neuroticism. Siegelman concluded that the differences in parental relationships between homosexual and heterosexual men found in earlier studies were 161 related to differences in neuroticism rather than to homosexuality per se. Researchers of the mothers of lesbians have similarly failed to produce consistent findings, although some investigators have reported mothers of lesbian women to be dominant and fathers to be inferior or weak (Bell et al., 1981; Bene, 1965a; Kaye et al., 1967; Newcombe, 1985).

From the perspective of classic social learning theory, which has focused on the development of childhood sex-typed behavior rather than on adult sexual orientation, the two processes that are important for children's gender development are differential reinforcement and modeling (Bandura, 1977; Mischel, 1966, 1970). There is much empirical evidence to suggest that parents of preschool children do treat their sons and daughters differently, although the extent to which they are producing sex-typed behavior rather than simply responding to preexisting differences between boys and girls remains unknown (Lytton and Romney, 1991; Maccoby and Jacklin, 1974). Right from birth, parents interact with their infants differently according to whether they are male or female (Moss, 1967; Parke and Sawin, 1980; Power and Parke, 1982; Rubin et al.,

1974). They dress their girls in pink, decorative clothes and their boys in blue, functional ones (Shakin et al., 1985), and they surround them with sex-typed toys and furnishings (Rheingold and Cook, 1975). And from as early as twelve months, infants are encouraged to play with sex-typed toys and to avoid play activities that are considered more appropriate for children of the other sex (Snow et al., 1983). The differential encouragement of sex-typed activities in boys and girls becomes even more apparent as infants grow into toddlers (Fagot, 1978; Langois and Downs, 1980). Differential reinforcement by parents, however, seems to decline once children reach school age (Fagot and Hagan, 1991; Lytton and Romney, 1991). At this stage of a child's development, friends take on a more important role. Peers consistently and strongly reinforce sex-typed toy choice and play and punish cross-gender activities (Carter, 1987).

According to classic social learning theorists, boys and girls also learn sex-typed behavior by imitating models of the same sex, particularly the same-sex parent. However, the idea that children acquire sex-typed behavior by directly imitating same-sex parents is now thought to be rather simplistic, and a modified version of social learning theory has been proposed (Bandura, 1986; Bussey and Bandura, 1984; Perry and Bussey, 1979). It seems that children learn which behaviors are considered to be appropriate for males and which for females by observing many men and women and boys and girls and by noticing which behaviors are performed frequently by females and rarely by males and vice versa. Children then use these abstractions of sex-appropriate behavior as models for their own imitative performance. Thus, children observe a wide variety of role models in their daily life and tend to imitate those whom they consider typical of their sex. Friends, in particular, appear to be important role models; school-age boys and girls show a strong preference for same-sex peers (Maccoby. 1988). But it is gender stereotypes rather than specific individuals that seem to be most influential in the acquisition of sex-typed behavior. Gender stereotypes are pervasive in our society, and children are aware of these stereotypes from as early as two years of age (Martin, 1991; Signorella et al., 1993; Stern and Karraker, 1989).

Like social learning theorists, cognitive developmental theorists have focused on the development of childhood gender identity and role rather than on adult sexual orientation. For cognitive develop-

162

mental theorists, the role of parents is a minor one. A central tenet of this approach is that children play an active part in their own development; they seek out for themselves information about gender and socialize themselves as male or female. Parents are viewed as simply one source of gender-related information.

Early studies of cognitive developmental processes focused on children's developing understanding of the concept of gender (Kohlberg, 1966; Stagnor and Ruble, 1987). Basic gender identity is established at about two to three years. By this age children know that they are male or female and can correctly label other people as male or female as well. It is not until they reach the stage of gender stability a year or two later, however, that they realize that gender is stable across time. Gender constancy, the understanding that gender is a characteristic that does not change, is the final stage in the development of the gender concept and is reached at about five or six years of age. According to Kohlberg, it is when children reach the stage of gender constancy that they begin to identify with their own gender, seek out information associated with their own gender, come to value the characteristics and behaviors associated with their own gender, and engage in gender-related activities. Although these behaviors may increase when gender constancy is reached — **163** for example, gender knowledge increases in content and complexity throughout childhood (Martin, 1991), and children are more likely to imitate models of their own sex once they have reached gender constancy (Slaby and Frey, 1975) — children know a great deal about gender and consistently show a preference for toys and activities associated with their own gender by the time they achieve basic gender identity at about two to three years (Maccoby and Jacklin, 1974; Martin and Little, 1990).

Gender schema theorists have examined the way in which children organize knowledge about gender (Martin, 1989, 1991; Martin and Halverson, 1981). Gender schemas refer to organized bodies of knowledge about gender and are functionally similar to gender stereotypes. Gender schemas influence the way in which we perceive and remember information about the world around us so that we pay greater attention to — and are more likely to remember — information that is in line with our gender schemas than opposing information. From as early as two to three years, soon after they begin to consistently label themselves and others as male or female, children organize information according to gender. If told that a person is male or female, children will make gender-related predictions about that person's behavior (Martin, 1989; Martin et al., 1990), and children as young as five years have been shown to have a better memory for events that fit gender stereotypes than those that do not (Liben and Signorella, 1980; Martin and Halverson, 1983; Signorella and Liben, 1984).

So what can we predict from these various psychological theories about the consequences for gender development of being raised by a lesbian mother or a gay father? Traditional psychoanalytic theorists, stressing the importance of the presence of heterosexual parents for the successful resolution of the oedipal conflict, would expect that the lack of a father figure, together with the mother's atypical female role, would influence the gender development of children brought up in lesbian families. Specifically, it has been argued that boys will not identify with the male role and will therefore be less masculine and that girls will identify with a mother who does not conform to the traditional female role and will thus be less feminine. Similarly, it would be predicted that the gender development of the sons and daughters of gay fathers would be affected by the father's atypical male role. Boys, in particular, would be expected to be less masculine than their counterparts with heterosexual fathers. Although researchers of children raised in heterosexual families have failed to produce empirical evidence to demonstrate that the quality of parent-child relationships influences the development of children's sexual orientation, psychoanalytic theorists would predict that a gay or lesbian identity would be particularly likely for boys with a close relationship and girls with a hostile relationship with their lesbian mother and for boys with a hostile relationship and girls with a close relationship with their gay father.

From a social learning theory perspective, it could be expected that different patterns of reinforcement may be operating in homosexual than in heterosexual families such that young people in lesbian and gay families would be less likely to be discouraged from engaging in nonconventional sex-typed behavior or from embarking on lesbian or gay relationships. Whereas contemporary social learning theorists are less likely than classical social learning theorists to emphasize the importance of the same-sex parent as a role model, it could be argued that by virtue of their nontraditional family, the sons and daughters of lesbian mothers and gay fathers may hold less rigid stereotypes about what constitutes acceptable male

164

and female behavior than their peers in heterosexual families and may be more open to nonconventional gender-role behavior or to involvement in lesbian or gay relationships themselves. It is important to remember, however, that social learning theorists believe that individuals other than parents are also important role models and reinforcers of sex-typed behavior for the child.

Finally, cognitive developmental theorists place even less emphasis on the role of parents in the gender development of their children. According to this theory, children integrate information about sexual identity from their wider social environment, actively constructing for themselves what it means to be male or female. It would not be predicted that children raised by lesbian mothers or gay fathers would differ in this process from children in heterosexual families. Cognitive developmental theorists, like social learning theorists, have focused on childhood sex-typed behavior rather than on adult sexual orientation. To the extent that cognitive processes are contributing to the adoption of a heterosexual or homosexual orientation, it would seem that young people seek out information in their social world that is in line with their emerging sexual orientation and come to value and identify with those characteristics that are consistent with their view of themselves as heterosexual or homosexual. **165**

Empirical Evidence

The gender identity of children raised by lesbian mothers is in line with their biological sex. In none of the children studied to date, estimated by Patterson (1992) to be more than 300, has any child shown evidence of gender identity confusion; none of the children wished to be the other sex or consistently engaged in cross-gender behavior (Golombok et al., 1983; Green et al., 1986; Kirkpatrick et al., 1981). In terms of gender role, no differences have been found between children in lesbian and heterosexual families for either boys or girls. Examination of preferred toys, games, activities, and friendships has shown the children in both types of family to be quite conventional (Golombok et al., 1983; Green et al., 1986; Kirkpatrick et al., 1981). Lesbian mothers' greater preference than heterosexual mothers' for an equal mixture of masculine and feminine toys for their children appears to have little impact on the toys and activities chosen by their daughters and sons (Hoeffer, 1981).

Data on the gender-role behavior of children of gay fathers come from a small survey of eleven gay fathers and ten lesbian mothers (Harris and Turner, 1986; Turner et al., 1990). In comparison with the more-feminist lesbian mothers in this survey, gay fathers were more likely to report that they encouraged their children to play with sex-typed toys. The lesbian mothers and gay fathers reported that their children generally seemed to be developing typical sex-role identification and that their behavior was no different from that of other children of the same age and sex.

While researchers have demonstrated a link between boyhood gender identity disorder and adult homosexuality (e.g., Green, 1987; Zuger, 1984), suggesting that feminine boys — and possibly masculine girls — in lesbian or gay families may be particularly likely to develop a sexual orientation toward partners of the same sex, none of the sons or daughters of lesbian mothers or gay fathers investigated so far has shown marked cross-gender identity of the type associated with a later lesbian or gay sexual orientation.

One of the most commonly voiced assumptions about lesbian families is that the children will themselves grow up to be lesbian or gay, an outcome generally considered undesirable by those involved in decision making in courts of law. Until recently, studies of lesbian families have focused on children rather than adults, and sexual orientation has not been assessed. An exception is Gottman's (1990) study in which the fantasies and sexual object choice of adult daughters of lesbian mothers, but not actual sexual behavior, were examined. In a longitudinal investigation of the sexual orientation of adults who had been raised in lesbian families (Tasker and Golombok, in press-a, in press-b), it was found that while similar proportions of young adults from lesbian and heterosexual families reported feelings of attraction toward someone of the same sex, those from lesbian families were more likely to consider the possibility of having same-sex partners and to actually do so, particularly if their childhood family environment had been characterized by an openness and acceptance of lesbian and gay relationships. Nevertheless, the large majority of children who grew up in lesbian families identified themselves as heterosexual in adulthood. Only 8 percent of young adults raised by lesbian mothers reported a sexual orientation toward partners of the same sex, which is consistent with general population norms (Patterson, 1992).

The most extensive study of the sexual orientation of children of gay fathers is that of Bailey et al. (in press). Fifty-five gay fathers were asked whether each of their eighty-two sons over the age of seventeen is heterosexual, bisexual, or homosexual. Forty-three of the sons were also interviewed. Most of the sons were heterosexual, with only 9 percent classified as homosexual or bisexual. No association was found between the sons' sexual orientation and the number of years they had lived with their father, the frequency of contact with their father, their present acceptance of their father's gay identity, or the quality of the father–adult son relationship.

Other studies of the sons and daughters of gay fathers also support the general picture that most children of homosexual parents are heterosexual. None of the children over twelve years old in the study by Turner et al. (1990) was reported by their gay father to have shown any interest in having gay or lesbian relationships, and Miller (1979) found that only one of twenty-one sons and three of twenty-seven daughters were believed by their gay father to be homosexual or bisexual. Of the nineteen children of gay fathers interviewed, two sons identified as gay and one daughter as bisexual (Bozett, 1987a).

Children's Emotional and Social Development

167

Background

The assumption that children of homosexual parents may be more likely to experience emotional and behavioral problems than children of heterosexual parents stems from the finding that some childhood family experiences have been shown to carry an increased risk of psychiatric disorder. Of particular relevance to children of lesbian mothers and gay fathers is the children's experience of parental divorce and whether the children are being reared in a single-parent household.

A number of researchers have examined the psychological adjustment of children whose parents divorce, the most noteworthy of which is the longitudinal investigation by Hetherington and her colleagues (Hetherington, 1988, 1989; Hetherington et al., 1982, 1985). Children of divorced parents in mother-custody families were compared with children of nondivorced parents at two months, one year, two years, and six years following divorce using a variety of observational, interview, and rating-scale measures of the children's behavior at home and at school. It was found that in the first year, the children from divorced families showed more behavioral problems. They were more aggressive, more demanding, and more lacking in self-control than their counterparts in nondivorced families. By two years following divorce, the girls had adapted to their new situation and had a positive relationship with their mother, providing she had not remarried. The boys, although slightly improved, still showed problems in adjustment and difficulties in their relationship with their mother. By the time of the 6-year follow-up, some of the mothers had remarried so that these children were living with their mother and a stepfather. The mothers who had not remarried continued to have good relationships with their daughters and difficult relationships with their sons. This pattern was reflected in the children's behavior. The daughters were functioning well, whereas the boys were more likely than boys in nondivorced families to be noncompliant, impulsive, and aggressive. In families where the mother had remarried, however, the situation was rather different. After the early stages of remarriage, the boys had fewer problems than boys in nonremarried families. If the stepfather was supportive, boys developed a good relationship with him. The girls, on the other hand, had more difficulties with family relations and adjustment than girls whose mothers had not remarried and continued to

168 reject their stepfather no matter how hard he tried to develop a positive relationship (Vuchinich et al., 1991).

When intense marital conflict continues after the divorce, it can have a more harmful effect than when it occurs in intact families (Hetherington, 1988, 1989). Wallerstein and Kelly (1980) also found that children with difficulties are those whose parents remain in conflict after the divorce and concluded that whether children's problems diminish is a function of whether divorce improves parental relationships. The quality of the child's relationship with parents is also an important determinant of the child's psychological adjustment. Children who have good postdivorce relationships with their parents are less likely to suffer negative effects (Hess and Camara, 1979; Hetherington, 1988).

About 90 percent of single-parent families are headed by a mother rather than a father (Roll, 1992), and in studies of single-parent families, children raised by their mother alone have generally been compared with children in two-parent families. It is commonly assumed that differences between these two groups are directly attributable to paternal influences. However, the effects of father absence are difficult to disentangle from those of the absence of one parent. Although in much of the early research it was found that father absence had negative consequences for children's cognitive, social, and emotional development, the methods used were often inadequate, and the findings of the more–carefully conducted studies tended to be inconsistent (Biller, 1974; Herzog and Sudia, 1973). A major problem has been the failure to take account of factors that may be associated with father absence but not directly related to it. This is highlighted in a study of a nationally representative sample of families in the United Kingdom in which children in one- and two-parent families were compared (Ferri, 1976). Children in one-parent families were found to be less well-adjusted than those with two parents. However, the children raised by a single parent experienced a number of disadvantages, such as lower social class, poor housing, and economic hardship. When these factors were taken into account, there was little difference in emotional adjustment between the two groups of children. So the absence of a parent in itself was not adversely related to the child's social adjustment. Instead it was the poverty and social isolation that accompanied single parenthood that had a negative effect. Similarly, large studies in the United States found no impairment in IQ for father-absent children after controlling for social class **169** (Broman, et al., 1975; Svanum et al., 1982).

Another problem has been the failure to take account of the reason for becoming a one-parent family. In a comparison between children whose parents had divorced or separated and those who had lost a parent through death, a higher incidence of behavioral problems was found among the children who had experienced divorce or separation (Rutter, 1971). Discordant family relationships, rather than the loss of a parent, were responsible for the children's difficulties. Further evidence of the importance of factors that pre-date the transition from a two-parent family to a one-parent family comes from longitudinal studies that allowed comparisons to be made between the behavioral problems of children whose parents divorced or separated between the first and second assessment and the behavioral problems of children whose families remained intact (Cherlin et al., 1991). It was found that behavioral problems and family difficulties that were present before the parents' separation or divorce were strongly associated with the children's difficulties after the families had broken up. Thus it is not only what happens to children after their parents separate but also their circumstances beforehand that influence the impact of becoming a one-parent family on the emotional and social adjustment of children.

It has often been argued that the lack of a father as an identification figure or role model will result in atypical gender-role behavior in children, particularly for boys. For this reason much of the research on father absence has focused on children's sex-typed behavior. Again, the empirical findings relating to this issue are contradictory and inconclusive (Biller, 1974; Herzog and Sudia, 1973; Stevenson and Black, 1988). Most children raised by a single mother show typical gender-role development, but there may be a slight effect on some behaviors and attitudes. Father-absent boys of preschool age tend to show less-stereotyped choices of toys and activities. Older father-absent boys appear to be more stereotyped in their behavior than their father-present age mates. This effect is strongest for aggressive behavior, however, which is common among boys who have experienced parental divorce. Although the effects of mother absence on children's gender development has not been directly studied, investigators of families with highly involved fathers indicate that these children hold less-traditional attitudes about male and female roles (Radin, 1982; Sagi, 1982).

170   Neither parental divorce nor single parenthood are *directly* related to rearing in a lesbian or gay family. The expectation that being raised in a homosexual family would, in itself, increase the likelihood of psychiatric disorder in children arises from the assumption that the children would be teased about their parent's sexual orientation and ostracized by their peers. The concern is that this situation would be deeply upsetting to children and that it would have a negative effect on their ability to form and maintain friendships. There is wide agreement in the psychological literature that satisfactory relationships with peers are important for positive social and emotional development (Dunn and McGuire, 1992; Kupersmidt et al., 1990).

Empirical Evidence

The assumption that children raised in lesbian households would experience emotional or behavioral difficulties as a result of their upbringing has been examined in two studies (Golombok et al., 1983; Kirkpatrick et al., 1981). The presence of psychiatric difficulties in the child was assessed by means of a standardized interview with the mother in the study by Golombok et al. (1983). The interview had been specifically designed for this purpose, and its ability to reliably detect the most commonly occurring childhood disorders had been demonstrated in previous research (Graham and Rutter, 1968). For each child a rating was made of whether there was evidence of psychiatric disorder, and when a disorder was present, a diagnosis of the type of disorder was given. In order to avoid bias, these ratings were made by a child psychiatrist who was "blind" to the child's family type. No differences in psychiatric state were identified between the children of lesbian mothers and those of heterosexual mothers. In addition to the interview with the mother, schoolteachers were asked to complete the Rutter "B" Scale (Rutter et al., 1970), a questionnaire measure of children's emotional and behavioral problems. Again, there was no difference in the incidence of difficulties between the two groups of children, and in relation to general population norms, the sons and daughters of lesbian mothers were no more likely to show emotional or behavioral problems than children in heterosexual families. As the mothers may have wished to conceal their children's problems, the information obtained from schoolteachers provided validation of the mothers' reports.

Similar findings regarding children's emotional well-being were reported by Kirkpatrick et al. (1981). Ratings of psychiatric disorder, based on information obtained during a standardized interview with the mother, were made by a child psychiatrist who was unaware of the child's family background. There was no difference between groups in the proportion of children rated as showing a disorder, with approximately 10 percent of children in both lesbian and heterosexual families receiving a psychiatric diagnosis.

In the longitudinal study of adults who had been raised as children in lesbian families (Tasker and Golombok, in press-a, in press-b), no evidence of adverse effects on psychological well-being in the long term were identified. Men and women raised by lesbian mothers were no more likely than their peers from heterosexual single-parent homes to experience anxiety or depression and, for both groups of young adults, their scores on standardized depression and anxiety inventories fell within the normal range. Furthermore, young adults from lesbian families were no more likely than those from heterosexual single-parent backgrounds to have sought professional help for psychiatric problems.

An aspect of human development closely related to psychological well-being is the development of self-esteem. No differences in levels of self-esteem have been demonstrated between the offspring

171

of lesbian and heterosexual mothers either in childhood (Puryear, 1983) or in adolescence (Huggins, 1989).

It seems, therefore, from research on emotional well-being during childhood and on self-esteem during childhood and adolescence, that children in lesbian families are at no greater risk for emotional or behavioral problems than children raised in heterosexual households.

To date no study has focused directly on the psychological well-being of children with gay fathers. However, there are no indications, either from fathers' reports or from the limited number of interviews with the children themselves, that children who remain in contact with their gay father experience serious emotional or behavioral problems. Any problems gay fathers presented were attributed to parental divorce rather than to having a gay parent (Turner et al., 1990). It should also be noted that no study has assessed whether children of gay fathers or lesbian mothers who lose custody or visitation rights are adversely affected by the loss of contact with their homosexual parent.

With respect to children's peer relationships, systematic information on children's interactions with peers was obtained by interview with lesbian mothers in the study by Golombok et al. (1983), and these data were rated "blind" as to the knowledge of family type. No differences in quality of friendships were identified between children raised in lesbian and heterosexual single-parent families. Only two children in each group showed definite difficulties involving personal distress, social impairment, or restricted activities, and a further one third in each group showed minor difficulties associated with shyness, difficulty in maintaining friendships, or quarreling. At follow-up, the grown-up children from lesbian families reported close friendships during adolescence (Tasker and Golombok, in press-a, in press-b). Furthermore, they were no more likely than their counterparts from heterosexual single-parent families to experience peer stigma during adolescence, and most were able to integrate close friends with family life. However, they did tend to be more likely to recollect peer-group teasing about their own sexuality. In Green et al.'s (1986) investigation, no group differences were found for children's perceptions of their popularity with peers or for mothers' ratings of their children's sociability and social acceptance. It seems either that stigmatization by peers is not a major problem for children of lesbian mothers or at least that exposure to teasing or ostracism does not prevent them from forming meaningful and rewarding friendships.

Estimates vary as to how likely children with gay fathers are to experience stigma and relationship problems with peers or adults outside the family. Wyers (1987) reported that 74 percent of children of the thirty-two gay fathers in his questionnaire survey were believed by their father to have experienced some relationship problems as a result of his homosexuality. However, many of these problems concerned what to tell others about their father's sexual orientation or the worry that they might be ostracized by their peer group, and only 20 percent of the fathers reported that their children had experienced actual discrimination.

Data from interview studies with gay fathers and their children suggest that the children are less likely to experience prejudice than Wyers's (1987) survey indicates. Bozett (1987a) argues that although the possibility of peer-group stigma is a major concern of many children with gay fathers, they use a variety of strategies to cope. They may decide not to tell anyone about their father's sexual orientation, or they may carefully select those whom to tell. Furthermore, children are able to compartmentalize their lives to avoid having friends meet their father or, alternatively, to prevent their father's behaving in ways they feel make his sexual orientation public. For example, some children may try to persuade their father **173** not to wear any jewelry or avoid being seen with him and his partner outside the home. How children deal with the possibility of homophobia depends on how obvious they believe their fathers' sexual orientation to be, how much they identify with his sense of being different, their age, and whether they live with him. Neither Bozett (1987a, 1987b) nor Miller (1979) recorded many instances of homophobia directed against children of gay fathers. This seemed to be because the children were generally able to discern who could be trusted with knowing about their father's gay identity and also because gay fathers handled this issue sensitively.

Parenting Ability

Background
It is well-established that children's social and emotional development is fostered within the context of parent-child relationships (Darling and Steinberg, 1993; Maccoby, 1992). By far the most accepted and comprehensive explanation of the processes involved in the development of parent-child relationships comes from attach-

ment theory, put forward by Bowlby (Bowlby, 1969, 1973, 1980) and Ainsworth (Ainsworth, 1972, 1982; Ainsworth et al., 1978). According to this theory, interactions between the parent and the child form the basis of attachment relationships, and the type of attachment an infant develops (i.e., secure or insecure) largely depends on the quality of interaction between the parent and the child, such that parents of securely attached infants are responsive and sensitive to their infant's needs (Ainsworth, 1979). Recent research provides empirical evidence in support of this view (Grossmann et al., 1985; Isabella and Belsky, 1991; Izard et al., 1991; Pederson et al., 1990; Smith and Pederson, 1988). For example, it has been demonstrated that secure attachments in infancy are fostered by synchronous interactions, in which mothers are responsive to their infant's vocalizations and distress signals (Isabella et al., 1989).

Although theory and research on attachment has largely focused on the child's attachment to the mother, it is now generally accepted that children also form attachments to their father (Lamb, 1986). It has been shown that a similar proportion of infants are securely attached to the father as to the mother (Fox et al., 1991). Just like mothers, fathers who engage in frequent social interaction with their babies and who respond readily and sensitively to them have strongly attached infants (Cox et al., 1992).

Researchers have traditionally focused on the development of attachment in infancy. In recent years, however, attention has turned to the examination of attachment relationships in the preschool and school-age years. As a result, interest has grown in representational aspects of attachment. Through their early experiences with attachment figures, children are believed to form internal representations of their attachment relationships (Bowlby, 1969, 1973, 1980). Bowlby refers to these internal representations as "internal working models." According to Bowlby, the child's internal working model of an attachment figure — for example, as available and responsive in the case of securely attached children or as unavailable and unresponsive in the case of insecurely attached children — will influence the child's expectations of and behavior toward that person. The child's internal working models of attachment relationships are also believed to influence the child's internal representation of the self. Thus, a child who represents attachment figures as responsive and emotionally available is likely to hold an internal model of the self as lovable, whereas a child with internal models of attachment figures as unresponsive and unavailable is likely to represent the self as unworthy of being loved. The child's internal representations of attachment figures and of the self are believed to have a profound influence on the individual's relationships with others in childhood and in adult life. There is growing empirical evidence in support of Bowlby's view that individuals form internal models of their attachment relationships (e.g., Main et al., 1985). It has also been demonstrated that a connection exists between working models of attachment figures and the working model of the self (Cassidy, 1988).

Thus, it appears that the most important factor for a secure parent-child relationship is the quality of interaction between that parent and the child. Children in homosexual families would therefore be expected to have a positive relationship with their lesbian mother or gay father providing that the lesbian or gay parent is responsive to them and sensitive to their needs. It is important to note that the quality of the parent-child attachment relationship is not fixed for life and can change for better or worse according to family circumstances (Thompson et al., 1982, Vaughn et al., 1979). So insecurely attached infants can become more secure over time if, **175** for example, the parent experiences less stress. The opposite is also possible if the parent's situation makes him or her less accessible and less responsive to the child.

Empirical Evidence

Although security of attachment between homosexual parents and their children has not been directly investigated, a number of researchers have addressed the quality of the parent-child relationship in lesbian and gay families in a more general way. In courts of law lesbian mothers and gay fathers have been deemed unsuitable as parents on a number of grounds: It has been argued that they are not maternal or paternal, respectively; that they are emotionally unstable and prone to psychiatric disorder; and that they or their partner might sexually abuse their children. In fact, there is no evidence in support of any of these claims. It has been demonstrated that lesbian mothers are just as child-oriented (Miller et al., 1981), just as warm and responsive to their children (Golombok et al., 1983), and just as nurturant and confident (Mucklow and Phelan, 1979) as their heterosexual counterparts. And contrary to the view expressed in a number of custody cases — that the relationship with their female partner would take priority over child care — the day-to-day life of lesbian mothers is just as centered around their children as that of heterosexual mothers (Kirkpatrick, 1987; Pagelow, 1980).

As adults, men and women from lesbian families report positive relationships with their mother and her partner (Tasker and Golombok, in press-a, in press-b). The findings of the follow-up study indicate that children from lesbian homes had been able to forge closer relationships with their mother's new female partner than had children from heterosexual households with their mother's new male partner. It seemed that children from lesbian households could more easily add a stepparent into their family constellation, since their mothers female partner could be regarded as an addition to their resident parent rather than as a direct competitor to their absent father.

Researchers who have compared gay and heterosexual fathers have not shown detrimental effects of homosexual sexual orientation on parenting ability. Bigner and Jacobsen (1989) found that gay and heterosexual fathers did not differ on reported degree of involvement or level of intimacy with their children, although on average the gay fathers seemed to be more responsive to their children's needs. In comparison with heterosexual fathers, gay fathers tended to be more strict and set more consistent limits for their children's behavior. However, they were also more likely to provide their children with explanations for the rules and regulations they set up and to ask their child for his or her opinion in family decisions. The gay fathers in Harris and Turner's (1986) study generally reported very positive relationships with their children, rating their communication, cooperation, discipline, and enjoyment of their children very highly. Interview data from the same study revealed that gay fathers devoted a considerable amount of their available time to their children and tried to foster positive relationships with them and to create a stable home environment (Turner et al., 1990). Furthermore, none of the gay fathers interviewed reported any difficulty in reconciling their gay lifestyle with their parenting role.

Having a lesbian mother or gay father does not mean that children are deprived of contact with adults of the opposite sex. After divorce lesbian mothers are more concerned than heterosexual mothers that their children should have contact with men (Kirkpatrick et al., 1981), and children raised in lesbian families following divorce see their father more frequently than do children raised by divorced heterosexual mothers (Golombok et al., 1983). Turner et al. (1990) reported that gay fathers tended to have better relationships with their ex-spouses than lesbian mothers. In comparison with the single heterosexual parents who responded to their original survey, fewer gay and lesbian parents found visits with their child's other biological parent to be a problem (Harris and Turner, 1986).

The question of why lesbian women, and in particular gay men, married and had children sometimes arises in custody disputes. Wyers (1987) and Turner et al. (1990) reported that most gay men and women married for the same reasons as heterosexual men and women: they fell in love with their prospective spouse, they were influenced by personal and social expectations and wanted to adopt a heterosexual lifestyle, or they wanted to have children. Women appear to be less likely than men to be aware of sexual feelings toward others of the same sex before they marry. Many men, however, recognized their homosexual feelings but reported hoping that these would end with marriage (Wyers, 1987). Although the majori- **177** ty of gay fathers interviewed by Miller (1979) had experienced sex with another male before they married, most did not acknowledge this as a salient part of their identity.

Lesbians and gay men, whether or not they are parents, are at no greater risk for psychiatric disorder than are heterosexual women and men (e.g., Bell and Weinberg, 1978). In addition, there is no evidence to suggest that children in lesbian or gay families are at risk for sexual abuse. None of the ninety children in Miller's (1979) sample of children with gay fathers was reported to have been approached sexually either by their father or his gay friends. Furthermore, Bigner and Jacobsen (1989) reported that in comparison with heterosexual fathers, gay fathers were less likely to hug or kiss their partner in front of their child. Although there are no empirical studies of the sexual abuse of children by lesbian mothers, it is important to remember that in the large majority of cases of sexual abuse, the perpetrators are men (Finkelhor and Russell, 1984).

Perhaps the most important question concerning the parenting abilities of lesbian mothers and gay fathers is how children feel about being brought up by a homosexual parent. In comparison with gay fathers, lesbian mothers who take part in research are more likely to have been open with their children about their sexual orientation (Wyers, 1987). Results from our longitudinal study showed no difference between the recollections of young adults raised by lesbian mothers and young adults brought up by heterosexual divorced mothers with respect to their feelings during adolescence about their nontraditional family (Tasker and Golombok, in press-a, in press-b). Interviewees raised in lesbian families, however, were more likely to say that they were proud of their family of origin when asked for their current views.

Researchers of gay fathers found that many gay fathers experience considerable anxiety about coming out to their children (Bozett, 1987b; Miller, 1979). Indeed, many gay fathers keep their sexual orientation secret because they fear it will damage their relationship with their children (Bigner and Bozett, 1990). However, it is unusual for children to reject their father when they find out that he is gay, although they may not necessarily approve of his gay identity. Indeed, some father-child relationships have benefited from greater openness after the disclosure of the father's sexual identity (Bozett, 1987a; Miller, 1979). Miller reported that daughters tend to be more accepting of gay fathers than are sons, although Bozett argued that most children, regardless of their age or sex, respond positively.

Little is known about men who have sex with male partners but continue to identify as heterosexual and live with their wife. Even less is known about women in this situation (Coleman, 1990). Ross (1990) estimated that 2 percent to 4 percent of married men may be homosexually active. Some husbands are able to develop a bisexual identity and create a stable heterosexual marriage in which their bisexuality is acknowledged by their wife and sometimes by their children as well (Matteson, 1987). Many men, however, keep their sexual encounters with other men and their heterosexual lives separate so that they appear to have a typical heterosexual home life (Matteson, 1987; Ross, 1990). More-general research on the impact of AIDS on the gay community indicates that gay men may disclose their homosexual relationships to their heterosexual family only when they realize that they have HIV or become ill (Barret and Robinson, 1990; Lovejoy, 1990).

178

Planned Lesbian and Gay Families

Background

A major limitation of existing investigations of homosexual families is that the children were conceived within the context of a hetero-sexual relationship and spent their early life in a heterosexual family. To the extent that *early* family experiences are important determinants of later social, emotional, and gender development, we cannot generalize from the conclusions of the studies discussed above to children raised by lesbian and gay parents from birth. It could be argued, for example, that any influence of lesbian mothering or gay fathering on gender development would occur before age three, since basic gender identity and gender-role behavior are established by this age.

A growing number of lesbians are becoming parents after coming out, and studies of children raised by lesbian mothers from birth are now beginning to appear. Although some women embark on motherhood alone, many couples plan a family together and share the parenting role (Patterson, 1992). But however much the couple wish to share in the upbringing of the child, in most lesbian families only one mother may be the legal parent. For this reason, a common problem facing lesbian coparents is that the nonbiological mother is not viewed as being a "real" parent (Green, 1987). Pregnancy is sometimes achieved through heterosexual intercourse, but more commonly donor insemination is chosen as the method of conception. Some women prefer to use semen from an anonymous donor. Many donor-insemination clinics, however, refuse to accept lesbians — even when they are allowed by law to do so — and a growing number of women are choosing self-insemination instead. Self-insemination is also the preferred method of conception for women who wish to conceive without the involvement of the medical profession. The donor may be a friend, a relative, or an acquaintance of the biological mother or her partner and may or may not remain in contact with the family as the child grows up. (For a discussion of the issues surrounding self-insemination and an account of the experiences of women who have followed this route to motherhood, see Saffron, 1994.)

Many of the men who volunteer to donate sperm for women who wish to have a baby through self-insemination are gay men. Some men donate as a favor for a friend or out of political solidarity, know-

179

ing the difficulties lesbians face in becoming pregnant. These biological fathers do not wish to have emotional or practical involvement with their offspring. A variety of other arrangements exist
between donors, mothers, and partners so that some biological
fathers occasionally or regularly spend time with the child. In other
cases gay men and lesbians agree to set up coparenting arrangements so that children are brought up in both lesbian and gay families (Martin, 1993; Saffron, 1994).

The options for gay men who wish to become primary parents are
more difficult and involve surrogate motherhood or adoption. In a
surrogacy arrangement a woman agrees to be inseminated with the
sperm of the man who will parent the child and she then gives up
all parental rights at the time of the birth. In the United Kingdom
commercial surrogacy is illegal and noncommercial arrangements
are apparently rare. Both commercial surrogacy through various
agencies and private arrangements are sanctioned in many
American states and are possible routes to parenthood for gay men
who wish to be genetically related to their child. Martin (1993)
pointed out that although surrogacy is often expensive and may be
extremely difficult both emotionally and legally, it is not necessarily
more problematic for gay men than are other routes to parenthood.

Lesbians and gay men may also become parents through adoption (Ricketts and Achtenberg, 1987). However, in most countries
and in most American states, lesbian and gay couples are not permitted to adopt a child together in the way that heterosexual couples can, so that only one partner can become the legal parent. And
in some places it is illegal even for a single lesbian woman or gay
man to adopt a child. Legislation that permits lesbians and gay men
to adopt does not guarantee that this will be an easy process. Even
in the states of California and New York, where it is illegal to reject
a prospective adoptive parent on the grounds of sexual orientation,
social workers who are opposed to lesbians and gay men becoming
adoptive parents may find other ostensible reasons for not placing
a child in a lesbian or gay household (Martin, 1993).

Empirical Evidence
In the United States an investigation of preschool children found no
differences in the presence of emotional problems or in difficulties
in separation from the mother between children born to lesbian couples by donor insemination and children born to heterosexual cou-

180

ples (Steckel, 1987). The children in heterosexual families, however, were found to be more aggressive, and the children of lesbian mothers, more affectionate and responsive. Similar findings for preschool children were reported in an uncontrolled clinical study by McCandlish (1987). The children formed secure attachments to both mothers and showed no evidence of psychological difficulties.

In addition, children between the ages of four and nine years who had been born to or adopted by lesbian mothers were not found to differ from children of heterosexual parents on measures of social competence, behavioral problems, gender-role behavior, or the extent to which they saw themselves as aggressive, sociable, or likely to enjoy being the center of attention (Patterson, 1994). Two differences between the children of lesbian and heterosexual parents were shown: Children in lesbian families reported more negative reactions to stress (such as anger and fear) and a greater sense of well-being (joy and contentment) than did children in heterosexual families. Patterson suggested that these differences may result either from greater stress in their everyday lives or from their greater ability to acknowledge both positive and negative aspects of their emotional experience. Steckel's (1987) finding that children of lesbian mothers saw themselves as less aggressive and more **181** sociable than children of heterosexual parents was not replicated in Patterson's investigation.

In Europe two studies of the psychological development of children born to lesbian mothers by donor insemination are currently under way. The first is being conducted in Belgium (Brewaeys et al., 1993). Of particular interest, in view of the current debate about whether children conceived by donated gametes should be told about their origins (Daniels and Taylor, 1993), is that lesbian mothers were found to be much less secretive about the child's genetic origins than heterosexual parents of children conceived by donor insemination. We are carrying out the second study in the United Kingdom. As yet there have been too few studies of the children of women who had come out as lesbian before becoming mothers to give a clear picture of the similarities and differences between these families and other family forms. The evidence so far, however, does not point toward psychological difficulties for children raised from birth by lesbian mothers.

References

Ainsworth, M. D. S. (1972). Attachment and Dependency: A Comparison. In J. L. Gewirtz (Ed.), *Attachment and Dependency* (pp. 97-137). New York: Wiley.

Ainsworth, M. D. S. (1979). Attachment as Related to Mother-Infant Interaction. In J. Rosenblatt, R. A. Hinde, C. Beer, and M. Busnel (Eds.), *Advances in the Study of Behaviour,* (Vol. 9, pp. 1-51). Orlando, Florida: Academic Press.

Ainsworth, M. D. S. (1982). Attachment: Retrospect and Prospect. In C. M. Parkes and J. Stevenson Hinde (Eds.), *The Place of Attachment in Human Behaviour* (pp. 3-30) New York: Basic Books.

Ainsworth, M. D. S., Bleham, M., Waters, E., and Wall, S. (1978). *Patterns of Attachment.* Hillsdale, New Jersey: Erlbaum.

Bailey, J. M., Bobrow, D., Wolfe, M., and Mikach, S. (in press). Sexual Orientation of Adult Sons of Gay Fathers. *Developmental Psychology.*

Bandura, A. (1977). *Social Learning Theory.* Englewood Cliffs, New Jersey: Prentice Hall.

Bandura, A. (1986). *Social Foundations of Thought and Action: A Social Cognitive Theory.* Englewood Cliffs, New Jersey: Prentice Hall.

Barret, R. L. and Robinson, B. E. (1990). *Gay Fathers.* Lexington, Massachusetts: Lexington Books.

Bell, A. P. and Weinberg, M. S. (1978). *Homosexualities: A Study of Diversity Among Men and Women.* New York: Simon & Schuster.

Bell, A. P., Weinberg, M. S., and Hammersmith, S. K. (1981). *Sexual Preference: Its Development in Men and Women.* Bloomington: Indiana University Press.

Bene, E. (1965a). On the Genesis of Female Homosexuality. *British Journal of Psychiatry, 111,* 815-821.

Bene, E. (1965b). On the Genesis of Male Homosexuality: An Attempt at Clarifying the Role of the Parents. *British Journal of Psychiatry, 111,* 803-813.

Bieber, I., Dain, H., Dince, P., Drellick, M., Grand, H., Gondlack, R., Kremer, R., Rifkin, A., Wilber, C., and Bieber, T. (1962). *Homosexuality: A Psychoanalytic Study.* New York: Basic Books.

Bigner, J. J. and Bozett, F. W. (1990). Parenting by Gay Fathers. In F. W. Bozett and M. B. Sussman (Eds.), *Homosexuality and Family Relations* (pp. 155-175). London: Harrington Park Press.

Bigner, J. J. and Jacobsen, R. B. (1989). Parenting Behaviors of Homosexual and Heterosexual Fathers. In F. W. Bozett (Ed.), *Homosexuality and the Family* (pp. 173-186). New York: Harrington Park Press.

Biller, H. B. (1974). *Paternal Deprivation.* Lexington, Massachusetts: D.C. Heath.

Bowlby, J. (1969). *Attachment and Loss. Vol. 1. Attachment.* London: Hogarth Press.

Bowlby, J. (1973). *Attachment and Loss. Vol. 2. Separation: Anxiety and Anger.* London: Hogarth Press.

Bowlby, J. (1980). *Attachment and Loss. Vol. 3. Loss.* London: Hogarth Press.

Bozett, F. W. (1987a). Children of Gay Fathers. In F. W. Bozett (Ed.), *Gay and Lesbian Parents* (pp. 39-57). London: Praeger.

Bozett, F. W. (1987b). Gay Fathers. In F. W. Bozett (Ed.), *Gay and Lesbian Parents* (pp. 3-22). London: Praeger.

Brewaeys, A., Ponjaert-Kristoffersen, I., Van Steirteghem, A., and Devroky, P. (1993). Children From Anonymous Donors: An Inquiry Into Heterosexual and Homosexual Parents' Attitudes. *Journal of Psychosomatic Obstetrics & Gynaecology, 14,* 23-35.

Bromam, S. H., Nichols, P. L., and Kennedy, W. A. (1975). *Pre-school IQ: Parental and Early Development Correlates.* Hillsdale, New Jersey: Lawrence Erlbaum.

Bussey, K., and Bandura, A. (1984). Influence of Gender Constancy and Social Power on Sex-Linked Modeling. *Journal of Personality and Social Psychology, 47,* 1292-1302.

Carter, D. B. (1987). The Roles of Peers in Sex Role Socialization. In D. B. Carter (Ed.), *Current Conceptions of Sex Roles and Stereotyping* (pp. 101-121). New York: Praeger.

Cassidy, J. (1988). Child-Mother Attachment and the Self in Six-Year-Olds. *Child Development, 59,* 121-134.

Cherlin, A., Furstenberg, F., Chase-Lansdale, P., Kiernan, K. E., Robins, P. K., Morrison, D. R., and Tettler, J. O. (1991). Longitudinal Studies of Effects of Divorce on Children in Great Britain and the United States. *Science, 252,* 1386-1389.

Coleman, E. (1990). The Married Lesbian. In F. W. Bozett and M. B. Sussman (Eds.), *Homosexuality and Family Relations* (pp. 119-135). London: Harrington Park Press.

Cox, M. J., Owen, M. T., Henderson, W. K., and Margand, N. A. (1992). Prediction of Infant-Father and Infant-Mother Attachment. *Developmental Psychology,* 474-483.

Daniels, K. and Taylor, K. (1993). Secrecy and Openness in Donor Insemination. *Politics and Life Sciences, 12,* 155-170.

Darling, N. and Steinberg, L. (1993). Parenting Style as Context: An Integrative Model. *Psychological Bulletin, 118,* 487-496.

Dunn, J. and McGuire, S. (1992). Sibling and Peer Relationships in Childhood. *Journal of Child Psychology and Psychiatry, 33,* 67-105.

Editors of the Harvard Law Review (1990). *Sexual Orientation and the Law.* Cambridge, Massachusetts: Harvard University Press.

Evans, R. (1969). Childhood Parental Relationships of Homosexual Men. *Journal of Consulting and Clinical Psychology, 33,* 129-135.

Fagot, B. I. (1978). The Influence of Sex of Child on Parental Reactions to Toddler Children. *Child Development, 49,* 459-465.

Fagot, B. I., and Hagan, R. (1991). Observations of Parent Reactions to Sex-Stereotyped Behaviors. *Child Development, 62,* 617-628.

Falk, P. J. (1989). Lesbian Mothers: Psychosocial Assumptions in Family Law. *American Psychologist, 44,* 941-947.

Ferri, E. (1976). *Growing Up in a One Parent Family.* Slough: National Foundation for Educational Research.

Finkelhor, D. and Russell, D. (1984). Women as Perpetrators: Review of the Evidence. In D. Finkelhor (Ed.), *Child Sexual Abuse: New Theory and Research* (pp. 171-187). New York: Free Press.

Fox, N. A., Kimmerly, N. L., and Schafer, W. D. (1991). Attachment to Mother/Attachment to Father: A Meta-Analysis. *Child Development, 62,* 210-225.

Freud, S. (1953). Three Essays on the Theory of Sexuality. In J. Strachey (Ed. and Trans.), *The Standard Edition of the Complete Psychological Works of Sigmund Freud.* (Vol. 7, pp. 125-263). London: Hogarth Press. (Original work published 1905).

Freud, S. (1955). Beyond the Pleasure Principle. In J. Strachey (Ed.), *The Standard Edition of the Complete Psychological Works of Sigmund Freud.* (Vol. 18, pp. 3-68). London: Hogarth Press. (Original work published 1920).

Freud, S. (1933). *Psychology of Women: New Introductory Lectures on Pscychoanalysis.* London: Hogarth Press.

Golombok, S., Spencer, A., and Rutter, M. (1983). Children in Lesbian and Single-Parent Households: Psychosexual and Psychiatric Appraisal. *Journal of Child Psychology and Psychiatry, 24,* 551-572.

Gottman, J. S. (1990). Children of Gay and Lesbian Parents. In F. W. Bozett and M. B. Sussman (Eds.), *Homosexuality and Family Relations* (pp. 177-196). New York: Harrington Park.

Graham, P., and Rutter, M. (1968). The Reliability and Validity of the Psychiatric Assessment of the Child: II. Interview With the Parent. *British Journal of Psychiatry, 114,* 581-592.

Green, R. (1987). *The "Sissy Boy Syndrome" and the Development of Homosexuality.* New Haven: Yale University Press.

Green, R. (1992). *Sexual Science and the Law.* Cambridge, Massachusetts: Harvard University Press.

Green, R., Mandel, J. B., Hotvedt, M. E., Gray, J., and Smith, L. (1986). Lesbian Mothers and Their Children: A Comparison With Solo Parent Heterosexual Mothers and Their Children. *Archives of Sexual Behaviour, 15,* 167-184.

Grossmann, K. E., Grossmann, K., Spangler, G., Suess, G., and Unzer, L. (1985). Maternal Sensitivity in Northern Germany. In I. Bretherton and E. Waters (Eds.), *Growing Points of Attachment Theory and Research: Monographs of the Society for Research in Child Development, 50,* 233-256.

Harris, M. B. and Turner, P. H. (1986). Gay and Lesbian Parents. *Journal of Homosexuality, 12,* 101-113.

Herzog, E. and Sudia, C. E. (1973). Children in Fatherless Families. In B. M. Campbell and H. N. Ricciuti (Eds.), *Review of Child Development Research* (pp. 161-231). Chicago: University of Chicago Press.

Hess, R. D. and Camara, K. A. (1979). Post-Divorce Relationships as Mediating Factors in the Consequences of Divorce for Children. *Journal of Social Issues, 35*(4), 79-96.

Hetherington, E. M. (1988). Parents, Children and Siblings Six Years After Divorce. In R. Hinde and J. Stevenson-Hinde (Eds.), *Relationships Within Families* (pp. 311-331). Cambridge: Cambridge University Press.

Hetherington, E. M. (1989). Coping With Family Transitions: Winners, Losers, and Survivors. *Child Development, 60,* 1-14.

Hetherington, E. M., Cox, M., and Cox, R. (1982). Effects of Divorce on Parents and Children. In M. E. Lamb (Ed.), *Nontraditional Families: Parenting and Child Development* (pp. 233-288). Hillsdale, New Jersey: Lawrence Erlbaum.

Hetherington, E. M., Cox, M., and Cox, R. (1985). Long-Term Effects of Divorce and Remarriage on the Adjustment of Children. *Journal of the American Academy of Psychology, 24,* 518-530.

Hoeffer, B. (1981). Children's Acquisition of Sex-Role Behavior in Lesbian-Mother Families. *American Journal of Orthopsychiatry, 5,* 536-544.

Huggins, S. L. (1989). A Comparative Study of Self-Esteem of Adolescent Children of Divorced Lesbian Mothers and Divorced Heterosexual Mothers. In F. Bozett (Ed.), *Homosexuality and the Family* (pp. 123-135). New York: Harrington Park.

Isabella, R. A. and Belsky, J. (1991). Interactional Synchrony and the Origins of Infant-Mother Attachment: A Replication Study. *Child Development, 62,* 373-384.

Isabella, R. A., Belsky, J., and von Eye, A. (1989). Origins of Infant-Mother Attachment: An Examination of Interactional Synchrony During the Infant's First Year. *Developmental Psychology, 25,* 12-21.

Izard, C. E., Haynes. M., Chisholm, G., and Baak, K. (1991). Emotional Determinants of Infant-Mother Attachment. *Child Development, 62,* 906-917.

Kaye, H., Beri, S., Clare, J., Eleston, M., Gershwin, B., Gershwin, P., Kogan, L., Torda, C., and Wilbur, C. (1967). Homosexuality in Women. *Archives of General Psychiatry, 17,* 626-634.

Kirkpatrick, M. (1987). Clinical Implications of Lesbian Mother Studies. *Journal of Homosexuality, 13,* 201-211.

Kirkpatrick, M., Smith, C., and Roy, R. (1981). Lesbian Mothers and Their Children: A Comparative Survey. *American Journal of Orthopsychiatry, 51,* 545-551.

Kleber, D. J., Howell, R. J., and Tibbits-Kleber A. L. (1986). The Impact of Parental Homosexuality in Child Custody Cases: A Review of the Literature. *Bulletin of the American Academy of Psychiatry and Law, 14,* 81-87.

Kohlberg, L. (1966). A Cognitive-Developmental Analysis of Children's Sex-Role Concepts and Attitudes. In E. E. Maccoby (Ed.), *The Development of Sex Differences* (pp. 82-173). Stanford: Stanford University Press.

Kupersmidt, J. B., Coie, J. D., and Dodge, K. A. (1990). The Role of Poor Peer

Relationships in the Development of Disorder. In S. R. Asher and J. D. Coie (Eds.), *Peer Rejection in Childhood* (pp. 276-305). Cambridge: Cambridge University Press.

Lamb, M. E. (1986). *The Father's Role: Applied Perspectives.* New York: Wiley.

Langois, J. H. and Downs, A. C. (1980). Mothers, Fathers and Peers as Socialization Agents of Sex-Typed Play Behaviors in Young Children. *Child Development, 51,* 1237-1247.

Liben, L. S. and Signorella, M. L. (1980). Gender-Related Schemata and Constructive Memory in Children. *Child Development, 51,* 111-118.

Lovejoy, N. C. (1990). AIDS: Impact on the Gay Man's Homosexual and Heterosexual Families. In F. W. Bozett and M. B. Sussman (Eds.), *Homosexuality and Family Relations* (pp. 285-316). London: Harrington Park Press.

Lytton, H. and Romney, D. M. (1991). Parents' Differential Socialization of Boys and Girls: A Meta-Analysis. *Psychological Bulletin, 109,* 267-296.

Maccoby, E. E. (1988). Gender as a Social Category. *Developmental Psychology, 45,* 513-520.

Maccoby, E. E. (1992). The Role of Parents in the Socialization of Children. *Developmental Psychology, 28,* 1006-1017.

Maccoby, E. E. and Jacklin, C. N. (1974). *The Psychology of Sex Differences.* Stanford: Stanford University Press.

Main, M., Kaplan, N., and Cassidy, J. (1985). Security in Infancy, Childhood and Adulthood: A Move to the Level of Representation. In I. Bretherton and E. Waters (Eds.), *Growing Points in Attachment Theory and Research, Monographs of the Society for Research in Child Development, 50*(1-2, Serial No. 209), 66-104.

Martin, A. (1993). *The Lesbian and Gay Parenting Handbook.* New York: HarperCollins.

Martin, C. L. (1989, April). *Beyond Knowledge-Based Conceptions of Schematic Processing.* Paper presented at the Society for Research in Child Development, Kansas City, Missouri.

Martin C. L. (1991). The Role of Cognition in Understanding Gender Effects. In H. Reese (Ed.), *Advances in Child Development and Behavior, 23,* 113-164. New York: Academic Press.

Martin, C. L. and Halverson, C. (1981). A Schematic Processing Model of Sex Typing and Stereotyping in Children. *Child Development, 52,* 1119-1134.

Martin, C. L. and Halverson, C. (1983). Gender Constancy: A Methodological and Theoretical Analysis. *Sex Roles, 9,* 775-790.

Martin, C. L. and Little, J. K. (1990). The Relation of Gender Understanding to Children's Sex-Typed Preferences and Gender Stereotypes. *Child Development, 61,* 1427-1439.

Martin, C. L., Wood, C. H., and Little, J. K. (1990). The Development of Gender Stereotype Components. *Child Development, 61,* 1891-1904.

Matteson, D. R. (1987). The Heterosexually Married Gay and Lesbian Parent. In F. W. Bozett (Ed.), *Gay and Lesbian Parents* (pp. 138-168). London: Praeger.

McCandlish, B. (1987). Against All Odds: Lesbian Mother Family Dynamics. In F. W. Bozett (Ed.), *Gay and Lesbian Parents* (pp. 23-36). New York: Praeger.

Miller, B. (1979). Gay Fathers and Their Children. *Family Coordinator, 28,* 544-552.

Miller, J. A., Jacobsen, R. B., and Bigner, J. J. (1981). The Child's Home Environment for Lesbian vs. Heterosexual Mothers: A Neglected Area of Research. *Journal of Homosexuality, 7,* 49-56.

Mischel, W. (1966). A Social Learning View of Sex Differences in Behavior. In E. E. Maccoby (Ed.), *The Development of Sex Differences* (pp. 56-81). Stanford: Stanford University Press.

Mischel, W. (1970). Sex-Typing and Socialization. In P. Mussen (Ed.), *Carmichael's Manual of Child Psychology* (Vol. 2, pp. 3-72). New York: Wiley.

Moss, H. A. (1967). Sex, Age, and State as Determinants of Mother-Infant Interaction. *Merrill-Palmer Quarterly, 13,* 19-36.

Mucklow, B. M. and Phelan, G. K. (1979). Lesbian and Traditional Mothers' Responses to Child Behavior and Self-Concept. *Psychological Reports, 44,* 880-882.

Newcombe, M. (1985). The Role of Perceived Relative Parent Personality in the Development of Heterosexuals, Homosexuals and Transvestites. *Archives of Sexual Behavior, 14,* 147-164.

Pagelow, M. D. (1980). Heterosexual and Lesbian Single Mothers: A Comparison of Problems, Coping and Solutions. *Journal of Homosexuality, 5,* 198-204.

Parke, R. D. and Sawin, D. B. (1980). The Family in Early Infancy: Social Interactional and Attitudinal Analyses. In F. Pedersen (Ed.), *The Father-Infant Relationship: Observational Studies in a Family Context* (pp. 47-70). New York: Praeger.

Patterson, C. J. (1992). Children of Lesbian and Gay Parents. *Child Development, 63,* 1025-1042.

Patterson, C. J. (1994). Children of the Lesbian Baby Boom: Behavioural Adjustment, Self Concepts, and Sex Role Identity. In B. Greene and G. M. Herek (Eds.), *Lesbian and Gay Psychology: Theory, Research and Clinical Applications* (pp. 156-175). Newbury Park, California: Sage.

Pedersen, D., Moran, G., Sitko, C., Campbell, K. Ghesquire, K., and Acton, H. (1990). Maternal Sensitivity and the Security of Infant-Mother Attachment: a Q-Sort Study. *Child Development, 61,* 1974-1983.

Perry, D. J. and Bussey, K. (1979). The Social Learning Theory of Sex Difference: Imitation Is Alive and Well. *Journal of Personality and Social Psychology, 37,* 1699-1712.

Power, T. G. and Parke, R. D. (1982). Play as a Context for Early Learning: Lab and Home Analyses. In E. Sigel and L. M. Laoss (Eds.), *The Family as a Learning Environment.* New York: Plenum.

Puryear, D. (1983). *A Comparison Between the Children of Lesbian Mothers and the Children of Heterosexual Mothers.* Unpublished doctoral dissertation, California School of Professional Psychology, Berkeley, California.

Radin, N. (1982). Primary Caregiving and Role-Sharing Fathers. In M. E. Lamb (Ed.), *Nontraditional Families: Parenting and Child Development* (pp. 173-204). Hillsdale, New Jersey: Lawrence Erlbaum.

Rheingold, H. L. and Cook, K. V. (1975). The Content of Boys' and Girls' Rooms as an Index of Parents' Behaviour. *Child Development, 46,* 459-463.

Rickets, W. and Achtenberg, R. (1987). The Adoptive and Foster Gay and Lesbian Parent. In F. W. Bozett (Ed.), *Gay and Lesbian Parenting.* New York: Praeger.

Rivera, R. R. (1991). Sexual Orientation and the Law. In J. C. Gonsiorek and L. D. Weinrich (Eds.), *Homosexuality: Research Implications for Public Policy* (pp. 81-100). Newbury Park, California: Sage.

Roll, J. (1992). *Lone Parent Families in the European Community.* London: European Family and Social Policy Unit.

Ross, M. W. (1990). Married Homosexual Men: Prevalence and Background. In F. W. Bozett and M. B. Sussman (Eds.), *Homosexuality and Family Relations* (pp. 35-57). London: Harrington Park Press.

Rubin, J. Z., Provenzano, F. J., and Luria, Z. (1974). The Eye of the Beholder: Parents' Views on Sex of Newborns. *American Journal of Orthopsychiatry, 44,* 512-519.

Rutter, M. (1971). Parent-Child Separation: Psychological Effects on Children. *Journal of Child Psychology and Psychiatry, 12,* 233-260.

Rutter, M., Tizard, J., and Whitmore, K. (1970). *Education, Health and Behaviour.* London: Longmans.

Saffron, L. (1994). *Challenging Conceptions.* London: Cassell.

Sagi, A. (1982). Antecedents and Consequences of Various Degrees of Paternal Involvement in Child Rearing: The Israeli Project. In M. E. Lamb (Ed.), *Nontraditional Families: Parenting and Child Development* (pp. 205-232). Hillsdale, New Jersey: Lawrence Erlbaum.

Shakin, M., Shakin, D., and Sternglanz, S. H. (1985). Infant Clothing: Sex Labelling for Strangers. *Sex Roles, 12,* 955-963.

Siegelman, M. (1974). Parental Background of Male Homosexuals and Heterosexuals. *Archives of Sexual Behaviour, 6,* 89-96.

Signorella, M. L., Bigler, R. S., and Liben, L. S. (1993). Developmental Differences in Children's Gender Schemata About Others: A Meta-Analytic Review. *Developmental Review, 13,* 106-126.

Signorella, M. L. and Liben, L. S. (1984). Recall and Reconstruction of Gender-Related Pictures: Effects of Attitude, Task Difficulty and Age. *Child Development, 55,* 393-405.

Slaby, R. G. and Frey, K. S. (1975). Development of Gender Constancy and Selective Attention to Same-Sex Models. *Child Development, 46,* 849-856.

Smith, P. B. and Pedersen, D. (1988). Maternal Sensitivity and Patterns of Infant-Mother Attachment. *Child Development, 59,* 1097-1101.

Snow, M. E., Jacklin, C. N. and Maccoby, E. E. (1983). Sex-of-Child Differences in Father-Child Interaction at One Year of Age. *Child Development, 49, 227-232.*

Socarides, C. W. (1978). *Homosexuality.* London: Longmans. New York: Jason Aronson.

Stagnor, C. and Ruble, D. N. (1987). Development of Gender Role Knowledge and Gender Constancy. In L. S. Liben and M. L. Signorella (Eds.), *Children's Gender Schemata: New Directions for Child Development, No. 38*(pp. 5-22). San Francisco: Jossey Bass.

Steckel, A. (1987). Psychological Development of Children of Lesbian Mothers. In F. W. Bozett (Ed.), *Gay and Lesbian Parents* (pp. 75-85). New York: Praeger.

Stern, M. and Karraker, K. H. (1989). Sex Stereotyping of Infants: A Review of Gender Labeling Studies. *Sex Roles, 20,* 501-522.

Stevenson, M. R. and Black, K. N. (1988). Paternal Absence and Sex Role Development: A Meta-Analysis. *Child Development, 59,* 793-814.

Svanum, S., Bringle, R. G., and McLaughlin, J. E. (1982). Father Absence and Cognitive Performance in a Large Sample of Six- to Eleven-Year-Old Children. *Child Development, 53,* 136-143.

Tasker, F. and Golombok, S. (1991). Children Raised by Lesbian Mothers: The Empirical Evidence. *Family Law, 21,* 184-187.

Tasker, F. and Golombok, S. (in press-a). Adults Raised as Children in Lesbian Families. *American Journal of Orthopsychiatry.*

Tasker, F. and Golombok, S. (in press-b). *Growing Up in a Lesbian Family.* New York: Guilford Press.

Thompson, R. A., Lamb, M. E., and Estes, D. (1982). Stability of Infant-Mother Attachment and Its Relationship to Changing Life Circumstances in an Unselected Middle-Class Sample. *Child Development, 53,* 144-148.

Turner, P. H., Scadden, L., and Harris, M. B. (1990). Parenting in Gay and Lesbian Families. *Journal of Gay and Lesbian Psychotherapy, 1,* 55-66.

Vaughn, B., Egeland, B., Sroufe, L. A., and Waters, E. (1979). Individual Differences in Infant-Mother Attachment at 12 and 18 Months: Stability and Change in Families Under Stress. *Child Development, 50,* 971-975.

Vuchinich, S., Hetherington, E. M., Vuchinich, R., and Clingempeel, W. G. (1991). Parent-Child Interaction and Gender Differences in Early Adolescents' Adaptation to Stepfamilies. *Developmental Psychology, 27,* 618-626.

Wallerstein, J. S. and Kelly, J. B. (1980). *Surviving the Breakup: How Children and Parents Cope With Divorce.* New York: Basic Books.

Wyers, N. (1987). Homosexuality in the Family: Lesbian and Gay Spouses. *Social Work, 32,* 143-148.

Zuger, B. (1984). Early Effeminate Behavior in Boys: Outcome and Significance for Homosexuality. *Journal of Nervous and Mental Disease, 172,* 90-97.

The Men in My Life
by Lisa Orta

Introduction

When (at last) I was seriously pregnant and saw our unborn child swimming gleefully inside me on the ultrasound screen, I was most anxious to see what the technician called "the baby's pelvic area." As it came into full view, I nearly whooped with joy — there were those three visible points that gave a good indication the baby was a boy. A boy! My dream, my wish, my most powerful desire had come true. The news helped alleviate my deepest fear, that in becoming a mother, I would re-create the complex and unsatisfying relationship I have with my mother, a relationship much like the one my mother had with her mother and one that an astrologer warned me years ago it was my task to resolve. In being "the other," in being a boy and in not being a girl, my son set me free. A lesbian with no brothers, I welcomed my son's and my differences with an open heart. And as I created myself as a mother in our early years together, it was my son's "otherness" that showed me the way to a truly unconditional love, a love that began to heal some of the deep, deep wounds of my childhood. What I had not counted on was that he would also bring me back to family connections in ways that are most precious to me. In these pieces, written when Gary was three years old, I write about ways in which, through my son, I have been able to hold on to the men who are beloved to me. In pieces yet to be written, I will write about the ways loving my son prepared me for loving my daughter with no fear, no doubt, no hesitation. I will write about how this mother love finally showed me how to love myself as a woman, as a mother, and, at long last, as a daughter.

The Real Meaning of Family

When Gary was born, sacks of cards and packages were delivered to our house. We felt like the whole world — *our* whole world — was vibrating with joy. One of the most important cards we received was from Karen's father. It wasn't the Hallmark message that was so remarkable, it was the signature. I remember the sting of tears in my tired eyes as I read the words GRANDDAD BART in his scrawly handwriting. I let go of the fears I harbored about how Karen's family was going to deal with our new child. A man of principle and honesty, Bart was sending us a calculated, deliberate signal. I heard it loud and clear — I love you, I am proud to have another grandchild, everything's okay on this end.

This is a lesbian mother's dream, that her father-in-law will embrace not only her but also her children. With Bart there was never a question that he embraced all of us. I remember a letter he wrote to Karen in anticipation of our visit to their home early in our relationship. Basically he said, "Be happy, and then I will be happy too." So we jumped in the car (with the dogs) and drove to Arizona. We were welcomed with open arms and put up in the same bedroom. All that was left was for me to compliment him on his cooking, the praising of which took absolutely no effort, I promise.

Karen's father died suddenly one summer, and there was no way to express the grief. I was sad for Karen, for Bart's loving family, and for me. This was a big loss. I was also sad for Gary, his grandson. Bart had a sense of humor and irreverence that I wanted Gary to know but that Gary was still too young to appreciate. Gary and his granddad will never live out the conspiracy that grandparents and their grandchildren get to create — the undercover chocolate bars, the silly in-jokes, the furtive winks across the dinner table. With our kinds of families, these traditional gestures take on more importance. They scream of acceptance and validation, of love and connection.

We had planned to invite Bart and Phyllis, Karen's stepmother, to meet us at spring training camp in Phoenix the next summer. We anticipated a really good time — watching baseball and getting to know each other better. I fantasized about Gary and Bart wandering off to the coffee shop together, hand in hand, recounting some awesome play or missed opportunity. We still may go — and Phyllis may join us. And next to us on the bleachers will be this ghost, this great guy who with one small gesture — a wink, a nod, a chuckle — could spell out the real meaning of family.

Naming Our Children

Karen was away on business last night, so Gary eagerly crawled into her spot in our bed. I tucked him in with his doll, his stuffed dog, his "footie-foot-foot" and his "nippie-nip-nip" and leaned over

189

for a nice, big hug. He smiled and said, "Mommy, you love me so much, you love me more than anything else in the whole world." Later, as I was drifting off to sleep next to him, he reached out and put his little hand in mine and gave it a squeeze.

Ten years ago, in 1984, my best friend, Gary Lee Watson, died of AIDS complications. His was one of the first AIDS cases in San Francisco. His nine-month illness precipitated incidents of homophobia and discrimination that will never leave me. I also live with memories of a friendship that was so deep and so real that there is a sign planted on the kindest, softest spot of my soul that reads, GARY WAS HERE.

Gary wanted to adopt a child back in the '70s. A social worker took offense to the essay he had to write on his religious views. He wrote about his anger at Catholicism (it was a homophobic priest that ran Gary out of his hometown when he revealed his homosexuality), and the social worker buried his case. Another social worker found Gary's folder one day, reactivated his file, and called to tell him she had found a child for him. But her call came too late. Gary was already sick.

I remember preparing my talk for his memorial service, overcome with grief for the person who had taught me the intimacy of friendship and shown me the true value of love and trust. I swore to his memory that I would name my child for him. I knew I was right to make this promise, but I was a little scared of how it would play out. What would it do to my child to carry the weight of someone else's name?

Years later, when the doctors lifted a child from my womb, the first thing I heard was Karen saying, "Hi, Gary." And there he was — the same but different. It hasn't been difficult to differentiate between the two Garys in the least; instead it's completed the circle. I witnessed the exit of one wonderful guy and facilitated the entrance of another. Gary Watson used to call me every morning. I would pick up the phone, and in his best sing-song–sarcastic voice, he would say, "Wake up, little Susie." This morning, when I opened my eyes, there was a smiling, curly-headed boy with ping-pong–ball cheeks looking over at me. "Let's wake up," he said, and so we began our day.

Wings
by Janell Moon

It wasn't just that I left his dad
or that I was lesbian
although my son couldn't stand the women
in and out
watching my focus on one after another
getting hysterical.

I should have believed in us
believed we could be caught
but I had tumbled into a darkroom
too deep, never seen pictures for this life
no scenes of how to do it, scenes of hope.
I let him go to his fathers, a nice man
with no doubts.

My lover packed us up to move and cut her hand.
It throbbed for several days.
That was the first of it. That night my car
was totaled. We were robbed the morning
we went out for the paper. I fell
hurt my wrist when I was fixing the windows.
My lover lost her wallet and I lost
my sense of humor. When my son came to visit
we were all bandaged up
and he didn't want to stay.

My lover sank into quiet.
I couldn't keep on talking, couldn't
find a smile. Finally she moved out.

My son and I would have these strange
weekends where neither of us had any fun.
He wanted to play basketball, but we had no yard,
tried to sleep in but the flat was too noisy.
He'd beg to watch TV but I'd drag him out
to go exploring. He'd shuffle along
behind me, whining.
I had no money to buy us anything.

We'd return home and I'd stir up some homemade soup
but he was used to Campbell's and salt.
We'd get flat tires, parking tickets.

I don't know how we got through it; how
this time of our life ended.
I stopped trying so hard,
found a job, took a rest
from women. He learned
to move between his father and me,
such different worlds,
played baseball, studied hard,
worked at the grocery store.

Now my son's in Thailand helping
families stay together, earn enough money
to keep their daughters at home,
away from Bangkok, away from AIDS.
He calls me each Tuesday, says he's learning
the language pretty well, has to change
to tones, learn a new alphabet.
It's hard but he can do it.
Says I'm the one who taught him,
the one who knows him,
been through it with him.
He's glad he stuck to me
even in the falling times. Now he's better,
time of wings.

Lesbians, Sons and the Courts
by Kate Kendell

Polls show that most Americans do not believe that lesbians or gay men should be fired from their jobs but that an equal number also don't think we should be parents. The issue of family is one on which the lesbian and gay community is vulnerable. For a long time we ourselves didn't think we should be parents. We had our own concerns about those issues because that is what we heard. We could do anything we wanted as long as we didn't become involved with kids. I think the issue of our families is the last, most difficult hurdle to overcome. It's all the radical right has left to hang on to, and they're going for it, big time. We are now seeing the right wing supporting those who oppose our families in the courts.

The issue is one of becoming more and more visible. Lesbian and gay parents are asserting their right to custody regardless of their sexual orientation, and because there is an increase in the number of cases, there is an increase in our losses from years previous. In many areas of the law, we're doing well. In seventeen states, courts have granted second-parent adoptions. More lesbians and gay men are able to adopt than was previously the case. More lesbian couples are creating children in the context of their own relationship, as are gay-male couples through surrogacy and adoption. But when we encounter a situation in which a previously heterosexual marriage dissolves and the woman or the man comes out as lesbian or gay and is challenged for custody, we are probably at this point losing more than we're winning. Clearly there are many cases that are decided at the trial-court level that we never hear about that are successful. On balance we're moving forward, but we still lose cases based on sexual orientation and custody. Maybe in five to ten years we'll be there, but we're not there yet.

There are generally three concerns courts have in custody cases involving lesbians raising children: 1) that the child will face ostracism and harassment from other children; 2) that they will grow up to be lesbian or gay, and 3) that they will grow up with psychological problems and gender-identity confusion. In effect, it's as if they have three levels to their prejudice: 1) they think we're perverts and we're dangerous; 2) they think we're not perverts but we need a man; and 3) the enlightened position — the only issue is whether we're good parents.

While I can't prove that lesbians raising sons are more at risk for discrimination than lesbians raising daughters, the reasons for the courts' scrutiny are different regarding male children. My gut reaction is that if a child is male and the judge buys into the stereotype that a gay or lesbian parent creates a gay or lesbian child, they'll be much more protective of a male child being negatively influenced than a female child. The concern about proper gender orientation and behavior that is consistent with one's gender is heightened when boy children are involved. Whether the child will have gender-identity issues is more often articulated when there is a boy involved because the court is concerned that the lesbian parent is going to model "inappropriate" affectional relationships and "inappropriate" sexual relationships, causing the child to be confused about his own gender identity. This is because there is more rigidity regarding gender identity for our male children: What mainstream society views as appropriate behavior for a male is much more severely defined than for females.

194

If you dig deep enough to look at what the facts are in the particular cases, you can see that this increased scrutiny is going on for families with boys. On the other hand, if the court believes that the parent's sexual orientation will influence the child's sexual orientation, they will try to take the child away regardless of the gender of the kids. If the parent is lesbian or gay, depending on where they live and the homophobia of the judge, they're just as likely to lose custody of a boy or a girl child. It's just that the reasons are somewhat different.

Most lesbian and gay parents who are good parents are generally more progressive and generally less concerned with rigid sex-type behavior in their children than are heterosexual parents. Our children grow up with very healthy gender-identity orientations, and they generally grow up to be heterosexual — but they are much more tolerant of differences, and they have a much higher level of self-esteem around gender issues and sexual orientation issues because there's a wider range within which gay parents accept behavior. Lesbian parents are more likely to let the kids be kids and grow up in a way that's comfortable, rather than imposing on them mainstream society's version of how boys and girls should act.

One unfortunate thing I see happening is that lesbian or gay parents are often concerned about a child's being lesbian or gay. They're overly concerned about gayness being the result of their child rearing, and they usually overcompensate for this. They have their own homophobia around being parents. There's almost a pressure to think, *I'm as good as you because I can raise a heterosexual too.* We've bought into society's stamp that not only do we raise lesbian or gay kids but that there's something wrong with that. We've bought into two things: 1) that it happens, which is not true and 2) that even if it did, it would be an undesirable result. Either one of those impressions would be unfortunate, but we, and obviously some judges, adopt this bias.

Clearly there is a special responsibility on lesbians raising sons because men raised wrong do a whole lot of damage. Clearly men are going to have predominant power and decision-making control in our society for the foreseeable future. Lesbians who are good parents raising sons will ultimately have a tremendous impact on how the world goes.

195

An Unsent Letter
by Martha Miller

Dear Son,

When you were a little boy and things were different with us, you used to climb onto my lap every time I sat down. You were slender, and your narrow butt fit in the rocking chair with me comfortably. You would kick at your brother if he came near, as if to say, "This is my mom and my time — stay away." I remember you as a very blond, very angry child who tested the limits of everything and whom no one could handle but me. You wouldn't mind your father. You fought constantly with your brother, and you tricked the baby-sitters into opening shaken-up bottles of soda. I went back to work when you were a baby. I remember waking you early in the morning, packing a diaper bag, and sending you and your brother, sleepy and full of fruit-flavored cereal and peanut butter, to a day-care center. When I picked you up at night, we were all tired and angry. Day after day droned on that way. I thought I would never get you to tie your shoes, never get you to drink from a cup. Evenings, our living room was always scattered with toys, the washer was always running.

Sometimes I wonder what you remember of me from that time. I know what you've told your counselors — that you don't remember much at all. That I was never home. But I have pictures of us together. I can prove that our lives touched. And I know that every time I sat down, you climbed onto my lap. I would sit there, smoke cigarettes, drink tequila, and press my nose in your dry, sun-bleached hair. You drew up your bony knees and folded into my arms. Until you were almost four years old, you sucked your thumb. Everyone told me to break you of that sooner, but it was a comfort to you, and I had so little comfort to give.

The day you asked if you could play T-ball, there were tears in your eyes. You could have asked for the world with that look, and I would have tried to give it to you. I signed you up and saw to it that you got to your games. I remember the one I went to. I was impressed. You were good. I wish I would have come more.

I know I don't do as good as some parents. I also know I don't do as bad as others. I don't do as bad as the ones I had. I was the alcoholic daughter of an alcoholic father who did not sober up until you were half grown. Long past your T-ball days, somewhere in the middle of Cub Scouts, I came home from the hospital with a clear head and found an angry little boy with a messy room who was always in trouble at school. You wouldn't let anyone close. I vowed to do better by all of you, but there were a lot of things about myself I didn't know. Less than two years later, your father moved out of our home and a woman moved in. From then until the morning you ran away, I remember only a very rocky road for us.

I really wanted for us to be a family. I believed that was possible. I didn't understand anything about what was about to happen to us. I hung on and did the best I could. I fought your father, who tried to take you away from me. I fought with Suzie, who wanted me to let you go. And I fought with the rest of the world, who thought it was wrong for lesbians to raise children. Then I woke up one morning, and your bedroom curtains were billowing inward. And your bed was empty.

When I first took Suzie as my lover, there was a big adjustment. I don't think about it much these days, but it was painful in the beginning. We couldn't hold hands walking down the street. She couldn't put her arm around my shoulders in the theater. When the women at work talked about their husbands and boyfriends, I sat quietly. Those sorts of sociological dysfunctions do something to a relationship. Lack of support and acknowledgment erodes the bonds. If validation is a kind of cement, it's no wonder lesbian relationships, on the average, are so short.

Suzie didn't like men. Here I was with two sons who were ready to enter adolescence, and I let a woman who felt that way into our lives and our home. I didn't see it then. That's my only excuse. She later turned out to be abusive to all of us, you and me and your brother. I watched you knock yourself out trying to make friends with her. Then I listened to her scream at me after you'd gone to bed, that I spoiled you, that I loved you more than her, that she hated you — that she would like to kill you. I tried to quiet her. You always claimed not to hear her tirades. You got so good at it, you managed not to hear my screams the night she tried to strangle me, during the last fight. Your room was ten feet away.

I am angry — at her and at me. Those were very hard years for us, dealing with her hostility at home and the hostility of the outside world. Later you told me, "Mom, I was just trying to survive with Suzie."

It is said that in ancient times gays were the chosen people. It was believed that we were closer to the gods because we lived in both worlds, male and female. But ancient times don't help me now.

Nor do they help you.

I told your brother that I was gay when he was twelve. I thought he was old enough to know. But you were younger. I figured I had a couple of years. Then I was cleaning your room and found a poem:

When I was a kid
at ten
My dad got divorced
he told me
That my mom was gay
And that was sad.
And now he has me pass
his joints all around
To Steve, and Del, and Jennifer...

198   I talked to you that night. I explained that all *gay* meant was that I loved Suzie the way I used to love your dad.

It was a lie. To you — and to me.

I really thought that that was all it meant.

As it turned out, it also meant that the neighbors would throw trash in our yard, people would stare at us when we took walks in the evenings during the summer, the neighbor's children would call us homos, your father would hire a lawyer and try to take you both away from me, your brother would go live with him, and — worst of all — your friends would tease you.

I think it's normal for kids at some point to be ashamed of their parents, but I handed it to you gift-wrapped.

I remember pulling out of the driveway one afternoon. Our friend Stuart had been over. He had a new motor scooter and had given us all rides. You asked me, "Is Stuart gay?"

"Yes," I said. "Beau is his lover."

You said softly, "Am I gay?"

"Probably not," I replied, shrugging. "Most people aren't."

I smiled to myself, having handled it so well.

I should have pulled the car over. I should have embraced you. I should have offered you more comfort. What a question! How quickly I had forgotten the pain of asking myself that question.

"Am I gay?" How can I be when I just feel like me. When I don't feel like a queer, like a joke. "Am I gay?"

Maybe at that point you thought it was like the color of your eyes. Inherited. I could have told you that both my parents were straight and that I didn't inherit that. I could have told you that being gay doesn't feel very strange. It's like having a different preference. It's liking chocolate ice cream when everybody else likes strawberry. It shouldn't make you a criminal, though in many states it does. It shouldn't make you lose your job or lose your children.

When you were fourteen and ran away the first time, I was scared and angry. It was later that I saw the pure genius in your act, and I wished I could have gone with you. How many times had I felt like throwing a duffel bag in the trunk of the car and driving as far as the gas would take me?

Suzie had been gone for several months, and I had met a new woman. I know you thought the new woman meant more abuse, even when I promised you I'd never let that happen again. I know you thought that because with every new woman that followed, you came a little more unglued. Maybe it wasn't just the abuse from Suzie that was too much — after all, she was gone. Maybe it was the added abuse from everyone around you that made it all unbearable. For many years all you said about my lifestyle was, "It's your business." The healthiest thing I ever saw you do was sit in a room on the psych ward (it took a fucking psych ward!) with your counselor and a nurse and tell me, finally, that you had some problems with my lesbianism. It was a hard thing for me to hear, but I knew you needed to say it and deal with it. I wish I could have said, "If you have a problem with it, I will try to change it." But that's impossible. It's not a choice. It's who I am.

In the long, long hours after I discovered you'd run away, I wondered whether you were dead or alive and whether I'd ever see you again. Then you called me and told me what you had done and that you were coming home.

I said, "I'm coming to get you."

I took off work and left that night. For the whole long trip, I was afraid. Were you all right? Obviously you weren't all right if you needed to do this. When I pulled into that little hick town in Arkansas and saw first the car, then you, I thanked the God I had been praying to that whole trip.

199

Driving home through Silver Dollar City and past Six Flags, I remembered all the times I told you we would take a trip together and all the times I'd gone without you because Suzie had insisted. The times I told you the car wouldn't make it or we couldn't afford it.

You got your trip. The car made it.

I brought you home to a waiting policeman and handcuffs. I called the police because I saw the courts as a way to get the help for you that my insurance company had already refused to pay for. You were fourteen years old and out of control. You had stolen my car. I was afraid. I didn't know what else to do.

The day, sometime later, you told me you had a problem with my lifestyle, I was scared. It occurred to me that I could lose you, that you would go live with your father like your brother had.

I reluctantly offered.

You shook your head. "I don't even know him."

I waited, watching you.

"Mom, it embarrasses me," you said at last. "I've lost friends. I don't want to bring them home."

I nodded. I could believe it. The sun shone through the hospital window. Particles of dust swirled in the air. I remembered an old woman talking. "Gay life, now there's a funny word for it," she had said. "It isn't very gay at all. Relationships are short. Society and your family rejects you..."

One weekend, when you were about sixteen, you went with me to help my friends Cara and Kathy and their son Josh, who is just younger than you, to move. Several gay friends were helping. The man in the apartment next door was drunk. Josh came and told me that the man was shouting insults about gay men and lesbians.

I looked at him and sighed. I didn't know what to do.

One of the gay men said, "I don't mind it for myself, but this is bad in front of the kids."

A painful knot tightened in my throat. How could he not mind? Are we so used to quietly sitting by that we think we don't mind? Have we listened to so many jokes in silence that we've stopped feeling? Are we better at cowering under the abuse than taking what is rightfully ours? Or is it that we just don't know how? I've seen us in numbers, in parades, at music festivals — God, if we would just stand together, just say, "Enough!"

"I'm calling the police," Kathy said.

200

I was scared then. I didn't want to deal with sneering policemen. But what else could we do? I thought the worst thing you could see us do was nothing. I wondered what you felt, tried to talk to you on the way home. You wouldn't discuss it.

It was several days later when Cara told me that you'd stood on the balcony and screamed, "Ignorant redneck!" And when the man tried to answer, you shouted, "Enough! I've heard enough!"

Sometimes I try to put it all together. Where we've been. Where we're going. This isn't what I thought raising a child would be like. I knew it took a long time and a lot of energy. I just didn't know that it took so long and so much energy. I didn't count on things changing with me as much as with you. I didn't know what it would be like to need to be a parent to you on days when I thought my own life was falling apart. You were in a lot of pain that I couldn't see during the divorce, during the years with Suzie, who was openly malicious toward you. You tried to tell me in your own way, but I had my own pain and couldn't hear.

When you and your brother were born, the one thing I knew about parenting was that I didn't want to make the same mistakes my parents made. And I haven't. I went out and found some new mistakes of my own.

201

I look at you now, a tall, blond, handsome young man whose smile does not come easily. Oh, I can still see your anger. And I know you've asked for many things I didn't give you. Knowing that, I send you this request. Down this long, long path of pain, I know that you have loved me. And I want for us to find a way to live together in quiet dignity, putting my many and your few mistakes in the past. I want this letter to be one last new beginning. A start of something right and strong between us.

Can we please both say, "Enough — we have hurt enough"?

I love you,
Mom

Choices
by Tryna Hope

Can you believe it? I don't remember the exact date I left my son, Jonah. So much was going on. I had come out as a lesbian; I had moved into my own apartment with my two children; my father-in-law had died of lung cancer; I wasn't speaking to my parents; my youngest brother had died unexpectedly at the age of twenty-two; and I was no longer observing the daily rituals of the Orthodox Jewish community I had been raised in. It was 1973.

Change finally occurred after years of stagnation, unhappiness, and loss of spirit inside my body. It's hard to remember what came first, what caused what. Were there casualties? Yes. The woman I was before 1973 was dead. So was the marriage I was in for nine years and the heterosexual family I helped create. Dead too was the expectation that families always stay together — and that mothers never leave their kids.

I left Jonah in winter. I know this because he told me one day on the telephone, shortly after I moved away. He said when he grew up he planned to live with his dad. It would have been easier, he thought, if the decision had been mine. Or his father's. Somehow Jonah and I both believed we had a choice.

Jonah had been unhappy ever since I came out as a lesbian. Gone was the structure and security of keeping kosher, of synagogue, of dad home every night. No longer was my exclusive focus on him and his older sister, Miriam. I was running around, eating all kinds of new food, meeting new women. Male culture, men, and male dominance were no longer underlying themes in our home. It was hard on both kids, but it was especially hard on Jonah. He had gotten more out of the heterosexual structure than Miriam. Although she too had trouble with the changes, she loved the adventure and spontaneity. She would have done anything to stay with me. And she did. Not so Jonah.

One night he exploded. He was only six years old and a most pleasant child, which made this night all the more eerie and unusual. It made his behavior something to reckon with. I was on his back about something. Maybe I wanted him to pick up his room or wash up before bed. He was tired. I took his hand to go do the task I'd asked him when he abruptly pulled away from me.

"Leave me alone!" he boomed in a voice I did not recognize.

"No," I said, "you have to do what I asked you."

"No, I don't," he said. "I don't have to do what you tell me."

His voice was deep, like a man's. His body seemed rigid. He looked older than six.

"If you're going to live here, you've got to follow the rules."

"I don't want to live here. I don't have to live here. I want to go live with Dad."

A little afraid, I reached out to touch him. He had never been like this. I thought he was possessed. I thought someone else was speaking through him. I was frightened of what was happening.

"You live with me now," I said.

"No! I don't want to live here. I want to go live with Dad, and if you don't let me, I'll tell the judge and he'll make you let me. I hate it here. I'm going to leave."

"Jonah, let's talk about it in the morning. Please. When we're both not so tired."

"Okay. But I'm not going to change my mind."

"Okay, okay," I said.

I lifted him up and took him to his room. I laid him on his bed, and I sat down next to him. When he fell asleep I went to my room. I did not sleep that night. When Jonah woke up in the morning, he had his sweet young voice back. But he was saying the same things. Within a week he went to live with his father.

By my current social-worker standards, I didn't handle it well. No closure, not much talking. And soon I left the state, the region, my family, and my son for good. Although Jonah and I have spoken and exchanged some letters over the twenty years, we have not seen each other since 1973 — except in my dreams, where he is still six years old.

Writing this, I began to wonder about something that the pain has kept me from thinking about until today. Can you imagine? Twenty years later. This is what I wonder: *How did Jonah know about judges and courts? How did he know? My husband must have been priming him, pushing him, putting words into his mouth, encouraging him to leave. Why didn't I know that then?*

People, family, and friends cajoled, warned, and threatened me when I decided to leave my husband, my community, observant Judaism. Oh, the terrible things they said would happen to me. Don't forget, I had been born during the Holocaust. It was frightening what happened to Jews, what the world didn't protect us from. If I left the safety and protection of my community, I would die, be killed, be raped. Even in 1973 it didn't feel safe.

But I was at a point in my life when I just didn't care. My life felt like death to me, anyway. What could I lose?

But I was scared too. The thing that scared me most were these words: "You'll be sorry." What did that mean? Up front I made the decision to take responsibility for my life. Underneath I decided that in order to leave I had to be sorry. I believed that I should pay for my decision.

So I paid. I believed I deserved the derision, the hurtful remarks, the silence and accusations that surrounded the subject of my son, even in the lesbian community. I didn't deserve to talk about missing him or to miss him. I had lost the right to wonder how he was doing, whether he was crying for me. I couldn't let anyone see me crying for him. Maybe I didn't even have the right to cry for him. Why? Because I left him.

Some people say I left my son because I wanted to, because he was male, because I hated all males. I wanted my life in my own hands. So I paid.

Lilith had to pay too. She gives birth to a thousand children every day and has to eat them, kill them, for refusing to obey Adam. That's me. Every day I give birth to Jonah, and every day I leave him. Over and over. Because I don't want to obey Adam.

Let's try a new view. What if this weren't my doing? What if I'm not disgusting? What if the way I've been thinking about this is wrong? What if I love my son, didn't want to give him up?

What if this weren't my choice? What if I had no choice? What if my husband would have taken Jonah away from me regardless of what I wanted? What if Jonah had never been mine, only borrowed in a way that my daughter never was? What if I had been only a caretaker?

I had my first big shock at Jonah's bris, his ritual circumcision. I was twenty-three years old, steeped in Jewish culture, unaware that any other life existed. Jonah was eight days old. I knew Jewish boys had to be circumcised, but I was unprepared for my reaction. I began to cry hysterically. I ran away and hid in the bathroom. They were hurting my son; I had no control. I was out of control. I couldn't stop them — they wouldn't listen. Men did this to my baby. Why?

Later I understood that they were marking him as theirs, not mine. I would take care of him that night, that week, for years. But at age thirteen that would be it. He would be mine no longer. He'd have a bar mitzvah, become initiated into Jewish manhood, maybe be sent away to a yeshiva. I'd have no more control over that than over the bris. How did I know that? Listen to this story I grew up with.

When my father was thirteen, my grandfather decided to send him to a yeshiva far away. My grandmother cried. She begged him, please don't send him. He's too young — he still needs his mother, his family. My grandfather yelled and slammed doors. Maybe he hit. He was an angry, violent man.

One day when my father came home from school, my grandfather met him at the door with a suitcase. My grandmother was not there; it was market day. Pulling my father by the arm, my grandfather dragged him to the bus station. He put my father on the bus for the Chicago yeshiva. No good-bye, no kiss, no proud send-off. How my grandmother must have wept when she came home and found him gone. My father did not see his mother until Passover of the following year.

Could I have kept Jonah? I doubt it.

But what about *this*? What if I did not want to raise Jonah anymore? What if I didn't want to be a mother anymore at all? What if I knew, deep down, that by being tied to my children, I was tied to a community I could no longer live in? What if I somehow knew that it was easier to join the lesbian community without children? After all, lesbians worked very hard to accept the idea that women did not have to be mothers.

This was long before artificial insemination was called alternative fertilization and made available to lesbians. This was before lesbians were having babies and spending time at parties and conferences discussing where to get sperm, whether their children should know who their fathers are, and whether fathers should know who their children are. This was before lesbians were considering how to raise a boy to be loving to women. Back then we took pride in cre-

205

ating lesbian-only space. Where was a boy to fit in here? Where did *children* fit?

I was so tired of giving my whole life over to someone else. Sick and tired. What if I really wanted to leave all that behind and just "do my thing?"

Perhaps *this* is the shame I've spent twenty years covering up: that I wanted out in a big way. If I had kept the kids, I would have had to keep everything that went with them. And they made my access to the lesbian community harder.

The truth is, I didn't see how I could be a lesbian *and* a mother. If my daughter hadn't fought so hard to live with me, if she had not made it clear that she wanted to go with me wherever I was going, I have to say I probably would have left her too. Should I be ashamed to admit this? I am. But it's the truth.

I was controlled through my children. That's how men do it. They get at you through the kids. You have these kids, and you love them. And then men own you. If you do this, if you do that, if you don't do this or that, they'll take away your kids. So what do you learn? To make the attachment so almighty important that you look down on anyone who does something different. Or to detach.

206 Want to hear a cruel hoax? I left my son; I thought it was my choice. It *is* what I wanted. But it was the only choice I had. I once asked my Aunt Ida why she chose to stay in a bad marriage. "Choose, schmoose," she said. "I had no choice. So I decided to stay." Me? I had no choice either. So I decided to leave.

Fighting for Our Children: An Interview With Sharon Bottoms
by Tzivia Gover

Seated on her living room floor wearing black leggings and an oversize T-shirt, Sharon Bottoms flips through the pages of her family photo album on a Sunday afternoon in early September. "He was always laughing and cooing," she says, pointing to pictures of her son, Tyler Doustou, cradled in her arms when he was an infant. There are pictures of baby Tyler wearing a baseball cap and sunglasses, Tyler's first Christmas, and Tyler learning to walk. "This is his first taste of salt," Bottoms says, explaining a snapshot in which Tyler wears an expression of surprise.

Next there's a picture of her son standing beside a bare mattress the day the two of them moved in with April Wade, Bottoms's lover of four years. "He was helping," the 26-year-old Bottoms says, explaining the hammer in the toddler's hands. She turns to the next page — an image of Tyler looking full-face into the camera, his eyes serious. "Here's how he looked the day we went to court."

From here the family memories become loaded with frustrations and regrets. Bottoms and Wade have been fighting since March 1993 to regain custody of Tyler, who is now five years old, from Bottoms's mother, Kay Bottoms. The latest court decision allows Sharon Bottoms to see her son only every other weekend at her home — and Wade cannot be present.

The case, which has been heard in Virginia's court of appeals and the state's supreme court, is perhaps the most highly publicized example of what can happen when, because of their sexual orientation, the fitness of lesbian or gay parents is challenged in court. "As long as we have the judges we have, I won't get Tyler back," Bottoms says. So on August 15 she announced that she would no longer fight for custody and instead focus on visitation. "When I told my attorneys I needed to stop, I didn't know how to explain it. I still don't know. It's just that when you have the judges saying one thing after another about you..." Bottoms falls silent, as if no words can explain what is going through her mind.

For now the case will go no higher. It can't reach the U.S. Supreme Court, since Bottoms hasn't exhausted the appeals process in Virginia and has been warned that she could face court sanctions if she appeals again in the state. Besides, Bottoms says, her decision to stop fighting for now also involves Tyler. "He's in school now," she says. "He needs things to be stable."

Although there is nothing she can do to change the court's opinion at this point, Bottoms isn't ruling out another appeal in the future. But right now she and Wade are just coping, and this is where Bottoms is unable to articulate her grief. Wade steps in: "It's beyond painful. On a scale of one to a billion...it's a billion-plus." Long-simmering rage and newly mounting resignation mix in Wade's voice: "The decision to stop was just as difficult as the decision to fight."

For three years Bottoms has been the national poster child for lesbian and gay custody issues. So as she and Wade back out of the public arena, other gay parents are left to assess what this struggle has meant. Has progress been made in changing the way the courts handle custody cases involving gay men and lesbians? Or are gay parents simply losing their children? Judging from recent news coverage of cases in the courts, it is easy to feel we are slipping backward. Just as Bottoms has been stymied in her struggle, another lesbian custody case — one that seems to sum up the worst of what gays and lesbians can face in court — made headlines when a mother lost custody of her child to her ex-husband, a convicted murderer.

These are the cases that grab headlines, but all over the country gay men and lesbians fight — sometimes successfully, sometimes not — to keep their children. "The American public thinks we're asking for special rights," Wade says. "But I don't think it's a special right to raise a child. It's a special thing to raise a child, but it's not a special right." Yet polls indicate that most Americans are not ready to grant gays the same rights as straights when it comes to family issues. While there are no widely known statistics on how Americans view homosexuals as parents, less than 40 percent support legally sanctioned gay marriages, according to a report published in September 1996 in *The New York Times* — far fewer than those who support equal rights for gays at work (about 85 percent).

"Family issues are where gay men and lesbians are most vulnerable," says Kathryn Kendell, executive director of the National Center for Lesbian Rights. It also seems that family issues are

208

where gays and lesbians are most visible. Since September 1996 Bottoms's story aired as an ABC made-for-TV movie, *Two Mothers for Zachary,* starring Valerie Bertinelli; the Defense of Marriage Act was signed into law; and closing arguments were heard in Hawaii's gay marriage case — with attorneys for the state using the so-called best interests of the children as ammunition against allowing lesbians and gay men to marry.

Diana Maldonado, a thirty-year-old woman who is appealing a decision that gave her ex-husband custody of their eight-year-old son, says her relationship with another woman tipped the scales against her. She had previously been granted custody and had raised her son for five years but was suddenly deemed unfit in September 1996. According to Maldonado, her ex-husband, John Wade Hall, was some $28,000 behind in his child-support payments when he was granted custody. It seemed that Hall had only to utter the *L* word to win in court. "His attorney screamed, 'Lesbian, lesbian, lesbian,' " Maldonado says. "The whole hearing consisted of my sexuality. I haven't been allowed to see my son for months. I go from being completely angry to feeling completely lost and alone."

Now the American Civil Liberties Union is taking up her cause. "I **209** was appalled when I heard about her case," says Joann Bell, executive director of the ACLU in Oklahoma. "There are several areas where I think her rights have been violated." Maldonado, who moved to Vermont for a job as a union electrician, realizes that she could face a battle as public and as trying as the one Bottoms waged. "I'm not up to date with any issues," she says. "I've just kept to myself, working overtime to support my son." But, she adds, "I feel like I have to do this. For this to happen to me or to Sharon or to anybody else is wrong."

Brian, a newly out gay man living in Florida who asked that his full name not be used to protect his children's privacy, is feeling the sting of a similar injustice. A computer analyst who left his wife for another man, Brian knew that telling the truth about his sexual orientation could cause problems for himself. Still, he chose not to lie to his wife of twenty years. His honesty wasn't rewarded: Even though Brian's teenage daughters told the court through a therapist that they preferred to live with Brian and his partner rather than moving to another state with their mother, the court awarded custody to the mother.

Brian fumes when he reviews his divorce judgment, which reads: "The Husband...has embarked upon a new lifestyle and a new location with a new significant other and his future is unpredictable." On the contrary, says Brian; he remained in the same community where his daughters had been living, while six days after the decision in her favor, Brian's ex-wife moved across the country with their daughters. She didn't know where they would live or what school the girls would attend. "Apparently, the fact that I'm gay negates all the constants in my life," Brian says. "It pretty much tells me what I already knew: that our [sexual] orientation becomes a big issue."

Gay men are hit with a double whammy when it comes to custody issues, says Wayne Steinman, president of Gay and Lesbian Parents Coalition International and an adoptive parent. "Everything that happens to the [lesbians] happens to the [gay] men — but double," he says, "because there's a stereotype that women make better parents." One reason women's cases come to the public's attention more is that women are more often seeking custody, while men, who after separation have traditionally been the noncustodial parents, are more often battling for visitation. But there is common ground for gay men and lesbians: As they fight to maintain their rights as parents, their sexual orientation is used against them.

210

Still, legal experts express optimism when it comes to assessing the gains being made in courtrooms and the implications for the gay civil rights movement as a whole. But, they warn, the way toward consistently fair decisions in custody cases is more a zigzagging path than a steady ascent.

In the summer of 1996, Kendell fought two cases that illustrate the back-and-forth progress she sees. In one case Valerie Maradie, a lesbian who was appealing a custody ruling against her, won her petition to have her case retried when Florida's first district court of appeals ruled that her sexual orientation alone was not sufficient reason to deny her custody. This advance was offset soon after by the ruling against Mary Ward, the lesbian who lost custody of her daughter to a convicted murderer. After the good news from the Maradie decision, the outcome of the Ward case was "devastating," says Kendell, who adds, "It does feel like two steps back, but there is no doubt that there is a trend in this country that judges are adopting better attitudes about gay and lesbian parents."

Florida is one of some thirty states where a parent's sexual orientation alone cannot be used as the basis to deny custody, says

Denny Lee, an ACLU representative. But the Bottoms and Ward cases — both tried in states on that same list — illustrate that even this protection doesn't mean a gay parent's case will be heard without bias. "[Judges] now try to say their decision is based on some other behavior," says Abby R. Rubenfeld, a Tennessee lawyer who has won many custody cases in favor of gay and lesbian parents.

This was the situation in the Bottoms ruling, where everything from the fact that Bottoms didn't complete high school to the fact that she accepted a deal with ABC to make a television movie about her life was cited in the judge's decision against her. Ten years before Bottoms lost custody of her son, precedent for such cases had been set for judges in Virginia by the *Roe* v. *Roe* decision. In this 1985 case a gay man was denied custody of his ten-year-old daughter because he lived with his male lover. By contrast, the Bottoms decision explicitly states that a lesbian or gay relationship alone is not cause to deny custody, yet the careful wording still did not alter the outcome.

"In a perverse way the Bottoms case is an advance for Virginia state law," says Nancy Polikoff, a legal scholar who has been writing about lesbians and the law since the '70s. "As horrible as it is for Sharon, they didn't say that she didn't get custody because she's a lesbian living with her lover — amen." This may seem a mere matter of semantics, but Polikoff insists that it is significant: "The [Virginia] rule before Bottoms was the very worst in the country. So this is a step forward."

In the highly publicized Ward case, the decision, again, was worded to emphasize that John Ward, who was convicted twenty-two years ago of murdering his first wife, did not win custody because Mary Ward is a lesbian. "The focus of this case is not on the mother's sexual orientation but on the interests of the child," the decision reads. Instead the judge cited "unusual and inappropriate statements and behavior" as the basis of the decision. These problems, reported by John Ward and his current wife, Rita, included the fact that the girl allegedly pointed to Rita's crotch and asked if her father "fucked" her "there." Also listed were the child's "poor bathroom hygiene," bad table manners, and the fact that she prefers men's cologne. "Had these been the behaviors of a child who had two heterosexual parents," Polikoff says, "I don't think there would have been any question that this wouldn't be a reason to change custody."

But similar family issues have been fought with better results — and increasing levels of success — over the past twenty years. Until the mid '70s gay men and lesbians rarely, if ever, dared contest a custody decision if there were any chance their sexuality would become an issue, Polikoff notes. After 1974, the year the American Psychiatric Association removed homosexuality from its list of mental disorders, the climate changed for lesbian and gay parents. More cases began to appear in the courts, since lawyers now had backing for their argument that gay men and lesbians could be fit parents.

The battle to end discrimination against gay parents has been helped further by studies showing that children of gay parents have no more problems than those raised by heterosexuals, Polikoff explains. Evidence that gays and lesbians can raise healthy children continues to mount. In 1995 the American Psychological Association published a pamphlet examining the effects of gay and lesbian parenting on children. Not only was there no proof of problems based on parents' sexual orientation, but the report also noted that by being open with their children about their relationships and by living with their same-sex partners, gay men and lesbians

212   increase the chances that their children will grow up well-adjusted.

But this information is only slowly trickling down to the trial-court level, lawyers say. "The attitudes in some states are as bad as they were twenty years ago," Polikoff says. Because custody decisions leave so much to the judge's discretion, it is difficult to predict results. Attitudes vary not only from state to state but from region to region. "If Mary Ward lived in California, this wouldn't have happened," says Kendell, who attributes the ruling against Mary Ward to the "misfortune of geography." Bottoms also sees her geography as her downfall. Commenting on the baby boom among lesbians and gay men in light of her own experience, Bottoms laughs. "More power to them — and don't move to Virginia," she says.

The arbitrary nature of custody rulings doesn't affect only lesbians and gay men. In some states, including Tennessee, judges can take children away if a parent lives with someone out of wedlock. But gays are still at a disadvantage. "Heterosexuals can cure that problem by getting married," Rubenfeld says. "We don't have that option." Because the family court is an arena where negative stereotypes about gay men and lesbians are articulated, what happens there is indicative of how lesbians and gays are viewed in society as a whole. Unfounded stereotypes of gays as pedophiles and perverts tend to surface during custody hearings, says Ruthann Robson, a professor at City University of New York law school. "Even if you don't have a child or if you don't live with a child," she says, these issues that come up in court touch the lives of all gays.

And since custody cases define the extent to which homosexuals are viewed as parents, decisions made in family courts can serve as warnings about how lesbians and gay men might be viewed or treated in jobs, such as teaching, that require interactions with children, Robson notes. Although at times it may seem as though society is moving backward on these issues, the attention recent court decisions have garnered hint at a silver lining. Now that this type of homophobia has been addressed, Robson says, "people are more outraged over these cases, and that's a good sign."

Bottoms and Wade have a tangible reminder of that sentiment. Stowed in their living-room closet is a black satchel bursting with letters of support from people around the country. "When you have a judge sitting on the bench, you think he's speaking for the people," Wade says. "We found out that that's not the case." The couple also keep a collection of videos that record their court appearances and interviews with Connie Chung and Larry King, among others. **213** These also document sympathetic reactions from the national press and talk-show audiences. Bottoms pops one of those tapes into the VCR. It's an episode of the *Sally Jessy Rapha'l* show filmed three years ago, after the first appeals hearing in which Kay Bottoms won custody of her grandson.

On-camera, Kay Bottoms accused her daughter of being an unfit mother, of being immature, of partying, doing drugs, and mistreating Tyler. Bottoms stops the tape every few seconds to set the record straight. Wade adds simply, "The only reason Sharon doesn't have Tyler is that she's a lesbian." Fast-forward to another segment. This time Sharon Bottoms stood before the cameras saying, "I'll fight until we win." Watching the footage again, just weeks after she decided to drop the custody fight, Bottoms leans into the corner of the sofa, frowns, and shakes her head, her shoulder-length blond hair falling in wisps around her face.

The loss of her son, Bottoms says, has affected every aspect of her life. She's missed work because sometimes it has been too difficult to face another day without Tyler. She and Wade have learned to rage and cry rather than suffer silently or shut each other out.

Bottoms complains that she has gotten too thin and can't gain weight. She wonders if the stress from these years of fighting are responsible. And each time Bottoms returns her son after a visit and drives away in her red Camaro with plates that read AL4TYLER, she feels the pain. She says, "When he gets out of the car, I take a deep breath and say, 'OK, I have to keep it together until I see him again.' "

Contributors

Shelley Adler is looking for a new publisher for her fifth book of poetry, titled *Poems of a Pervert*. She and her partner, Sue, have raised five children and are waiting for their infant daughter from China to become the sixth. Adler has been a teacher, counselor, barber, and taxi and school bus driver. "I also have three useless M.A. degrees," she says, and hopes to write more poems.

Before becoming a mother, **Harriet Alpert** edited the book *We Are Everywhere: Writing By and About Lesbian Parents*. Now, nine years later, she has written about her own sons, using pseudonyms, she says, to honor their evolving sense of privacy.

Sara Asch is a pseudonym used only to protect the privacy of her children in this entry. She is willing to correspond with anyone interested in furthering this dialogue and who writes to her c/o 55 Kenwood Ave., Wakefield, RI 02879.

Karen Bellavance-Grace founded Valuable Families, a lesbian, gay, and bisexual families group serving western New England. Her work has appeared in *The Family Next Door* and *The Journal of LGB Identity*.

Margaret Bradstock is a senior lecturer in English at the University of New South Wales in Sydney, Australia. She is also a writer, critic, and the editor of nine books, including *Beyond Blood: Writings on the Lesbian and Gay Family*.

Loree Cook-Daniels is a writer and the author of "Common Ground," a syndicated column on conflict analysis and resolution in the lesbian, gay, bisexual, and transgender communities. She lives with her partner of thirteen years, Marcelle (a female-to-male transsexual) and their toddler son, Kai, in Vallejo, California.

Sara Michele Crusade is a graduate student in counseling psychology at John F. Kennedy University, a freelance journalist, and a lesbian mom. She and her son, Dare, live in Northern California. "Lesbian Divorce" is dedicated to the memory of child therapist Leah Lagoy, MFCC.

Laura Davis is the lesbian mother of two sons, one nineteen and the other three. She is the coauthor, with Ellen Bass, of *The Courage to Heal* and *Beginning to Heal* and the author of *The Courage to Heal Workbook* and *Allies in Healing*. Her latest book, written with Janis Keyser, is titled *Becoming the Parent You Want to Be: A Sourcebook of Strategies for the First Five Years.*

Cheryl Deaner is the mother of a son, Jesse. She is the founder of the All Our Families Coalition, which provides support for families with lesbian, gay, bisexual, and transgendered members.

Lillian Faderman is the author of seven books, including *Surpassing the Love of Men, Odd Girls and Twilight Lovers,* and *Chloe Plus Olivia*. The book she is currently working on is titled *What Lesbians Have Done for America*. She was born in 1940 and has identified as a lesbian since 1956. Her son, Avrom, is twenty-one and is finishing his dissertation in philosophy at Stanford University. At age seventeen he graduated summa cum laude from the University of California, Los Angeles, where he was a member of Phi Beta Kappa. Faderman and her partner have been together for twenty-five years.

216

Susan Golombok's and **Fiona Tasker**'s work was originally published by the Society for the Scientific Study of Sexuality in Mount Vernon, Iowa.

Tzivia Gover is a freelance journalist and writer living in Massachusetts. Her work has appeared in a number of anthologies, journals and newspapers. She has an MFA in writing from Columbia University.

Ellen Grabiner is a painter, writer, and mother currently finishing up her book, *Piece of Cake: Memoir of a Lesbian Mother*. She lives with her lover in Cambridge, Massachusetts, where they are being raised by their son, Alex.

Laura K. Hamilton is a mother, writer, and educator striving to live serenely with her patient life partner and two wonderfully demanding sons — now bright and sensitive fourteen-year-olds.

Tryna Hope is a fifty-year old writer and social worker living in Hadley, Massachusetts. She grew up in Birmingham, Alabama. Her father is an Orthodox rabbi, and her mother was a socialist. She is the mother of two grown children. Tryna hosts a lesbian cable-TV talk show in Northampton, Massachusetts. Her work has been published in *The Tribe of Dina: A Jewish Woman's Anthology, Sinister Wisdom, Word of Mouth I* and *II,* and *Tues Night: Poetry and Fiction by Valley Lesbian Writers Group.*

Ilsa Jule is a writer living in New York City. As an undergraduate at Hunter College, she ran Sappho's Scribblers and hosted the radio talk show *Sappho's Squabblers.* She has been a mom for two years.

Kate Kendell received her Juris Doctor degree in 1988 from the University of Utah College of Law in Salt Lake City and served as staff counsel to the American Civil Liberties Union Foundation of Utah from 1992 to 1994. Prior to her ACLU work, she was an associate attorney at Van Cott, Bagley, Cornwall & McCarthy, a litigation practice in Salt Lake City. Kate joined the staff of the National Center for Lesbian Rights in November 1994 as legal **217** director. She is also an adjunct professor at Hastings College of Law, where she teaches Selected Problems in Civil Rights, a course focusing on constitutional law and lesbians, gay men, and the law. She is a board member of Bay Area Lawyers for Individual Freedom. She and her partner, Sandy, live in San Francisco with their infant son, Julian Lucas. Kate also has a daughter, age fifteen, who lives in Utah.

Leslie Lawrence is a recipient of a grant from the National Endowment of the Arts and is widely published (*Women on Women Vol. 1, Women's Review of Books, The Boston Globe, Colorado Review,* etc.) She lives in Cambridge, Massachusetts.

Jenifer Levin is the author of four novels: *Water Dancer* (nominated for the PEN/Hemingway First Novel Award), *Snow, Shimoni's Lover,* and *The Sea of Light* (nominated for a Lambda fiction award), and a story collection, *Love and Death, & Other Disasters.* She has written for *The New York Times, The Washington Post, Rolling Stone, Ms., Mademoiselle, Forward, The Advocate, The Harvard Gay and Lesbian*

Review, and many other publications. Her short fiction is widely anthologized. She lives in New York City with her partner and their children.

Audre Lorde, poet, novelist, essayist, educator, and activist, died of cancer in November 1992. She is the author of ten volumes of poetry, a novel, and numerous essays, which have been widely reprinted and translated. Her last book, published after her death, is *The Marvelous Arithmetics of Distance.*

Pearlie McNeill is an Australian author who suffered greatly as a child reared in a violent family. She has written mostly from personal experience, factually, fictionally, striving always for humor and optimism.

Martha Miller is a Midwestern mother of two sons. Her stories are widely published. She's had four plays produced and writes a monthly book-review column for lesbians.

Janell Moon won the 1995 Stonewall Competition for her chapbook, *Lesbian Speaker's Bureau.* She has won awards in the Wildwood Competition, the Whiskey Hill Prize, the Billie Murray Denny Contest, and the National Poetry Competition.

218

Robin Morgan is the author of two volumes of fiction, five volumes of poetry, and three volumes of nonfiction and the editor of three volumes, including the groundbreaking *Sisterhood Is Powerful.* An award-winning poet, political theorist, activist, writer, and until recently editor in chief of *Ms.* magazine, Robin has been at the forefront of this feminist wave from the first Miss America Pageant protest in 1968 to fights for abortion rights to the burgeoning of a global feminist consciousness and global action.

Carole Morton left New York City's Greenwich Village in 1976 for San Francisco, where her life and house went uphill. She's a therapist, public speaker, minister, and technical recruiter. Carole became a grandma on April 3, 1996.

Merril Mushroom has four sons and only one daughter. Somehow she finds time to write! Her work has appeared in many lesbian periodicals and anthologies.

Lisa Orta lives with her partner, Karen Rust; their two children, Gary (age five) and Geneva (age one); and their two dogs, Lucy and Ethel, in Oakland, California, where, on their block alone, there are gay and straight families of all different races and ages and an array of pets you wouldn't believe. Lisa and Karen published thirteen issues of *The Family Next Door,* a national bimonthly publication for lesbian and gay parents and their friends. Gary plans to be the first Major League Baseball player with openly lesbian moms; Geneva is already his most ardent fan.

Minnie Bruce Pratt's second book of poetry, *Crime Against Nature,* which is about her relationship as a lesbian mother to her two sons, was chosen as the 1989 Lamont Poetry Selection by the Academy of American Poets. It was also nominated for a Pulitzer prize and received the American Library Association's Gay and Lesbian Book Award for Literature. Her other books include *We Say We Love Each Other, Rebellion: Essays 1980–1991,* and *S/he,* stories about gender boundary crossing. She is currently working on a series of narrative poems, *Walking Back Up Depot Street.* She lives in Jersey City, New Jersey, with her lesbian husband, Leslie Feinberg.

Tara Prince-Hughes is writing a dissertation on Native American and lesbian literature through the University of Rochester. She teaches college English in Bellingham, Washington.

Cindy T. Rizzo is a writer and lesbian activist from Boston. She and her partner of eighteen years are the parents of two sons, ages ten and four. She is coeditor of and contributor to the anthology *All the Ways Home: Short Fiction on Parenting and Children in the Lesbian and Gay Communities.* She has written about lesbian parenting and other issues in *Gay Community News, Sojourner, Bay Windows,* and the op-ed page of *The New York Times.*

Ruthann Robson is the author of two novels, *Another Mother* and *a/k/a;* two short story collections, *Eye of a Hurricane* and *Cecile;* and several works of nonfiction, including *Lesbian (Out)Law.*

Christina Starr is a writer and editor as well as performer-producer of her own blatantly lesbian works. She lives in Toronto with her fabulously wonderful soon-to-be-seven daughter.

Karen X. Tulchinsky is a Jewish butch dyke writer. She is the author of *In Her Nature* and the coeditor of *Queer View Mirror: Lesbian and Gay Short Short Fiction* and *Tangled Sheets: Stories and Poems of Lesbian Lust.*

Jess Wells's seven volumes of work include the novel *AfterShocks* and the short-story collections *Two Willow Chairs* and *The Dress/The Sharda Stories.* Her work has appeared in many literary anthologies within the lesbian, gay, and women's movement, including *Lavender Mansions, The Femme Mystique, Queer View Mirror, Woman on Woman, Lesbian Love Stories,* and *When I Am an Old Woman I Shall Wear Purple.* Her work is also included in university curricula and textbooks. She lives with her partner and son in San Francisco.

Grace Woodacre is a pseudonym for a journalist and freelance writer in the San Francisco Bay area.